THE COMPLETE GUIDE TO COCKAPOO DOGS

David Anderson

Special thanks to Erin Hotovy
for her work on this project

LP Media Inc. Publishing

Text copyright © 2018 by LP Media Inc.

www.lpmedia.org

Publication Data

Anderson, David.

The Complete Guide to Cockapoo Dogs / David Anderson. ---- First edition.

Summary: "Successfully raising a Cockapoo dog from puppy to old age" --- Provided by publisher.

ISBN: 978-1792775321

[1. Cockapoo --- Non-Fiction] I. Title.

Design by Sorin Radulescu

First paperback edition, 2018

TABLE OF CONTENTS

CHAPTER 16

CHAPTER 1
Introduction to Cockapoos

"Cockapoos are people pleasers; they love nothing more than to make the people around them happy! They are a happy go lucky breed that is perfectly content snuggling on the couch with you, or taking a trek through the woods: they just go with the flow. They are also incredibly intelligent and there is no limit to the things that they can be taught!"

Jamie
Cute Cockapoos

Bringing a new dog into your life is an exciting occasion, especially if the dog is a Cockapoo! This breed is cute, cuddly, and so much fun to have as a companion. However, a new dog is a lot of work. Before you even get the chance to pick out your dog, you'll need to think about things like breeders, training, and supplies. Don't worry—this book will guide you through everything you need to know about owning a Cockapoo! We'll cover it all, from food and exercise to grooming and vet care. By the end, you'll be more than ready to open your home to a new best friend.

What is a Cockapoo?

The Cockapoo is not a single dog breed—instead, it's a cross between a Poodle and a Cocker Spaniel. On their own, both breeds are fine dogs, but together, they create a super-hybrid that you'll be sure to love. Like many Poodle crossbreeds, this breed has a curly, fluffy coat and can vary in size, depending on breeding.

A Cockapoo is often designated as a "designer dog". This means that there is no purebred standard for them. Instead, two breeds are crossed to take desirable traits from one breed and infuse it within another. Designer breeds have become increasingly popular in recent decades, and there are tons of different hybrids out there for potential dog owners to choose. But this varied lineage does not mean that designer dogs are mutts—they are carefully bred and adored by organizations dedicated to the hybrids.

Photo Courtesy of Jaci Ingham

Understanding the Cockapoo's Lineage

You'll find that a Cockapoo has the very best qualities of the Poodle and Cocker Spaniel. This breed has a curly coat with big, floppy ears. They have a lot of energy but are also intelligent and easy to train. To understand this cross breed, it helps to understand the common traits attributed to the Poodle and Cocker Spaniel as individual breeds.

Poodles are commonly used in crossbreeding designer dogs, and for good reason. Perhaps the most obvious desirable trait is their curly coat. A Poodle crossbreed's fur tends to mix textures with whatever breed it is crossed with. A straight-haired breed will yield wavy-haired offspring when crossed with a Poodle. Also, Poodles are bred to be different sizes, leading to some variation and choice when it comes to the Cockapoo. Standard Poodles can grow to be rather large, so the Miniature and Toy Poodle were created. When you see breeders advertise smaller-than-average Cockapoos, it's likely that the Cocker Spaniel is bred with one of these smaller types of Poodles.

While the Poodle is often stereotyped as being pompous and prissy, this is not the case with the breed. Poodles are one of the more intelligent dog breeds, meaning that training is easy with them. They are sensitive dogs, so they are able to take in a lot of information from their surroundings. This is a good thing when it comes time to train your dog, as a sensitive dog cares about the nonverbal cues their owner presents. A sensitive dog generally wants to please their owner, so they are able to better understand what you want and adjust their behavior accordingly.

Poodles also have a ton of energy and require lots of play and exercise. As with any intelligent breed, mental stimulation is just as important as physical exercise. This dog can get along well in a small home or apartment as long as the owner commits a few hours to exercise and play each day.

The Cocker Spaniel is much smaller than the standard Poodle and rarely grows to be larger than thirty pounds. This dog's coat is very thick with a slightly wavy texture. This is one of those breeds where frequent grooming is non-negotiable; without regular brushing and trimming, the coat will turn into a matted mess. This breed also has adorable floppy ears, which are prone to infection, especially if moisture is trapped underneath.

Cocker Spaniels are friendly dogs, and they are very much owner-oriented. They want to spend as much time as possible with their favorite people and dislike being left alone. They are moderately stranger-, kid-, and dog-friendly, though they are highly sensitive and may initially distrust others until they have the time to sniff them out. They may also bark at the sound of a doorbell, as they will want to protect their owner from whatever unknown danger is out there. With this breed, socialization is key because they need to learn how to get along with a variety of people and animals.

As is the case with other small breeds, Cocker Spaniels don't require as much exercise as larger dogs. They are playful and energetic, but not to the point where they are unmanageable. This dog is satisfied with a nice walk at the end of the day, with lots of cuddles and attention in between.

You'll find that the Cockapoo is really the happy medium between these two dog breeds. They're full of energy, but not constantly bouncing off the walls. They have a coat that requires grooming, but don't shed a lot of fur. They are cuddly and very friendly towards others. It's no surprise that this crossbreed has been popular for so many years.

Photo Courtesy of
Fiona Reid

Cockapoo History

Photo Courtesy of Lesley Gibbs

While Poodle crossbreeds have been extremely popular in recent years, the Cockapoo has been around longer than you'd think! This breed dates back nearly sixty years ago. It's not certain if the first Poodle/Cocker Spaniel was purposeful, but the breeder liked the result they got and it took off from there. Since then, breeders have continued to perfect this cross to produce the most desirable traits in this dog.

In 1999, the Cockapoo Club of America was created to promote a breed standard. Because this is not a pure breed that dates back to an era where dogs were workers, there were no official standards to aim for. Appearance and dispositional traits were mainly up to the individual, as there was no official kennel club designation to provide breeders with these standards and rules. This club prefers breeders to use Cockapoos in their crosses, instead of creating a first-generation Poodle/Cocker Spaniel pup, in order to maintain some consistency in the breed.

On the other hand, the American Cockapoo Club, founded in 2004, discourages members from crossing multi-generational Cockapoos with one another and promotes the breeding of Poodles and Cocker Spaniels. As you can see, there's more than one way to breed a Cockapoo! While both groups have differences in bringing about the perfect Cockapoo, both stress the importance of skilled and responsible breeding in order to keep the breed intact.

With these organizations and standards, breeders are able to produce litters of Cockapoos with similar characteristics. That way, when you buy a Cockapoo from a breeder, you have a good idea of what you're getting. Breed standards do not only affect the appearance of the dog, but also the behavioral characteristics.

Physical Characteristics

The standard Cockapoo is not a small dog. Often referred to as a "Maxi Cockapoo", these dogs are more than nineteen pounds and at least fifteen inches tall. This breed also has a single coat that can come in a range of textures. The curly or wavy coat is the most common, but straight-coated Cockapoos also exist. Generally, these dogs have a full, fluffy coat that does not require shaving to keep under control. However, when the fur occludes the eyes, a trim is needed to keep the dog looking neat and clean.

As is the case with many crossbreeds, there is a wide variety in coat colors, with some more common than others. Black, white, cream, brown, buff, and red are all coat colors seen in Cockapoos. Of course, some dogs have two or three of these colors in their coat. The variation is caused by the parents' coat colors, so if you're interested in buying a dog with a particular coat color, talk to your breeder about the possibilities of their puppies showing those traits.

This breed also comes in a variety of sizes. The standard Cockapoo is the largest and is over nineteen pounds. The next smallest is the miniature Cockapoo at thirteen and eighteen pounds and between eleven and fourteen inches tall. Smaller yet is the toy Cockapoo, which is less than twelve pounds and ten inches tall. And, if that isn't small enough for you, the teacup toy Cockapoo is also about ten inches tall but weighs under six pounds.

Photo Courtesy of Misty Reece

"Hypoallergenic Dogs"

One of the major reasons these dogs are so popular is because they are often referred to as "hypoallergenic." The Cockapoo definitely sheds less than a Cocker Spaniel and might create less of an allergic response in humans, but no dog is fully hypoallergenic.

Generally, the curlier the coat, the less likely the dog is to shed. When a dog doesn't shed excessively, that means that less of their dander spreads around your home. Since dander is often the thing that causes people to feel sneezy around pets, a dog with less of this is typically easier on the sinuses. For someone with less severe allergies, a dog with a curlier coat may be enough to keep one's allergies at bay entirely.

But if the owner has a moderate to severe dog allergy, they might not get away with having a Poodle crossbreed in their home. It's also possible to be allergic to a dog's saliva. And you may find that you're more allergic to some dogs but not others even within the same litter. So if you have a dog allergy, it may not be enough to buy a Poodle crossbreed. Their curly coat may prevent some issues and may keep your home cleaner than if you had a Cocker Spaniel, but there is no completely hypoallergenic dog.

Behavioral Characteristics

Though many choose their future dog based on appearance alone, temperament is important when selecting the right dog for your household. Luckily, this breed is easy-going and has a lot to offer for a variety of households. Cockapoos are generally friendly with just about anyone they come into contact with. They are companion dogs that want to make their owners happy and to be at their side as much as possible. Unfortunately, that means that these dogs may be prone to separation anxiety if left alone for too long.

Cockapoos are smart dogs that benefit from obedience training. They enjoy learning new skills and tricks. These dogs have plenty of playful energy, but not to the degree that a dog like a Poodle has. They are manageable for any owner who can provide them with a moderate amount of exercise.

Photo Courtesy of
Julie Bootle

Is a Cockapoo Right for Me?

Before you bring a Cockapoo into your household, it's important to have a thorough and honest look at your ability and willingness to provide everything a Cockapoo, or any dog, needs. The amount of attention, physical energy, and time varies from breed to breed, so it's a good idea to make sure you and your home are fit for a Cockapoo before bringing one home.

First, examine your housing situation. If you live in an apartment or small house, it might not be enough room for a standard Cockapoo. However, you can always consider buying one of the smaller variations, as they do not require as much room to roam. A backyard with a fence is also an added bonus for a dog, as it allows them more room to run and play in a safe environment. A little extra space can make a huge difference in your dog's overall happiness when it comes to their ability to burn energy. But, unlike many other breeds, a smaller home is not a deal breaker with this dog.

Next, think about your time commitments. These are companion animals and will want to be around you as much as possible. So, if you work a job where you're never home, you might want to consider a different pet that doesn't form as strong of a connection to you. It varies from dog to dog, but Cockapoos are susceptible to separation anxiety if they feel neglected. You'll want to have plenty of quality time to spend with your pup, especially in the early days.

This dog has moderate exercise requirements, so a few quick walks each day and some extra playtime is sufficient. Your dog will need this exercise no matter the weather, so you'll have to commit to walking for twenty minutes or more at a time. The smaller variations require a bit less exercise, if that makes a difference for you and your lifestyle.

Finally, you'll have to do some training with this dog. Cockapoos are generally pretty friendly, but their Cocker Spaniel genes might make them a little extra cautious. For this reason, it's important to get your puppy socialized and trained to behave around other animals, children, and strangers. This breed does best with some obedience training and regular practice. Training can be fun, but it can also be frustrating at times. Cockapoos are sensitive animals and respond best to positive training methods. Are you someone who can dedicate time to training and do so in an upbeat method? If so, you'll have no problem training this dog.

If you can read through this quick list of prerequisites for Cockapoo ownership and honestly say that you can fulfill each item, then it's time to start preparing for your new dog! If not, you may find that it's best to wait until you're at a stage in your life where you're better prepared to own a Cockapoo. Owning a Cockapoo is a lot of work, and everyone involved will be so much happier if you're fully prepared for the responsibility. But the great thing about Cockapoos is that they are generally easy to take care of.

Cockapoos make great pets for people of all ages and backgrounds. If you show them love and kindness, they will return the favor. When it comes to their appearance, there is so much variation that you have options when it comes to picking out the cutest. And their bubbly personalities will ensure that you immediately fall in love with them. There's still a lot of work to do before bringing home your new best friend, but by the time you reach the end of the book, you'll hopefully feel fully prepared for your new Cockapoo!

CHAPTER 2
Choosing Your Cockapoo

Now that you've settled that this is the right breed for you, it's time to figure out how to find the right dog. When choosing a new companion, there's more to it than just going to a pet store and picking out the cutest dog. You'll need to do some research and think about what's important to you when it comes to getting a new dog.

Buying vs. Adopting

Photo Courtesy of Samantha Harwood

The first choice to make is whether you want to buy or adopt your new dog. This decision should be made on what is best for you and your home. People will inevitably try to persuade you to go one route or the other; in the end, you know what's best for you.

There are lots of benefits to purchasing a dog from a good breeder. First, you'll have a good idea of what your future dog is going to look and act like because breeding is a science. Before the puppies are even born, the breeder will be able to tell you the traits of their pups because they've spent time with the parents and have gotten to know previous litters. While an inexperienced breeder may end up with sickly dogs with behavioral issues, a good breeder knows what traits are important in a Cockapoo.

Some owners like to start from scratch when it comes to raising their new dog. If you're the only influence on the dog from an early age, you'll have control over how the dog is brought up. If you start with a new puppy, you'll make the rules from Day One. If you adopt a dog that's had a previous owner, it's hard to know what the dog has learned from that person. Many times, the dog has no trouble adjusting to life with a new owner, but you may find that the dog has learned bad habits that take some work to undo.

Photo Courtesy of
Susie Thomas

On the other hand, there are also many benefits to adoption. Of course, perhaps the best aspect about adopting is knowing that you're giving a dog a much needed forever home. Many adoption advocates claim that a rescue dog is more appreciative of their owner. Whether or not this is true, it's undeniable how good it feels to give a dog a second chance at life.

Also, if you aren't interested in spending a thousand dollars or more on a Cockapoo puppy, adoption is much more affordable. Shelters generally charge a small fee, but this also includes veterinary services such as vaccination and spay/neuter surgeries. This allows you to save a little money to be spent on spoiling your pup with the best treats and toys!

Adoption is also beneficial if you're apprehensive about training a new puppy. Some adopted dogs will need a refresher course on basic training if they didn't come from a good home, but many surrendered Cockapoos come from good homes that fell into unfortunate circumstances. It's possible to get an adult Cockapoo that is potty-trained and knows some basic commands. Training a puppy is hard work and is very time consuming, so it can be nice to have a little help from a previous owner. Puppies are cute, but they're rambunctious and require a ton of care. You may find that a mellower adult Cockapoo is exactly what you need.

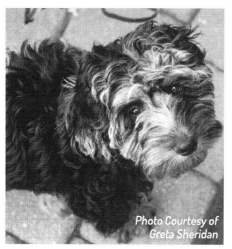

Photo Courtesy of Greta Sheridan

If you decide you want to buy a puppy, it's important to find the right breeder. Because Cockapoos are considered to be a designer dog, this is especially important. Inexperienced breeders often jump in on trends because it's an easy way to make extra money. Unfortunately, when people breed dogs without the right expertise, it leads to inconsistencies with the standard. It can result in dogs with genetic defects and bad behavioral traits. Essentially, you'll be sold an inferior product at a high price.

How to Find a Good Breeder

A good breeder knows exactly what they're doing and has the experience to back it up. These people breed dogs for the love of the breed, not just for money. They work with the best stock and produce puppies that win competitions. But you need to know how to identify a good breeder.

If you've come to love the Cockapoo, there's a good chance that you know someone else who has one. If the owner is happy with their dog, absolutely ask them who their breeder was. Breeders love to get referrals from satisfied customers. If you don't know anyone with a Cockapoo, you'll have to do a little extra research on your own.

Start out with a list of Cockapoo breeders in your area. If they have a website or social media page, look at the image they present. However, there's only so much you can tell about a breeder from their web presence. To know more, you'll have to ask questions and look at their facilities.

A good breeder will welcome any and all questions you can think of. They are passionate about Cockapoos and want to be able to share their knowledge with you. After all, they worked hard and spent a lot of time educating themselves on the breed.

During this information-gathering process, you should ask the breeder about health clearances. These are certificates that a breeder should provide to you to guarantee that your puppy will not experience genetic illnesses later in life. The parents of your new puppy should be in excellent health, as certified by a veterinarian. A less-reputable breeder may not have this kind of assurance

*Photo Courtesy of
Pat Johnson*

Photo Courtesy of
Judith Hathaway

available or may even try to hide that information. You may also want to ask for references of satisfied owners of the pups. Some breeders also require you to take the puppy to a veterinarian within the first few months after you bring your dog home, just to ensure that the buyer is happy with their dog's health. This protects the breeder if the buyer later decides they don't want the dog and they try to make excuses for a return. This practice is good for both the breeder and the new owner to ensure that the new puppy is as healthy as can be.

If possible, try to visit the breeder's home. The area where the puppies are kept should be clean and free of animal waste. They should have enough room to move around and spend time with their siblings, not locked in a tiny cage. If a breeder doesn't allow you to come to their home or seems secretive about how the puppies are looked after, you should stay away.

Finally, ask about certifications. A breeder should be eager to tell you about the Cockapoo associations they belong to or the different dog clubs they're a part of. Make sure they really care about the breed and aren't just trying to make a buck off of a fad.

Choosing Your Cockapoo

Once you've found the right breeder, it's time to choose the dog. It may be tempting to choose your new puppy based on a picture alone, but if you really want the pick of the litter, an in-person visit can help you find the right dog.

While a good breeder will do their best to make sure the puppies have the best temperament possible, you'll still notice subtle variation within a litter. Just like with human siblings, each puppy has their own unique personality. If you get the opportunity to pick from the entire litter, spend a little time playing with the puppies and observe how they respond to both people and the other dogs. Then, choose a dog that falls somewhere in the middle of the personality spectrum.

For example, you may notice that some puppies are very rambunctious, while others are submissive and shy. Neither extreme is best, so you want the puppy that is playful but also capable of being calm and sweet. An overly dominant puppy may turn into a stubborn dog, and a shy pup might develop anxiety or phobias. Of course, many behaviors are learned later on, but finding a pup that falls somewhere in a happy medium of personality traits might help you on your way to puppy parenthood. Also, don't underestimate your first instinct. If you find yourself bonding with a particular dog, that might be the one for you.

If a Cockapoo is your dream dog because you have allergies, it's especially important that you check the puppies out in person. You'll want to make sure you feel okay after spending some time around the dogs. You may even want to allow the puppies to give you kisses, just to make sure their saliva doesn't cause an allergic reaction either. Never assume a dog will not give you an allergic response just because it's advertised as hypoallergenic. Everybody is different, and what works for other people may not work for you.

Adoption Tips

If you decide that you'd rather go with the adoption route, there are a few ways to make sure you end up with the perfect Cockapoo. Local shelters can be hit-or-miss when it comes to having the right breed. This is where adoption and rescue websites come in handy. Websites like PetFinder.com allow you to search for specific breeds in your area. If you select a wider search radius, you can find all the Cockapoos within whatever distance you're willing to drive to adopt a dog. Or you can do your own search for Cockapoo rescues. These are organizations that collect Cockapoos from shelters and re-home them to good owners.

Don't assume that adopting a dog is as simple as paying a fee and picking up your new Cockapoo. Because these dogs were once surrendered, the volunteers who run these shelters are very particular about the homes they go to next. Too much change can be hard on a dog, so they want their next home to be their last home for the rest of their life. Especially with Cockapoo rescues, you can expect a detailed application form and even home visit. They'll want to know who lives in your home and if you have any other pets. They'll want to know where you live, what kind of experience you have with dogs, and if you have a backyard fence without any gaps for a dog to squeeze through.

If your web search brings up a dog, don't feel obligated to adopt it. Perhaps you had your heart set on an adult dog and the one in the shelter is a puppy. Or maybe it's documented to be bad with children and you have kids at home. It can be hard to wait for the perfect dog to appear in a shelter near you, but it's best not to force a dog into a situation that isn't right for you. You'll only end up with problems and will have to return the dog to the shelter. It may take a little time to find the right Cockapoo to adopt, but it will absolutely be worth it when you're able to bring your dog to their new forever home.

Once you decide you want a Cockapoo in your home, it's hard not to rush things and buy the first dog that's available. Take your time and explore all of your options. Not only does this allow you to get the best pup for you, but you'll have time to figure out what you need to make your future dog's life as perfect as possible. Support good breeders who use ethical practices instead of funding backyard breeding operations. Also, ask as many questions as you can think up! A breeder is a great source of knowledge for all things Cockapoo. Learn as much as you can from them so your dog's transition into your home is a smooth one.

*Photo Courtesy of
Dondra Blackwell*

CHAPTER 3
Preparing Your Home for Your Cockapoo

"I recommend to families, that their home should be child proof. As with any puppy, there an adjustment period; they need to acclimate to the new families' routine and smells."

Luann Woodard
Cockapoo Cottage

While you're in the process of finding the right breeder or shelter, it's the ideal time to start preparing your home for your new Cockapoo. Bringing a new dog into your home without any preparation is a good way to inflict unnecessary stress upon you and your new pup. Because you want your new dog's life with you to start out smoothly, you'll want to have everything in order before the big day. This means you'll need to get everyone in your household prepared for dog ownership, prepare spaces for the pup, and remove any hidden dangers in your home.

*Photo Courtesy of
Vikki Whitworth*

Adjusting Pets and Children

In time, your dog will learn how to socialize with people and other animals so that they can get along with everybody. Until then, it's necessary to teach the other people (and pets) in your household how to behave around a new puppy.

If this is your first dog and you have children, this is going to be a very exciting time for everyone. But unless your child has lots of experience with animals, they might not know how to behave around a dog. It's vital to teach kids how to act around dogs, because a dog will have little control over their instincts. They may be sweet as can be, but when faced with a perceived danger, they will act like an animal.

The Cockapoo is a very sensitive dog that tends to be friendly around kids, but still has its limits. Lots of loud noises may overstimulate or frighten this breed, especially if the dog has yet to get used to strange sounds. When dogs are scared, they usually try to remove themselves from the situation first. If this isn't possible, they might become aggressive.

For example, let's say your new Cockapoo is being poked and prodded in uncomfortable places by excited kids. Their first reaction may be to run away from the problem. But kids are persistent and may corner the pup and continue their rough petting. A frightened dog will growl and bare its teeth, but this may also go unnoticed by a young child who doesn't understand a dog's special language (or think it's funny or part of a game). Finally, the dog will snap—their final warning that they're stressed and need some space. Unfortunately, this can be very frightening and dangerous to a child and could create more issues for your household.

One way to prevent this type of situation from occurring is to teach your children your dog's warning signs. If they see their dog cowering away from them, tell them that the dog needs space, like a timeout. This way, both your dog and your children can take a moment to chill out.

Even the gentlest dog will not enjoy being poked and prodded with little fingers. It's not unheard of for a curious child to go poking around the eyes or ears, which can be very sensitive for a dog. The little wagging tail of your Cockapoo is irresistible, but your dog will not like being grabbed by it. Teach kids how to "pet nicely" by running a flat palm from the back of the neck to the base of the tail. This is a good way for young kids to bond with their new pet without the risk of getting bitten.

If you have pets, you'll want them to be acquainted with your Cockapoo early on. If your breeder allows you to take the pup away from their premises to meet your pets, that will help you out a lot in the long run. If you're adopting, the shelter or rescue will likely allow you (and encourage you) to take the Cockapoo home to check things out.

This process may take several steps before you're at the point where you're comfortable having your pets together. Dogs don't like to be forced into interacting with strange animals, and their resistance can set you back if things don't go well in the first meeting.

For your first meeting, choose neutral ground. Dogs are notoriously territorial, and even the best-behaved pup may act aggressively around a strange dog if they feel like their space is threatened. Your old dog may not get along with another dog if it's in his home. A park or a friend's backyard is a great place to set up this meeting, as neither dog will feel like they 'own' the space. You may even ask your breeder if it's okay to bring your dog to their home, as there will likely be a lot of room to roam around.

Now, it's time to call in reinforcements. Because it can be difficult to juggle two dogs, ask a friend or family member to help you with the introduction stage. Put each dog on a secure leash to prevent an incident from happening. Slowly approach your friend with the other dog and let the two pups sniff each other out. Remain calm and casual, and don't force the dogs to interact if they're not interested in it. Also, give the dogs plenty of time to sniff. There's a lot of information that can be gained from sniffing a behind, so allow them to make their full introductions in the manner that dogs usually do.

If this meeting goes without an issue, then you're on your way to making both dogs feel comfortable together. If not, give the dogs plenty of space and try again another time.

If your dogs passed the first step, it's time to reunite them in your house. You might even want to take another baby step and let the dogs check each other out in the backyard before moving to inside the home. Repeat the process with the dogs on separate leashes and give them the chance to get comfortable around the house. If everything goes well, you may even decide to let them play around a little. Be cautious and make sure that play doesn't turn into fighting. However, you may notice that your older dog may want to put the puppy in his place as the beta dog in the relationship.

If things don't go so well, that doesn't mean all hope is lost for a peaceful household! It may take some time for your dogs to feel comfortable around each other. Let your dogs have a little time and space apart and try again later. It can be frustrating when progress seems slow, but it's best to be patient so that everyone is happy and comfortable.

Photo Courtesy of
Karen Oakley

Household Dangers

Photo Courtesy of Susie Thomas

Once everything is squared away with your children and other pets, it's time to make sure your house is ready for your new dog. If this is your only dog, you may not realize that there are hidden dangers around your house for a canine. Spend a little time examining your home for things that could be dangerous for a new puppy. Think of it as "baby-proofing" your house for your new arrival.

Especially when dealing with puppies, just assume that everything your dog can reach will get chewed on. You may be in the habit of kicking your shoes off at the front door and leaving them there, but a dog will wait until you're not around and chew them to shreds. Start getting into the habit of picking up items that are within reach for a dog. Shoes, cords, and remote controls on coffee tables are all frequently-chewed items. These things can pose a risk for electric shock or choking if your puppy is a big chewer. Smaller items, like socks and underwear, can go missing and require a vet's help to retrieve them.

You'd be surprised at how crafty a Cockapoo can be. Their intelligence allows them to figure out how to get into the things they want. If cleaning supplies are in plain sight or even on top of the counter, it's feasible for a dog to get a hold of a bottle and ingest dangerous chemicals. Or if you have cleaning chemicals in your toilet bowl, a Cockapoo might want to have a little drink. Make sure that there's no way for your dog to access cleaning supplies, because a curious dog will want to try everything.

It's great to have a fenced-in backyard because you can let your dog spend time in the fresh air without constant supervision, but if you're not careful, your dog can become very sick from innocuous-looking plants. If you have a lot of landscaping in your yard, take a close look at what's planted out there. There are tons of common plants that can make your dog very sick if they decide to munch on one. Ivy, lilies, and hostas are common outdoor plants that are toxic to dogs. If a small Cockapoo eats one of these, it won't take much to make them sick. If you're concerned about growing any dangerous plants in your yard, do a search for plants that are toxic to dogs. Many websites contain lists and pictures to help you identify plants that are not safe for dogs to eat. Not all dogs will want to take a big bite out of your decorative plants, but it's good to be aware of some of these hidden dangers.

Also, do a sweep through your garage and garden shed before bringing your dog home. While they might not have a lot of access to these areas, in the event they do, you don't want certain items to be at snout-level. Basically, anything you wouldn't want a child to eat you will want to move out of reach for your dog. This includes pesticides, fertilizers, or rodent killers. The sticky mousetrap you put in the corner of the garage years ago and forgot about will easily be found by your dog. If you've gotten accustomed to life without a curious dog that is determined to get into everything, it's easy to overlook things that have never been a problem in the past. Take caution in the products you use around your yard and home, especially if your Cockapoo is going to be allowed to roam around the backyard alone on a frequent basis.

Preparing Spaces for Your Cockapoo

This is also the time to begin thinking about the spaces in your home that you're allowing access to. If you're planning on keeping your Cockapoo outside often, seriously consider where you spend the bulk of your time. Cockapoos need to spend a lot of time around their people. If you plan on keeping your dog outside all the time while you're inside, your dog will become very lonely. You don't necessarily need to let your dog sleep in your bed, but allowing your dog to spend time with you indoors is vital to your Cockapoo's happiness. This is not a breed that can be left outside all day long.

However, a puppy can wreak havoc in a house if left unchecked. Don't feel as though you need to let your Cockapoo have the run of the house. Close any doors that you don't want your dog venturing through and use gates to keep them from stumbling downstairs or wandering through hallways that are off-limits. You want your dog to have plenty of room to roam, but it's good to give your puppy boundaries early on.

One way to make your dog feel comfortable in your home is to give them some personal space. Designate a part of the house to keep your dog's bed or crate. The corner of the kitchen or living room is a good choice because it allows your social dog to be part of the family while also having some private room to relax.

Once you set up this space with comfortable blankets and toys, leave them alone. This teaches them that if they feel scared or uncomfortable,

Photo Courtesy of Emma Balsom

they can go to that spot for a little "time out". When your Cockapoo is ready to be around people, they'll let you know! Giving your dog their own space allows them to clearly tell you when they're stressed or annoyed. It can be tempting to bother them, but it's important to leave them be when they retreat to their bed or crate.

For example, you might have a dog that hates having their toenails cut. They may sit or wiggle around for the first few toenails, but at a certain point, they have reached their threshold of tolerance and need to escape before they act out. If they jump up and curl up in a ball on their bed, it can be tempting to pin them down and finish the job. You must resist this urge! If you violate their space, then they no longer have a safe spot to chill out. You can always wait until later to finish the job—let them have their moment and prevent them from acting out when they get agitated.

If you plan on letting your dog spend time outside without supervision, you may want to set up a comfy spot for them in the backyard as well. When the weather is nice, a lot of owners let their dog chill out in the fresh air for a few hours while they're away. Unfortunately, a change in weather can be unexpected. Make sure you have a spot in your yard that provides plenty of shade on hot, sunny days. If you don't have a lot of trees or shrubs for your dog to rest under, consider getting an awning or umbrella for your deck. This will also provide protection from the rain and snow.

A fence is vital if you want to let your Cockapoo run around in the safety of your own backyard while unsupervised. A Cockapoo owner will require different things when it comes to a fence, depending on the type of Cockapoo you have. If you have one of the smaller variations, you need to be very careful about making sure they can't squeeze out of any gaps. It doesn't take a lot of digging for a little Cockapoo to make a break for it. Or, if you have a short fence, you'd be surprised at how springy your standard Cockapoo is if they see a squirrel on the other side of the street. If you're installing a fence for your new Cockapoo, you might also want to consider choosing something that doesn't allow visibility through the fence. A chain-link fence may be a more affordable option, but consider how much your dog will want to bark at people in neighboring houses.

After teaching kids how to behave around a new dog, teaching dogs how to behave around the new Cockapoo, and doing a quick sweep of your home, you'll feel more prepared to bring the new puppy to their new home. Cockapoos are sensitive and can pick up on their owner's stress levels, so if you want your new puppy to feel calm, you need to feel calm too. Knowing that your dog will be safe in your home will go a long way to making you feel at ease with a new Cockapoo in the family.

Photo Courtesy of Maria McNamara

CHAPTER 4
Bringing Your Cockapoo Home

"The Cockapoo is an excellent breed for in-town living. They are not a 'high-energy' dog but still require a couple walks outside a day or a fenced backyard to play in."

Alisa Foerderer

Foerderer Horses and Cock-a-poos

The preparation is not over yet! You may be in the process of figuring out when you're going to bring your new Cockapoo home, but there's still some more work to do to ensure the transition into your home is as smooth as possible. It might seem excessive to go through all of these measures just for a dog, but you'll find that the preparation is absolutely worth it.

This chapter will walk you through a few important things to consider in the early days of having your new Cockapoo at home. It will discuss things you need to arrange early on, plus a few items you should have on hand. Finally, we'll break down the average costs of owning a Cockapoo in the first year of its life so that there are no surprises for you down the road.

Dogs are perceptive creatures, and the Cockapoo is even more so than other breeds. They have a way of noticing how you feel by paying attention to your non-verbal cues. They can tell when you're happy and they know when you're upset. Sometimes, dogs look to their people to tell them how they should feel. If you're happy and excited, then your dog will mirror that and respond similarly. If you're stressed out and overwhelmed, your dog may take that as a cue to panic because something is obviously wrong. They may not understand that their arrival is the cause of the stress, but they're still likely to feel some of that anxiety. So, the less stress you feel about your new arrival, the smoother things will go for everyone in the household.

Photo Courtesy of
Jenna Galpin

The First Night Home

The first night at home will likely be pretty rough. Your dog will be in a completely new setting without their mother or siblings. They will cry a lot and want you to soothe them. Also, if your Cockapoo is a puppy, they will also need to go to the bathroom frequently. If you're not used to getting up multiple times in the middle of the night, this will be a big change for you.

If you're crate training (which you should seriously consider), you may want to put the crate in a place close to where you sleep. That way, your dog will know that you are near and haven't abandoned them, and you can hear when they cry because they need to go to the bathroom or need to be comforted. Especially in the early days, prepare for your sleep to be interrupted by your dog. As your dog becomes more comfortable in your home, you can move their crate or bed further away. Some owners like to sleep with their dog in their bed. While this is completely up to personal preference, just remember that there will be times where you don't want your Cockapoo hogging your bed. You can push them off, but they might not understand why they can sleep there sometimes but not at other times.

If you want to prevent accidents during the night, prepare to get up every few hours to walk your dog outside. A puppy cannot hold their potty for more than an hour or two, so unless you want to clean up a mess in the morning, you'll have to get out of bed and go outside when they cry.

Nighttime is a good opportunity to close all the other doors in your house and set up gates. If you leave your home open to your dog, you may change your mind about that decision when you wake up the next morning. If you're not awake to supervise your dog's movements, you may discover that they like to explore and soothe themselves by chewing on your furniture. An unsupervised dog can get into a lot of trouble very quickly, so minimize risk by keeping the majority of your home off-limits at bedtime.

Your first night might be very stressful for your new dog, and this stress may not fully dissipate for a week or two. Your dog is learning how to live life with a new human in a new place without their family members surrounding them. Their cries at nighttime the first few days are no indication of their overall happiness with you—they're just getting used to their new home. Before long, they'll be sleeping through the night.

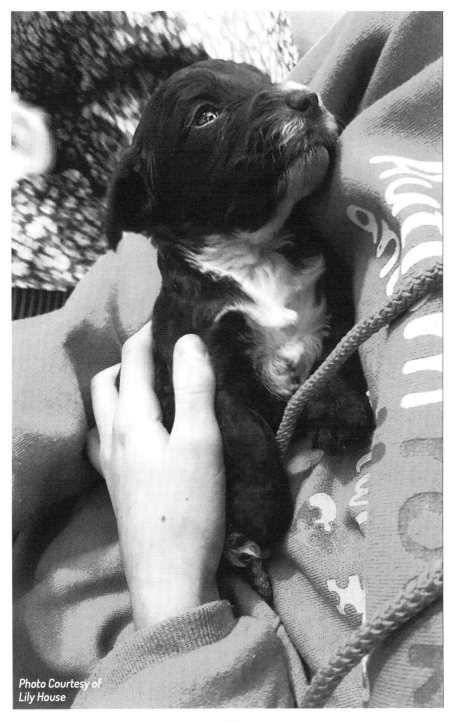

Photo Courtesy of
Lily House

How to Find a Vet

During the first week or two, it's important to decide where you are going to take your Cockapoo for their veterinary care. If you live in a city where there are plenty of choices, it can be hard to decide. Friends, breeders, rescue volunteers, and trainers are all good sources for referrals. Also, prices and services will vary from office to office, so you may need to do some "shopping" to find one that fits your needs. For example, the small clinic closest to your home may be a fine place for check-ups and general care, but they may not have a laboratory or surgical facilities. This means that if your dog needs advanced care, they would have to go to a different clinic. Either option is valid, but it's a good idea to know the full range of services before you settle on a vet.

If your regular vet does not have emergency services, it's recommended to find your closest emergency vet clinic and write down their contact information. You never know when something bad might happen to your Cockapoo, and you don't want to wait for an emergency to start your research. Keep the phone number and address stored in your cell phone so you can quickly contact and locate them if an accident happens.

Photo Courtesy of
Natalie McGuigan

Photo Courtesy of Katherine Hanke

Puppy Training

Also, within the first month or two of dog ownership, you'll want to find a puppy training class for your new Cockapoo. All dogs should go through some training course, but this is especially important for smart breeds like the Cockapoo. There are many benefits to continuous training, which will be covered in detail in later chapters.

A puppy training course is a good way to learn how to train a new dog, especially if you don't have a lot of experience with training. Every dog is different, and if you've trained a dog in the past, you might find that your Cockapoo has a different personality with a different learning style. A trainer-led session is great for picking up tips and tricks for turning your Cockapoo puppy into an obedient adult.

These classes will focus on the very basics of obedience. You'll likely practice walking your dog on a leash without pulling and simple commands like "sit" and "down". Your puppy is still learning on how to live with a human, so it takes a lot of practice for them to realize that they need to listen to you and follow your lead. A puppy class won't necessarily prepare them for the show ring, but it will give them a good foundation on which to build their training. Also, it gives the owner the opportunity to seek advice from an expert trainer. It's possible to train your dog without formal classes, but they're incredibly useful when working with a new dog.

There are tons of different trainers with different methods. If you do a quick search, you'll find trainers who conduct lessons at their home, trainers who work out of pet stores, and some that train dogs at a dog club. Any of these options are fine. When choosing a trainer, look for one that uses training methods that coincide with your values for your pup. For example, if you want to focus on using positive-only techniques, and you find a trainer that is stern and uses punishments, it's probably not a good pick. Choose a trainer that is knowledgeable and has a good reputation within the community or the club they work for.

Supplies

Before you bring your dog home, you should already have the necessary supplies on hand so you don't have to leave your dog at home alone to go shopping. It may seem like you're buying a ton of things all at once, but remember, some of these supplies will last you the entirety of your dog's life.

First, you'll need a sturdy collar and leash. A flat, buckled collar is good for daily use. You'll want something that fits snugly but is comfortable for your dog to wear every day. On this collar, you'll want to put a personalized tag on the front loop in case your dog gets lost and needs to be identified. When it comes to leashes, a four- or six-foot leash is all you'll need. Retractable leashes are popular, but they make it hard to control your dog. A strong, nylon leash that can withstand your dog's strength is perfect.

Next, you'll need dishes, food, and treats. Because Cockapoos have floppy ears, they get infected easily when they get wet. An elevated water dish allows them to drink water without it getting into their ears. Pet stores sell food and water dish platforms that lift the dishes far enough off the ground to prevent this problem. Or you might even decide to make one yourself! A good puppy formula is important for giving your Cockapoo the nutrients they need to grow into healthy adults. Later chapters will cover food and nutrition. Treats are vital to keep on hand at all times. A good treat can transform your Cockapoo from a wild animal into a perfect canine citizen. If you want to train your dog to do anything, you'll need to have some tasty treats.

Toys and chews are also important for your dog's upbringing. Cockapoos are extremely playful and love to have a good time. A variety of sturdy toys can keep their interest for hours, preventing them from acting out from boredom. You don't have to spoil your dog rotten, but a good selection of toys will make your best friend very happy. Choose a toy that's fun to chase around the yard, like a ball or a Frisbee, something that is interactive, like a tug rope, something that works their mind, like a food puzzle, and some-

*Photo Courtesy of
@cockapoograham on Instagram*

thing that gives into their animal instinct, like a squeaky toy. These basics will keep your dog from getting tired of the same old games every day.

It's also necessary for your dog to have something to chew on. Otherwise, they will gnaw on everything you own. It's only natural for dogs, especially puppies, to chew. It calms them down and keeps their mind busy. Teething puppies need to chew because it helps them work their new teeth through their gums. Choose a size-appropriate chew toy that won't break or splinter into small pieces that can be choked on. Pet stores sell different types of real and synthetic bones and animal materials to keep your dog busy.

Next, you'll need grooming supplies. A Cockapoo's fur needs to be brushed regularly to keep from getting matted. Because they don't shed a lot of fur and have a single coat, a basic pin brush should be enough to keep your dog's fur tangle-free and shiny. It might also be a good idea to keep a bottle of dog shampoo on hand in case your pup gets into something dirty or stinky. If you plan on cutting your dog's toenails, a good set of clippers will come in handy. Find a pair that cut the nail instead of crushing it. Some clippers even come with a guard that prevents you from cutting too much of the nail off if your dog gets squirmy. A toothbrush and toothpaste are also necessary for your dog's oral health. Pet stores sell brushes that are specially designed to fit a dog's mouth and come with toothpaste with dog-friendly flavors, like poultry or peanut butter.

Finally, you'll need a crate, a bed, or both for your dog's relaxation and security. A soft dog bed is a good place for your dog to chill out while she's hanging out with the family. Find one that's the right size for your Cockapoo and make sure it has plenty of padding. Crates also make excellent sleeping spots. When it comes to picking the right size, choose one large enough for your dog to be able to turn around in circles, but not so big that they can roam around. It should be like a cozy den, not a small room.

How Much Will This Cost?

All of these pet supplies can add up very quickly. When you start to factor how much your dog is going to cost you, it's enough to make your head spin. For this reason, it's important to budget for your new pet. Barring any medical complications, the first year of their life will probably be the most expensive for you. You'll have to buy all new supplies and take frequent visits to the vet for checkups and shots. Once you learn your Cockapoo's preferences, you'll be able to buy foods and treats in bulk, and you won't waste your time buying toys and chews your dog doesn't play with.

Prices for supplies and services vary from place to place. Also, it makes a huge difference in the budget if you buy a super expensive dog food compared to a bargain brand one. This estimation of how much your Cockapoo will cost in the first year of his life should be used as a general guide to give you an idea of how much you may need to spend. Of course, location and choices make a big difference in cost, but hopefully, you'll start to figure out how to budget for your pup.

First of all, to buy a Cockapoo from a good breeder, you will likely spend anywhere from $1,000 to $1,500. If you choose to adopt, you're looking at somewhere around $100 to$200, which often includes spay/neuter surgery, shots, and micro-chipping. If you buy your dog, a spay/neuter surgery is, on average, around $75.

Yearly veterinary costs will be around $200 to $500 a year for basic services. Not all vaccines are required on a yearly basis, so some visits will cost more than others. You'll also need to budget at least $100 on heartworm medication and flea and tick preventative.

Next, you'll have to buy many bags of dog food during the course of a year. The average dog eats about $400 worth of dog food per year.

Depending on which size of Cockapoo you get, you may get away with spending less than average. You'll also need lots of treats for training purposes, which will cost you about $100 a year.

Then, we have all the supplies you'll buy right away. Leashes, grooming equipment, and dishes will add up. You'll also need some fun toys and chews for your dog. In total, you're looking at spending approximately $200 around the time you bring your dog home.

It's hard to estimate how much your dog will cost you, but you could spend around $1,000 the first year, not including the dog. Over a dog's lifetime, it's said that the average person spends around $10,000 on their pup. This seems like a lot of money now, but once you get your dog adjusted into their new home, you'd spend all of your money to make your dog happy.

All of this preparation probably seems overwhelming, but you'll feel much better compared to if you didn't plan at all. It may seem like dogs require a lot of things, but they mostly just need the basics and lots of love and attention from you. In no time, you'll find yourself spoiling your little Cockapoo rotten with the best toys and the tastiest treats. After all, your Cockapoo is a member of your family now, and you'd do anything to treat them like your own.

Photo Courtesy of Glenda Stickler

CHAPTER 5
Puppy Parenting

"Two simple things are required to get a new puppy/dog. Love & patience, if you can do both of those two things, then you will do great and everything will fall into place!"

Daxon Weaver

Weaver Family Farms

Once your Cockapoo puppy is adjusted to their new home, it's time to get to work. Puppies require a little discipline so that they can grow up to be awesome adult dogs and not tiny terrors. Your aim is to be consistent, but gentle, while you show your dog how things work around your household. In the end, your Cockapoo pup will know exactly what you expect from them and will feel even more like a member of the family.

Photo Courtesy of Carolyn Long

Standing By Your Expectations

When starting out, it's so easy to come up with a list of expectations for your puppy, just to loosen the slack once you find out how much work it is to train your dog. Resist this urge to become complacent at the sight of your puppy's sweet face. You don't need to be a drill sergeant with your Cockapoo, but it's beneficial to have a clear set of rules that don't have exceptions.

For example, you may decide that you never want your dog to sleep on your bed. It's understandable that you'd want one place in your home to be clean and dog-free. So, when your puppy tries to jump on the bed, you shoo them off and teach them not to jump up there. But then you might decide that you want your pup to jump up there so you can take cute pictures on your nice bedspread. This change in the rules confuses your dog and makes them think that maybe it's okay to jump on the bed. Then, they're utterly confused when you shoo them off again later and get mad when they leave dirty paw prints on your bedding.

Dogs don't understand conditions like humans do. They can understand hard and fast rules (bed is forbidden), but they don't understand exceptions to the rules (bed is okay, only when the owner wants to take pictures). Because of this, if you make a rule for your dog, you should stick to it. Dogs do well with routine and consistency.

Crate Training

Crate training is an often-misunderstood practice that can be really beneficial to both you and your dog. Don't think of it as locking your dog in puppy prison; crates should be used to keep your dog comfortable and safe. When used correctly, a crate, or kennel, is a comfy spot to curl up and relax. It can double as a dog bed, with sturdy walls to make your dog feel protected. It's meant to be a place for your dog to sleep through the night and hang out for a few hours at a time otherwise.

Where owners go wrong is when they use it too much. Some will use it in place of human supervision and lock their dog up all day while they're at work or when the dog is misbehaving. This is not an ideal use because it teaches your dog that the crate is a bad place to go, and it could create anxiety in a Cockapoo. If your dog hates going in their crate, it has lost its utility as a safe spot for your dog to go when they get stressed.

It's normal for a puppy to be a bit wary of the crate at first, so it's your job to get them accustomed to hanging out inside. Never push them in; instead, give them space to explore on their own. Put a comfortable blanket inside and toss a tasty treat in there for your dog to snag on their own time. Do this a few times until they're ready to go inside. Next, practice spending longer quantities of time in the crate by putting food and water dishes inside. Your puppy will come to associate food time (good) with spending time in the crate. As your puppy becomes accustomed to hanging out in their crate, try closing the front gate and extend the amount of time you leave them in there. Your goal is to go a whole night without any issues.

Chewing

Especially with puppies, chewing is a necessary activity for dogs. It keeps them calm and entertained as well as cleans their teeth. Puppies will chew regardless if you want them to or not. So, it's best to redirect them from chewing on whatever they find lying around to a more suitable chew toy.

Inevitably, you will catch your Cockapoo chewing on something they shouldn't. When they do this, get their attention. You might clap loudly or say "hey" or "no" in a loud and firm voice. When they're distracted, give them a chew toy and let them continue with their appropriate chewing.

This kind of training requires you to constantly supervise your puppy. You must be watching them in order to correct their mistakes in the moment, because if you discover one of your items with old tooth marks, the teachable moment has passed. Catch your dog in the act, get their attention, and redirect them to a more appropriate item. And if all else fails, pet stores sell sprays that can be applied to furniture that are supposed to taste terrible to dogs. That kind of deterrent may help you if you turn your back on your dog for a moment.

When choosing a dog chew, make sure it's something appropriate for their size. If it's too big, a small Cockapoo won't be interested in gnawing on it. If the toy is too small, it can become a choking hazard for your dog. Pick a toy that will not break into small pieces easily. You might even consider buying different chews to keep your dog interested in chewing on bones and uninterested in chewing on your belongings.

Along with chewing, you will find that your puppy will try to bite you at one point or another. They don't do this because they want to hurt you, but because that's how they play with their puppy siblings. Over time, they'll learn how hard they can mouth another dog before it's painful, but as a puppy, they don't know that their teeth can hurt.

Photo Courtesy of Darian Mills

To correct this issue, act like a fellow puppy. If a puppy bites their brother too hard, it will respond with a yelp that signifies that the puppy caused pain. If your dog bites you, let out a high-pitched yelp or "ouch". They'll be surprised by this and will stop biting you, if only for a moment. Continue this every time their sharp puppy teeth nibble you, and they'll finally figure out that their teeth can hurt others.

Barking

Vocalizations are a dog's way of communicating with others. Your dog might bark to warn you that there's someone at the door because they sense a stranger and they want to protect you. However, it can get very annoying if your dog is constantly yapping at seemingly nothing. If you live in an apartment, it's important to teach your dog how to be quiet so you don't drive the rest of your building crazy. However, overriding your dog's natural instinct to bark at stimuli is easier said than done.

One way to deal with barking is just to eliminate all barking triggers. If your dog barks when your front blinds are open, simply shut the blinds and see if that helps. Your dog may be trying to communicate to you that they see something out there that you should be aware of (though they don't know that you're not interested in neighborhood stray cats). A doorbell is another big trigger for dogs because something exciting happens when they hear it. If your dog is a doorbell barker, teach them to lie on their bed or in their kennel when they hear the noise. This might keep them too busy to bark.

Some trainers even suggest that the best way to teach your dog not to bark is to teach them to bark on command. That way, they learn that they must be commanded to bark, and they'll understand the "no bark" command easier. However, these commands can be tough to teach to a puppy.

Another option is to get your dog's attention whenever they bark and surprise them into silence. For example, when your dog begins to bark, clap loudly or shake a bottle of pebbles. The sound will be so surprising that they'll stop barking for a second to figure out what's going on. When they're quiet, praise them and give them a treat. This will let them know that you like it when they're quiet.

*Photo Courtesy of
Vicki Kelly*

Separation Anxiety

Separation anxiety is a very real possibility with a Cockapoo. They're very family-oriented, companion-minded, sensitive creatures, so they don't like to be away from their people for very long. When they are apart from you, they can get so upset that they act out. While anxiety in dogs may take the form of crying and whining, it can cause your puppy to turn into a tornado of destruction, ripping apart furniture and going potty on the floor.

There are a few things you can do for your Cockapoo to minimize their separation anxiety. One of the biggest things you can do is be mindful of the way you exit and enter your home. If you say goodbye to your dog every time you leave and make a big show of it, it's going to get the dog wound up before you leave him alone for several hours. Or if you return from your day at work and get excited and talk in a high-pitched voice, this shows your dog that it's a big deal for you to return. Over time, this puts them on edge when you leave because they know it's serious for you not to be home. It's really fun to see your dog get excited when you come home, but the best thing you can do is act like nothing exciting is happening. Leave in the morning without hugging your dog goodbye, and return in the afternoon in a calm manner. If you pretend like there's nothing to you leaving and returning, your dog will get the idea that this is normal and there's nothing to worry about.

Another thing you can do is practice spending time apart from your dog and working up a tolerance for time spent alone. For example, if you usually let your dog ride along with you to the grocery store, leave them at home while you're gone for a little bit. When you return without incident, they'll start to understand that there's nothing to be worried about when you're away. Over time, prolong your absence until they can go a full workday without causing destruction.

Bedtime

The night can be a difficult time for your new Cockapoo puppy. They're used to being the center of attention all day, and then you ask them to be quiet for eight hours so you can get some sleep. This can be a little strange and confusing for a puppy that has been on their own schedule for they're whole life thus far.

You may decide that it's best for your dog to sleep somewhere near you so they know you haven't abandoned them. This also allows you to hear when they need to go to the bathroom in the middle of the night. However, this arrangement might not be a permanent option, as dogs tend to do things like lick themselves and scratch in the middle of the night, which can disrupt a light sleeper. As your puppy ages, start increasing the space between you and your dog at night.

Sometimes your puppy will not want to settle down when you're ready for bed, or they'll wake up and want to play shortly after retiring. To mitigate this issue, make sure your dog gets plenty of exercise before bed. Maybe go

Photo Courtesy of Mel Shaw

to the park or go on a walk in the evening to burn a bunch of energy, and then cuddle with your dog right before bed to calm them down. That way, they aren't full of pent-up energy, but they aren't still excited from playtime either.

It's also important to make sure your puppy goes potty immediately before bedtime. Their tiny bladders can only hold so much, so to increase the amount of time between potty breaks, you'll have to get them to go before bed. Using the bathroom before bed will help them get into a routine. They'll understand that going out at night is for their bathroom break, and then they'll settle down and go to sleep once they're inside.

Home Alone

A well-behaved adult Cockapoo can be trusted to stay home alone for a few hours, but puppies are another story. Puppies like to get into mischief and go to the bathroom where they please. If you have to leave your puppy home alone, here are a few tips and ideas for minimizing potential disasters.

Make sure your Cockapoo gets as much exercise as possible throughout the day. If you work away from home, take your dog for a quick walk in the morning to wake them up and get them moving. When you leave for the day, leave out fun puzzle toys for your dog to work at. This will keep them busy for a little while so they won't get bored. Chew toys are also great for entertaining your dog and they don't require your supervision. If you come home for lunch or have a sitter let your dog out, use this time to throw a ball and get your dog moving again. If your dog is tired, they are less likely to become anxious and may even nap while you're gone.

If you have issues with your puppy going potty in the house while you're gone, hiring a dog walker gives your dog the opportunity to go outside to use the bathroom midday. This means that you have fewer accidents to clean up when you get home, and your dog won't be so worried about being alone all day.

A new puppy takes a lot of work. It's easy to get frustrated at their behaviors, but they're still learning to assimilate to your household and your rules. It takes a little time for them to learn how to be a dog and how to be a pet. Be patient and stick to your training. In the end, all of your hard work in puppy raising will pay off when you have a great adult Cockapoo. Also, don't forget to enjoy your time as a puppy parent. Before you know it, your little puppy will be a grown dog!

*Photo Courtesy of
Lorraine Owen*

CHAPTER 6
Housetraining

"When housetraining your Cockapoo puppy, take note of the puppy's favorite places to relieve itself. Strategically place puppy pads or potty training pads in those favorite potty places. In addition, remember that a puppy will almost immediately urinate when it wakes up from a nap, so be prepared to pick the puppy up immediately and take him or her outside."

Alisa Foerderer
Foerderer Horses and Cock-a-poos

When you bring your new puppy home, housetraining is perhaps the top priority on your mind. Learning how to sit and stay can wait, because it's less than ideal to have little puddles of puppy pee on the carpet. It's said that a puppy can only hold their potty, in hours, for as many months are they are old. So, if your puppy is two months old, they can reasonably hold it for two hours. That keeps you on a very tight schedule of letting your dog outside to see if they need to go. Sometimes, they'll walk around on the grass and do nothing, but the second you bring them inside, they use the bathroom on your kitchen floor. It's an annoying and messy process to housetrain your dog, but if you use every moment as a lesson, you'll be past that stage in no time.

Photo Courtesy of Julie Blakeway

Different Options for Potty Training

Photo Courtesy of Sarah Vaughan

When it comes to places you let your dog go to the bathroom, outside is best. Cleaning up is easy and doesn't leave an odor behind for you to deal with. But it's not always possible to get your dog to go to the bathroom outside every single time. There are some options when it comes to housetraining.

Cockapoos are unique because they come in a wide range of sizes. If you have a mini or toy Cockapoo, their messes will be much smaller than a standard Cockapoo's. This makes the smaller versions perfect for apartment dwellers. But if you do live in an apartment, it's not so easy to find the perfect patch of grass every time your pup needs to potty. That's where potty pads and grass mats come into play.

There are products specifically designed to help little dogs do their business inside without causing a mess for you. Potty pads are absorbent sheets that you can lay on top of your floor. They contain special enzymes and smells that make your dog want to potty on it. When your dog feels the urge to go, they'll wander over to the potty pad instead of your couch. When their business is finished, all you have to do is throw the pad away. Think of it like a diaper for a dog. Even if you don't plan on indoor potty training your dog, these might be nice to have on hand, especially at night.

There are also products that are a cross between a litter box and the outdoors. These contraptions consist of a small frame with artificial grass (or real grass) inside. You teach our dog to use the mat, just as you would teach them to go potty outside. With enough practice, they'll divert all important business to their designated spot. You'll still have to clean up the mess when you get home, but at least all of the mess will be in one spot. This method is useful for owners of small dogs who cannot take them outside at their every whim.

There are some downfalls for teaching your dog to use the potty inside. While it can be very convenient, it's not ideal to have pet waste in your home. If you have a small space, the scent will eventually fill the air no matter how much cleaning you do. Also, it might be nice to have an indoor option to prevent accidents, but it might be harder to teach your dog to hold it until you get outside when he's a little older and has more control. The adjustment to the outside-only potty may be a bigger struggle than you initially anticipated.

The First Few Weeks

"I always tell people to immediately start with potty training. Cockapoos are incredibly smart so the more time you spend training them the better. Positive reinforcement and repetition are key to getting your puppy trained in a timely manner."

Jamie
Cute Cockapoos

Photo Courtesy of Linda Bareham

If you're buying your puppy from a breeder, you'll likely have your Cockapoo in your hands around the time they are two months old. This means that your puppy will want to eat and drink all the time to feed their growing body. This also causes them to turn into little waste-making machines that have very little control over their body.

Unfortunately for the owner, this means that you'll be spending a lot of those first few weeks either outside or cleaning up messes. Don't worry—with proper training, this stage will get much easier. Until then, stay vigilant about keeping an eye on your puppy.

If your puppy needs to go to the bathroom every two hours, this doesn't mean that you can set a timer for every two hours to make your trips. Your puppy does not run on an exact schedule, and accidents are bound to happen if they don't have the opportunity to go. Instead, plan to go out every hour, if possible. Walk them to their designated potty spot in your yard and let them sniff around. If they don't go, head right back inside and try again later.

You may feel like you're going outside way too often, but you'll find that you'll have fewer accidents if you maximize the opportunities for your dog to go potty.

Rewarding Positive Behavior

Cockapoos are sensitive dogs that respond well to positive reinforcement. Potty training is one of those high-stress moments that will test your patience. However, it's very important to keep your cool. Acting out in anger will confuse your poor pup and set them back in their training.

It's a common misconception that you can discourage your dog from having accidents by rubbing their nose in it. This is a harmful practice that will only make things harder on you and your dog. Dogs do not remember things in the same way humans do. If your dog has an accident and you find it after the fact, rubbing their nose in it and getting angry does not help them remember that what they did was forbidden. Instead, they'll associate their bodily function with your anger. This will lead to more accidents in hidden places because they think you'll get angry if they potty at all.

This means that you can only teach them in moments you are present for. If you find a mess when you come home from work, the only thing you can do is clean it up and try to be there for the next time your dog has to go. If you catch your dog in the process of going to the bathroom in your home, call attention to it. Clap your hands to get your dog's attention and make the effort to get them outside before they go. Over time, you'll start to learn your dog's cues that they need to go. Every time you get them outside to their special spot before they have an accident is a success and a teachable moment. Punishing them for something they did while you were not around will only cause more unwanted behavior.

Because this dog responds to positivity, you'll want to make your dog feel like the best dog in the world if they potty outside. Every single time they go to the bathroom outside, give them all the praise and affection you can. Keep yummy treats on hand to give them when their business is complete. This will reinforce the idea that they're supposed to go to the bathroom outside, so much so that the thought of going inside and not getting any treats or praise is unappealing. If your dog is play-driven, toss a ball around for a few minutes after a successful trip outside. Whatever you do, make sure they know you love it when they can make it outside to go potty.

When an accident happens, make sure to clean up the mess thoroughly. The smell of dog urine sticks around for a long time. That's why you'll notice that your dog goes to the same place in the yard almost every time. This smell signals them to return to their little bathroom time and time again. So, if you don't remove the odor from your home, they will come to know that spot as their indoor bathroom. Scrubbing will only get you so far, so remember to use a special pet mess cleaner that's designed to remove the enzymes that mark their territory. Otherwise, you'll find yourself cleaning up the same spot again and again.

Crate Training for Housetraining (and Other Tricks)

A crate is a wonderful tool that can be used for many reasons. If you are training your puppy to sleep in their crate, this can help cut down on accidents at night.

Though you may believe otherwise when your dog tears through your home, dogs are neat creatures when it comes to their own personal space. Generally, dogs dislike using the bathroom in their den. As long as the crate isn't too big for your dog, they're not going to want to go to the bathroom in there unless it is an emergency. They are more likely to wait until you let them out to go to the bathroom than they are to potty in their kennel if they can help it. This makes the crate a great place to keep them during the night. And if they do end up having an accident, you'll know exactly where you need to clean because it will all be contained within a small space.

*Photo Courtesy of
Liam Thompson*

If you don't want to crate train, you'll still want to limit the amount of space they have when you're not able to supervise them. A pen works well for these types of instances. If the space is confined enough, they will be less likely to soil their sleeping location. When you are home, give your dog plenty of room to roam around and explore. But if you have to leave for a bit, put your puppy in the pen to keep their messes under control.

Some owners also install doggie doors in hopes that their pups will be able to go outside and take care of their own business while their person is away. This can be a very helpful tool for people with a fenced-in backyard and a responsible puppy. However, if your dog requires a little more supervision, think about if you want your dog to be able to go in and out on their own accord. Puppies are adventurous creatures, and you may change your mind about the doggie door once they hunt their first baby animal and leave it for you as a present!

Especially in the first few months, you might find yourself wishing you had purchased an adult dog. Don't despair; the worst of your puppy training will soon be over. Then, you'll look back and miss the days that your puppy was so small! During this period, try to spend as much time as you can supervising your dog so you can create as many teaching moments as possible. If your dog has accidents (and they will) keep calm and clean it up. When your dog successfully uses the bathroom outside, let your dog know how loved she is. With lots of repetition, your Cockapoo will eventually get the hang of house-training and you'll never have to worry about an accident again.

CHAPTER 7
Socialization

Socialization is such an important part of raising a well-adjusted dog, but it is often forgotten about. With so many books and classes that talk about formal obedience training, owners forget there is more to a good dog than being able to sit when told.

When it comes to your dog, socialization is the ability of your dog to get along with others. This includes other people and dogs. This process is best done when your puppy is around 4-7 months old, but you can still work on socialization skills at any age. Cockapoos are usually friendly towards others, but your dog will still require a lot of practice around others.

Photo Courtesy of Carolyn Young

The Importance of Socialization

When you go out in public, you want your dog to be calm and get along with other people and dogs. You don't want your dog to be fearful or aggressive when a stranger wants to pet your Cockapoo. A trip to the dog park can be a nightmare if your dog can't get along with others. If your dog is not socialized, you'll find that you can't take them out in public because they won't respond well. You'll worry about how your dog will react if you have friends over. With a poorly socialized dog, it'll be hard to add another dog to your household in the future. In short, your life and your dog's life will be tougher if you don't take the time to socialize your pooch properly.

Cockapoos aren't typically fearful dogs, but they are sensitive. Sometimes, this sensitivity can manifest as fear if they're unable to make sense of the world around them. Your job as an owner is to help them apply some context to the things they see or hear. You want to show your dog that the world isn't so scary and that the things they're experiencing are perfectly safe.

Your attitude matters when it comes to keeping your dog calm. Dogs can pick up on non-verbal cues very well. Your posture, the tension on the leash, and even the tone of your voice send messages to your dog. For example, a soft, low voice may signal that you're calm. A stern voice can signal that you're not messing around. A high-pitched voice relays a message of anxiety or excitement. Some trainers say that your dog can read you through the leash. This is to say, if you're guiding your dog, think about the slight cues you're sending to your pup.

Treats are also very helpful when it comes to teaching your dog that something is okay. Dogs learn through conditioning, so if they're rewarded for specific behaviors, they will associate the action with the reward.

For example, maybe your dog gets nervous at dog parks and wants to run back to the car right after you get past the gate. You want your dog to be able to get exercise and play with other dogs, so you need to change their perception that the dog park is a scary place. When you get to the park, you might give your dog a treat for getting out of the car and staying calm. You can give your dog another treat when they make it to the gate, or they go inside and turn around and run. Every little step that your dog takes to face their fear, they get a reward for staying calm. With enough practice (and treats,) they should get to the point where they associate the formerly scary thing with an awesome reward.

Fear of everyday occurrences, like hanging around strangers or other dogs, is not good for your Cockapoo. Not only does stress negatively affect your dog's overall well-being, but it can be dangerous to others. Fear is not always expressed as cowering in the corner or hiding under

Photo Courtesy of
Jackie Meredith

the bed. Fear can be a dog on the edge that is willing to attack just to protect themselves from a perceived danger. A dog might not know how to play with other dogs, so when a friendly dog comes up to roughhouse with your dog, your dog might panic and attack because they haven't had the proper experiences. Or if a child runs up to your dog and wants to pet them on the head, your pooch may snap at their little hands because they don't know what's going to happen to them. In either case, your dog cannot learn that fighting back is an acceptable response to new experiences. The last thing you want is for your dog to hurt another human or animal.

But, if you expose your dog to enough different experiences in a positive manner, your dog will be less likely to act out of fear. Take your dog to different places and let them interact with different people and animals. Make them feel comfortable by keeping calm and behaving like everything is normal. Bring treats along and reward your dog when they're relaxed and responding to you. Start slow and let your dog hang out with one other dog or invite a friend over to meet your dog. If that goes well, increase the number of new people your dog meets. As long as your dog is doing well, increase the stakes until you're comfortable with your dog being anywhere.

Of course, try not to push your dog if they're not ready. It can be frustrating if your dog can't get along with others, but forcing them to do something they really don't want to do for the sake of progress can be dangerous. You may understand that your dog isn't in any real danger, but they don't understand that until they learn otherwise.

Behavior Around Other Dogs

While you may be confident that your Cockapoo is a precious angel who would never hurt a fly, you may not be so sure about all the other dogs out there. It's normal to be concerned about your dog when introducing them to other pups, but you have to keep your anxiety to a minimum for the sake of your dog. Otherwise, they will learn to be hesitant around others, too. Part of socialization practice is learning how to behave around your dog while they are learning how to behave around other dogs!

For your dog's safety, keep the dogs on leashes to start. That way, if a scuffle erupts, you can quickly separate the dogs and lead them to a space for them to calm down. But, this doesn't mean that you have to keep a tight leash and stand close to your dog while they sniff the other dogs. Give them their space and allow them to walk to the end of the leash to greet the other dog. It can be a natural reaction to have one hand on your dog to reassure them, but unless they're in danger, they can be given some space to socialize.

If that goes well, you can let your dog off their leash and let them play. As you'll find out, letting your dog run around with a friend is a great way for them to get the exercise and mental stimulation they need. Again, give your dog a little space, but watch all dogs involved for cues that things are headed in a rough direction.

For a new dog owner, it can be hard to distinguish between play behaviors and fighting behaviors. If you freak out and jump in when your

Photo Courtesy of
Sarah Johnson

63

Photo Courtesy of Morrigan Harvey

dog is just playing rough, you'll create some confusion.

As a general rule, if your dog is wagging their tail, that's a good sign. Dogs will also make a bowing motion towards other dogs that is like an invitation to play. Dogs will occasionally make biting motions towards another dog's neck, but this is done with a gentle mouth. You may even find that your dog isn't really making contact, but almost "pretend biting" at their friend. These are all cues that your dog is happy and having fun.

You'll need to watch out for the signs that your dog's not having a great time. These include sounds, such as snarling, snapping, and whimpering. A tail between the legs is another good sign that your dog is afraid. Bared teeth and raised hairs on the back of their neck are a sign that they're about to become aggressive. Because a fight with a dog can set their socialization back, try to intervene before things get too out of hand.

If your dog rolls over on their back and exposes their belly to another dog, it's a way of surrendering. This is a sign that your dog is not very comfortable with their role in the group of dogs. This signals to other dogs that your pup is not interested in their games and does not want to challenge anyone. The other dogs should understand this sign and leave your dog alone, as it is clear they do not want to participate in play.

If your dog does well with their socialization practice, make sure to reward them. But, you'll probably find that being able to play with a friend is enough of a reward for them. Even if you don't spend a lot of time around other dogs in your regular schedule, it's still important for your dog to get along with others. You never know when an opportunity will arise where your dog needs to be able to behave around others of his own kind. Because socialization is most effectively done while the dog is a puppy, you don't want to regret not taking your dog to the dog park for practice while you had the chance.

Properly Greeting New People

Unless you and your Cockapoo live under a rock, your dog will interact with other humans frequently. Whether your dog needs to greet a friend or the mailperson, you'll want them to be on their best behavior. But if your sensitive dog is occasionally anxious, they may be wary of a new smell and unfamiliar face. So it's important to teach them that it's okay to interact with all types of people.

Socialization with people is similar to socializing with dogs, but hopefully, people will be easier for you to control. If your puppy is a little nervous, it's a good idea to let strangers know this. That way, they'll approach your dog slowly and gently and not try to give them a big hug when your dog isn't ready for that kind of interaction.

When teaching your dog how to interact with people, have the person come towards your dog and have them offer the back of their hand for your dog to sniff. Have the person move slowly so your dog doesn't think they're about to be grabbed or tricked into doing something they don't want to do. If your dog is curious, let the person give them a treat or pet your dog's back. For some dogs, a head pat is too personal and only reserved for people they trust the most.

One way to get into socialization is to take your dog on a walk at places where you know you'll see other people. Bring treats along and ask passersby to give one of the treats to your dog if they are calm. You'll find that if you explain what you're doing, most people are more than willing to stop for a second to pet your adorable Cockapoo.

Once your dog has mastered this, take them somewhere with more people. Repeat this step until your dog can walk through a crowd without getting nervous. Outdoor shopping centers and farmers markets are great places to test your dog's ability to keep cool. You'll also need to remember that some dogs react differently to different people. For example, if you're a petite woman and your dog has only ever interacted with petite people or women, a large man wanting to pet your dog may freak your dog out. Make sure your dog has positive interactions with all sorts of different people, so when someone who looks a little different comes into your house, your Cockapoo won't panic.

It's best not to wait too long when it comes to the socialization process. Slowly start introducing your dog to other people and dogs in the first six months of their life. Otherwise, it's easy for them to get stuck in their own ways. If you have an adult Cockapoo that is nervous around others, not all hope is lost. You can still integrate your dog into polite society—it might just take a little extra work. Start slowly, be patient, and in no time, your dog will want to be the center of attention, no matter who they're around.

CHAPTER 8
Cockapoos and Your Other Pets

If your new Cockapoo is not your only animal, socialization is much more important than if they were an only pup. When you have other animals in your home all the time, the stakes are much higher for them to get along. Especially if you ever plan to leave your animals alone without any supervision, it's absolutely necessary for them to get along.

Introducing Your Puppy to Other Pets

A good introduction can go a long way. Introduce your new Cockapoo to your new pets before you even bring your dog home. Your old dogs may feel like they need to protect their turf if a new puppy suddenly waltzes in. This can create discord that lingers on, so it's best to make sure everyone is happy from the start.

As stated in the chapter about your puppy's first few weeks, it's good to start this process slow and have your pets meet in neutral territory. A park, a friend's house, or even your breeder's home is a good place to let your pets get to know one another. Then, once they feel comfortable and can behave themselves, let them get acquainted in your home.

During this period, supervision is a must. Your Cockapoo might be just fine when you're watching, but an animal's behavior can change in an instant when their owner isn't looking. Don't be surprised if you leave the room for a minute and come back to a commotion. Because you don't want any of your pets to be harmed by a simple misunderstanding, it's important for someone to be there at all times in the early days.

If you have a dog, this process may go smoothly. After all, your puppy will have spent a little time around other dogs. It's a lot less likely that your new Cockapoo has spent time with a cat, though. It's not impossible for cats and dogs to get along. Many times, they coexist in a home with no issues. However, it's likely that your dog has no idea how to act around a cat, and your cat will not be amused by a little puppy sniffing them and disrupting their peace.

The introduction between your Cockapoo and your cat may be a little different because many cats are generally disinterested in playing with dogs. If you can get them in the same space without a catastrophe, this is a win. Try to let your puppy get a good sniff of the cat so he can figure out what the heck that furry non-dog is, but not so close that he'll get his nose scratched.

*Photo Courtesy of
Kelly Collins*

With these interactions, you want to be positive that your Cockapoo is not going to think the cat is prey and try to give chase. A dog can seriously injure another animal. Always make sure your cat has an exit strategy if your dog gets too rough. A cat tree is good for keeping your cat out of reach, but a room that your cat can escape to is also great for the early months when your dog hasn't entirely figured out what cats are all about.

Over time, you'll feel more comfortable leaving your pets home alone for short periods of time. Remember to utilize all of the resources you have until then. Gates work well for separating animals that might not get along immediately. Also, pet sitting services or doggy daycares can be used to give your pup a little more supervision until they figure out how they're supposed to behave.

Pack Mentality

Though the dogs of today are far removed from their canine ancestors, a lot of trainers use concepts from how wolf packs operate for domesticated dogs. These rules of order amongst dogs are not hard and fast rules, but they may give you an idea of why your dog acts the way they do.

In a dog pack, there is a leader, or alpha. This alpha keeps the other dogs in line. He is dominant and puts the other dogs in place. Because there is a leader, the other dogs are followers with different degrees of submissiveness. These dogs do not try to take control, but follow along with the pack.

Dominance and submission in dogs is not necessarily a bad thing. People often mistake dominance for aggression and submission for fear. While it's possible for a dog to have both traits, they are not mutually exclusive. Some dogs just feel comfortable in different roles; it does not necessarily mean they are aggressive if they're a leader or a wimp if they're a follower.

Once your dog becomes integrated within their new "pack" of dogs in your home, you'll start to notice a hierarchy develop. One of your dogs may try to take control and make the rules. This is natural and perfectly fine as long as no one is getting hurt.

Remember if your dogs form their own pack with different levels of leadership, you still need to be the alpha dog. When you go on walks with your pack, you choose the direction. When it's suppertime, you should eat first before feeding your dogs. Small gestures show your pups that you're still in charge, even though the pack has new members.

Fighting

Sometimes you do everything right and you still notice your dogs fighting. When this happens, it's important to break it up quickly before things get dangerous. If you're around your dogs, it's likely that you'll notice the signs of an impending fight before it even happens. You may hear growling and see your dog's teeth bared. They will also be making eye contact with the dog they plan on fighting.

The first thing you want to do is to break the eye contact between dogs. It's not always safe to walk in between two dogs ready to brawl, so use your best judgment. Try making a loud noise to break the dogs from their trance. If this doesn't work, try to make a barrier between the two dogs or pull them away—anything to get them to stop staring at each other. Again, be careful, because you don't want to get caught in be-tween two dogs when they start fighting.

Photo Courtesy of
Neil Cauldwell

If you missed the warning signs and the dogs have started to fight, you need to safely separate them. If your dog happens to be on a leash, give a quick tug and lead the dogs away from each other. If they aren't on a leash, grab your dog's back legs and walk them away from the fight like a wheelbarrow. This keeps your hands away from their teeth and temporarily disables them from being an effective fighter. Once the dogs are separated, they need time apart to cool down. Send one dog to the backyard and keep the other one inside. Or, place the dogs in separate rooms so they don't have the opportunity to lock eyes again. When they've spent enough time away, let them return to the same area of the house and watch them closely. With any luck, whatever triggered the fight has been long forgotten. Don't worry about pushing your dogs together to "make up" after a scuffle. In this situation, it's best to just pretend like nothing happened.

The Dangers of Buying Littermates

If one new Cockapoo puppy is good, then two must be great, right? You may have decided that you would like to have two Cockapoos in your home. There's nothing wrong with having two dogs of the same breed and around the same age. These dogs make excellent companions to people and to each other. They can keep each other company and entertain each other while you're not home. But, it's not a good idea to take on multiple puppies from the same litter.

First of all, it's a ton of work to have just one puppy. Now, imagine doubling up on all the work you have to do. That's double the accidents, double the trips outside in the middle of the night, and double the tiny teeth marks on your furniture. It's not impossible to raise two puppies at once, but unless you have a ton of time, energy, and experience raising puppies, it's not ideal.

Also, many dog owners don't realize that owning two siblings from the same litter isn't a good thing. One might think that littermates would get along better than dogs from separate litters, but this is not often the case. Many trainers recommend not buying littermates because they can be difficult to deal with.

This is evident when it comes time to train your dogs. Littermates are often distracted by each other because they're so close. They just don't have the same focus as dogs from different litters do. If you sign up for a class, your trainer might not even let you bring both dogs to the same training session. You'll grow frustrated constantly split your time between pups just to teach them simple commands.

Photo Courtesy of
Marita Boast

Littermates also have increased separation anxiety if they have to be apart. For example, you might need to take one pup to the vet but not the other. In the meantime, both dogs are going to freak out because they're apart from their mate. This anxiety can make them difficult to work with or bring out destructive behaviors.

It's not impossible to raise littermates, but it's definitely not ideal. If you're set on getting two Cockapoos, consider buying one and getting them past the early puppy stage before buying another. This way, you don't have to spend all of your time raising puppies, and they won't suffer from Littermate Syndrome.

What if My Pets Don't Get Along?

It's not uncommon for an owner's pets to not get along with a puppy right away. Perhaps your dogs are older and feel the need to whip your puppy into shape. Or maybe there's something in your dog's DNA that makes it hard for them to get along with other dogs. Whatever the issue is, it's important to get everything settled before one of your pets gets hurt.

Try to create space between your pets. Maybe the issue is that they're cooped up in the same room and have to stare at each other all day. Give them separate parts of the house to hang out in so they don't feel like they're constantly competing for space. Crates and gates can help create distance in a small home. You might even take your dogs on separate walks or take them to separate training classes so they have some time apart (and quality time with you).

If nothing you've tried is working, it's time to come up with a plan to prevent the worst from happening. Consult with a trainer or dog behavioral specialist to meet your dogs and diagnose the problem.

If you absolutely can't keep your pets from fighting, you have a tough decision to make. It can be very hard to give up a dog, but their life may depend on it. If nothing you do is working, a new home for one of your dogs is better than having one get seriously injured by the other.

A Cockapoo can be an excellent addition to your dog-friendly household because the breed is good with other dogs. However, it's important to do whatever you can to make all pets feel loved and taken care of. Slowly work your new Cockapoo into your household so your other pets aren't threatened or confused. Once your new dog is home, watch everyone carefully to prevent altercations. Never force your animals to be together if they don't want to, and give them plenty of options for having their own space. Most importantly, keep calm and allow your dogs the time they need to become friends. If you show your old dogs that a new puppy is a good thing, they'll be more likely to believe you than if you constantly fret and hover over them. In no time, your pup will be the best of friends with the animals you already call family.

CHAPTER 9
Exercise

"Cockapoos are smart and can get bored easily which can lead to naughty behavior. It's vital to spend a lot of time playing with and exercising your puppy."

Jamie

Cute Cockapoos

Photo Courtesy of Stuart Baynham

When it comes to giving your dog something to do, exercise is non-negotiable. All dogs, no matter their size or breed, require some sort of activity to keep them moving. Daily exercise is an integral part of your dog's physical and mental health. Without it, they can pack on the pounds or even become anxious. Cockapoos are lively dogs, so they'll need an outlet for their energy to be happy and healthy.

The idea of frequent exercise can be daunting, especially if you're not so active yourself! Exercise for a dog doesn't necessarily mean going for a jog, though it's a quick way to burn energy in a hyper pup. Exercise can be a gentle walk, a long game of fetch, or an afternoon at doggy daycare roughhousing with friends. And if you're not in the best shape, a dog is the perfect motivation to get fit.

Cockapoos make great pets because they don't require a ton of exercise compared to other breeds. And the smaller the Cockapoo, the less exercise they will require because a toy Cockapoo's little legs can only go so far. You can still take these dogs on long walks, but they won't require as much exercise as a breed like a Border Collie might. This makes them a good pet for a first-time dog owner or someone with limited space in their home.

*Photo Courtesy of
Adele Donaldson*

Exercise Requirements

Try to get your dog outside a few times during the day. If you have a fenced-in backyard, you can allow your dog to get little spurts of exercise throughout the day. Otherwise, a walk in the morning and evening will suffice. These don't necessarily have to be particularly long walks either. After spending some time with your dog, you'll be able to determine how much exercise they need. A quick morning walk is a great time to get your dog to go to the bathroom after a long night of holding it. It also gives them the opportunity to stretch their legs and spend some time with you after they wait all night for you to wake up.

If your dog suffers from separation anxiety, some strenuous exercise can help them remain calm when you leave the house. A tired dog is the best-behaved dog because they don't have a ton of energy built up inside them. Exercise-starved dogs may be destructive because they don't have a positive outlet for their energy. If your dog is frantic when you leave the house in the morning, it might help to load up the early morning with exercise so your Cockapoo is more likely to rest after you leave for work. A longer walk, a quick jog, or even some time playing fetch will help your dog relax.

Then, in the evening, give your dog plenty of opportunities to play and burn some energy. If you're out of the house all day, they're going to want to play and be right by your side until bedtime. A long walk in the evening can get their legs going to the point where they'll be happy to snuggle next to you for the rest of the evening. In addition, a trip to the dog park or playing games in the backyard will make for one very happy Cockapoo.

When giving your dog exercise, make sure there is plenty of cool water available. Dogs don't sweat like people do, so they can overheat fairly easily. Also, dogs cannot tell you when they're feeling tired. Often, they're just so excited to be out and about that they don't show any signs of exhaustion until they really can't handle any more activity. If you live in a particularly hot location, consider waiting until a cool part of the day to give your dog the bulk of their exercise requirements. Also, if it's a hot and sunny day, feel the concrete with your bare feet. If it's too hot for you to walk without shoes, it's too hot for your dog to walk on the concrete. Dogs hide their discomfort very well, so you may not know your dog is in pain unless symptoms develop. When it comes to extreme weather, be mindful of your dog's comfort.

Photo Courtesy of Anne

Types of Exercise to Try

Dog exercise can be much more than going on walks. Switching up your dog's exercise routine can keep them from getting bored with one activity. There are so many fun things to do with your dog, so it's great to try a wide range of activities to see what your dog enjoys the most.

If you have a backyard or access to another large, grassy space, there are many games you can play to challenge your dog's coordination and skills. Tennis balls are a great toy to toss into the air to get your dog to practice their catching skills, or launch them as far as you can to see how fast your dog can run. Frisbee can also be a challenging game that will work your dog's coordination as well as your own. When choosing backyard games to play, you'll want to have a variety of toys on hand to keep your dog from getting bored with the same old stuff.

If you live near a body of water, swimming might be something your dog will enjoy. Not all dogs like water, so it's important to let your dog dip their toes in and decide how they feel before tossing them in. If your dog takes to the water like a fish, you might want to invest in a doggy life jacket to protect your furry friend. Even if your dog is a strong swimmer, they might overexert themselves and find themselves too far from shore. Life vests come in all sizes, so you should be able to find one that fits your

*Photo Courtesy of
Lee Carpenter*

Photo Courtesy of Karen Bird

Cockapoo. Of course, it's important to remember to dry their ears after a dip because trapped water can lead to infection.

If you enroll in training courses, you may find that your Cockapoo is awesome at organized sports for dogs. Your Cockapoo may not be the fastest or strongest dog out there, but that doesn't mean that they can't participate in fun competitions. These dogs are reasonably easy to train, so you might consider enrolling them in an agility course to test their skills. They'll practice running up and down ramps, weaving through pylons, and sprinting through tunnels. They'll get so much satisfaction in learning how to do the different obstacles and will love how excited you get when they do an awesome job. Most dog clubs offer beginning agility classes that can be a great opportunity to test your dog's ability. Flyball is another dog sport that your Cockapoo might enjoy. This is like a relay race for dogs. Each team has four dogs that take turns relaying a ball from one side of the room to the other. This sport is generally dominated by large, active dog breeds, but that doesn't mean that your Cockapoo can't participate. You might even be able to find a class that allows them to learn the skills they need to play the game.

Especially in the winter months when you might not be able to go outside very often, a membership to a dog club or an indoor dog park can be very beneficial. Your dog may have more energy in the cooler months, but if they don't have somewhere to go to burn that energy, they will come up with their own destructive games. A facility for dogs is nice for getting your dog out of the house and moving, especially when the weather is not suited for walks.

Mental Exercise

Photo Courtesy of Mandy Watson

Many dog owners don't take into account the mental energy their pooch has. With intelligent breeds like Cockapoos, it's necessary to make sure their minds are being worked as hard as their bodies. Intelligent breeds are fun to work with, but if they don't get the stimulation they need, they can become naughty. Because they get bored easily, they will make up their own games if they don't get what they need from you. These games often involve the destruction of your belongings because they're using whatever they can find as entertainment. If you have to leave your dog alone for any length of time, it's a good idea to make sure their minds are attended to as well as their physical needs.

Fortunately, there are a lot of products out there that can help you with this task. Try out a few different "food puzzles" for your pooch. The original Kong is a popular choice because it's fun for dogs of all abilities. This is a rubber toy that's something between a ball and a cone that can be filled with cheese, peanut butter, or little treats. Because of the toy's shape, it requires a little work to get the treats to fall out. Your dog will need to use their brain to figure out how to lick, toss, or drop the toy to get the treat out. Another food-driven toy, often used for fast eaters, is a ball that can be filled with their kibble. They must push the ball around with their nose to get a few pieces to fall out. One meal could take them thirty minutes of play to finish.

If your dog is looking for a challenge, there are puzzle boards that can be filled with treats to entice your dog to figure out how the contraption works. There are so many varieties out there, but many will require your dog to slide plastic disks, open drawers, and pull levers to get their prize. Raise the stakes and hide the highest-value treat you have to motivate them to work. When your Cockapoo has mastered one, try a new toy with different obstacles.

Training is also a good way to keep your dog's brain active. As long as you make training fun, your dog will enjoy learning and practicing new commands. If you spend 10 to 20 minutes a day working on commands, you'll be amazed at how many cool tricks your pup can learn. This makes them feel like they have a job and a purpose, which will prevent them from using that time for destructive behavior.

Especially when the weather prevents you from going outside, you might want to try to play hide and seek with your dog. Once they learn how to sit and stay, place them in one part of your house. In the meantime, hide in a different room and call them. Wait until they sniff you out, and then give them treats and praise. Repeat this until they get tired of the game. A variation of this game is to hide toys around the house and command them to find their toy. If they get good at this, you can try to teach your dog the names of several toys and command them to retrieve a specific one by name.

Tug is another activity that combines physical and mental exercise. Hand your dog one end of a rope toy and have them pull on the other end. It won't take long for your dog to figure out what to do. Wiggle the rope back and forth and try to trick them into letting up and allowing you to win. This will challenge them to outwit you and win the toy. Some dogs get pretty riled up with this game, so make sure your dog knows that you're in control. Always be the one to initiate the game and let them know when the game is over.

There are so many activities you can do with your Cockapoo that will keep them happy and healthy. Aim for at least thirty minutes of physical exercise and thirty minutes of mental exercise a day. Of course, your dog will want to play as much as possible. Especially in warm weather, keep an eye on your dog and watch for signs of exhaustion. Avoid pushing your dog beyond their capability.

Exercise doesn't have to be a chore for the owner, either. Having a dog is a great excuse to explore different places and to spend time out in nature. Your dog will enjoy getting out to see and smell new things, and you can relax while getting some gentle exercise. Your dog will love spending quality time with you, and you'll enjoy making your pooch as happy as can be!

CHAPTER 10
Training Your Cockapoo

"Schedule is very important, animals especially dogs run on nature's clock, when you choose a schedule roll with it and try to not change it! They will learn very quickly over time when it is time to go outside to use the bathroom, what time is chow time, and when it is bed time!"

Daxon Weaver

Weaver Family Farms

Photo Courtesy of Lucy Russell

One of the most important things you can do for your dog is obedience train them early in their life. There are many benefits to good training, but perhaps the most important is that it will make both you and your pup happy. It's easy to come up with a bunch of training plans in the early days, only to become complacent as life gets in the way. However, your relationship with your dog depends on their understanding of your expectations and their good behavior. Without training, your Cockapoo is just an animal.

If this is your first dog, it's easy to get overwhelmed. You might find that it's simple to get your dog to sit, but impossible to get them to walk on a leash. When your dog is misbehaving, it's too easy to get frustrated and want to give up. Stick with it! Some dogs need a little extra time with certain commands and behaviors. Positivity and patience will get you far when it comes to dog training.

82

Clear Expectations

In the beginning, decide what you want from your Cockapoo. This is totally up to you as the owner and your preference when it comes to their pet. You may decide that you want your dog to be able to compete in obedience competitions. Or you may just want your dog to be able to sit and stay when needed. Whatever you decide, come up with reasonable expectations for training. If you don't have the time to take classes or practice at home, it's not very reasonable to expect your dog to have perfect behavior. Or if you get angry at your dog every time they mess up, it's unlikely that they will want to learn new tricks. Understand that it will take a lot of time and effort into turning your new Cockapoo into a polite member of society.

Operant Conditioning Basics

Though it may appear that your dog can understand everything you tell him, dogs do not understand what we say like a human child might. When you're training a dog, they don't necessarily hear a command and know why you want them to do that thing. Instead, it's more of a knee-jerk reaction from practicing so many times. If you're familiar with basic psychological concepts, you'll know that dogs are trained through operant conditioning.

In short, operant conditioning requires a response for every action, either positive or negative. One classic demonstration of operant conditioning is done with rats in cages. A cage is outfitted with a lever. Obviously, the rat has never experienced levers before and doesn't know what to do with one. Eventually, the rat will meander over and push the lever. When this happens, a piece of food falls out. The rat will come to understand that every time they push the lever, they get food. Soon, they'll do nothing but work the lever until their little bellies are full of treats.

On the other hand, a second lever might be introduced. This one gives the rats a little shock when they push it. Because they don't like this, they'll learn that it's better to stick to the lever that gives them food. The shock is so unpleasant that they'll learn to avoid it, even though the other lever gives food. Soon, they'll learn which lever to push and which lever to leave alone.

Your dog's brain works in a similar manner. When you apply some type of reinforcement to their behavior, they will learn that some behaviors are wanted, and some are not. With enough repetition, you can apply a command and see a result from your dog. Remember,

Photo Courtesy of Maria McNamara

your dog doesn't hear "Sit" and understand the meaning of the word as if they suddenly understand human language. Instead, they've figured out that you like when they put their bottom on the floor when they hear that particular sound from you.

As your dog's primary trainer, you're the one in charge of handing out reinforcements to teach your dog how to behave. Because dogs respond best with positive reinforcements, these reinforcements are known as rewards. When your dog does something good, even by accident, you need to reward them to their brain can make the connection between the action and the reward.

If you're teaching your dog a basic command, like Sit, you'll want to manipulate them into the proper position. When they hit their mark, give them some type of reward. When you give the treat, you can say something like "Good sit!" Repeat this a few times, take a break, and repeat it again. When they do what you want, make sure they are rewarded with whatever motivates them the most.

Once your dog starts to understand what is going on, add the command. Say "Sit" and move them into the position. Then reward and repeat the command:"Good sit!" This process will take a while, so make sure to practice regularly. The end goal is for your dog to hear the command and do the action without any rewards needed—it should just become second nature.

Some dog trainers will also use negative reinforcements to prevent unwanted behavior. An example of this would be to use a pronged collar or shock collar when going on walks. The rationale behind this is that the dog is doing something dangerous on walks (like chasing cars) and will correct this behavior if an unpleasant deterrent is added. When your dog does something you don't like, they'll instantly be alerted with a negative response that they'll find uncomfortable and try to avoid the behavior that warranted that response. However, this practice is controversial amongst dog trainers. If done incorrectly, this method may have a negative effect.

Primary Reinforcements

Not all reinforcements are created equally when it comes to your unique Cockapoo. Once you start to get to know your dog, you'll learn which rewards make them go wild and which ones are ignored. Primary reinforcements are rewards that are good in and of itself. These rewards have immediate value to your dog. Treats, playtime, and toys are all examples of primary reinforcement.

The best reinforcement is something that really makes your dog go nuts. For some, this is a smelly dog treat. For others, it's a favorite toy. When your reward holds your dog's attention and can make them do whatever you want, you've found the right reward.

Photo Courtesy of
Louisse O'Neill

To really raise the stakes, try to find a special reward and make it scarce. If you use the same old treats or toys all the time, your Cockapoo might lose interest. You want something very special and exciting. While your dog may enjoy playing fetch with a tennis ball, is it as exciting as a stuffed animal that makes all kinds of exciting sounds? Are your training treats too similar to their usual food, or is it something extremely fragrant and tasty?

You'll find that most dogs respond to treats, but not all dogs will do tricks for just any edible thing. If your dog doesn't go for the basic treats, you'll have to find something extra special. You may go through a few different flavors before you figure out what your dog prefers. Moist training treats give off more odor than dry biscuits, so your dog might respond better to something with a little moisture in it because they can smell the reward and know what's at stake if they do a good job. Some owners even use cut up pieces of hotdogs as rewards because they're an extra special treat. Whatever you decide to use as your primary reinforcement, make sure it's exciting and always on hand.

Secondary Reinforcements

Secondary reinforcements are rewards that don't necessarily have intrinsic value but are still rewarding for a dog. You can think of secondary reinforcements as currency. On its own, paper money doesn't have any value. But we can give value to money when we trade it in for tangible items. Examples of secondary reinforcements in dog training include praise and clickers as markers of good behavior.

Because we're not made of an endless supply of dog treats, it's good to create rewards that don't always rely on food to get results. Auditory markers can let your dog know that they're doing something good without having to stop and hand over a treat. Over time, treats can pack on the pounds and can create a dent in your budget. However, this kind of training initially requires primary reinforcements to give meaning to the secondary reinforcements.

For example, a clicker is a small device that emits a sound when you push the button. When you start clicker training, give your dog a treat and a click when they do something good. Repeat the process until your dog learns that a click is meant as a reward. Then, you can give your dog just a click when they've done well, and treats can be used intermittently.

The same can be done with a voice cue. "Yes" is a common one because it's short and precise. When your dog sits, say "Yes" and give a treat. Over time, your dog will learn that your verbal cue means that they're doing a good job. That way, if you find yourself without a treat, you can reward them without giving them food.

Dangers of Negative Reinforcements

Negative reinforcements are part of operant conditioning, but you may decide that you don't want to use them with your dog. There is a thin line between self-correction and punishment, and you don't want to cross it.

Cockapoos are sensitive dogs, so they are less likely to require negative reinforcements. In fact, this kind of training may do more harm than good. Their sensitivity applies to their interactions with you. They are likely to respond to your happiness or anger. If they perceive your behavior as anger, they may become afraid of you. There are some breeds that hardly care if you're upset at them—the Cockapoo is not one of them. These little guys just want to make their owner happy, so if you do something that shows you're upset, they might get upset, too.

Photo Courtesy of
Lily House

Pain is a negative reinforcement and should not be used on dogs. This can lead to fear, which will ruin your training progress. Hitting a dog will not necessarily teach the dog to avoid bad behaviors. Instead, it will teach your dog to avoid you at all costs. If your dog is avoiding you out of fear, he is less likely to absorb your training lessons. You want your dog to be able to trust you and to feel safe around you. Once you go too far with negative reinforcements, you give your dog a reason not to trust you at all.

Hiring a Trainer and Attending Classes

Hiring a trainer or going to classes is absolutely beneficial for training your dog. Even if you have a general idea of how to train a dog, an expert can really boost your training practice. You may come across issues that you don't know how to resolve but your trainer has encountered many times before. Chances are that you've probably only ever worked with a few dogs in your life. Trainers, on the other hand, work with multiple dogs every day. They have the experience to help you with any problem that pops up along the way. They're also great at reassuring you when you're feeling stressed about your dog's behavior.

Group classes are also great for helping your dog socialize with others. Your dog doesn't necessarily have to get too close to the other dogs during class, but they'll have to relax enough to learn with lots of canine distractions around them. As you'll find when you work with your dog, it's one thing to train without distractions and another to train in a strange place with lots of people and dogs around.

There are many trainers to choose from, and all of them have slightly different ideas about the best way to train a dog. Some are good, while others will not be the right fit for you and your dog. If you're completely lost on where to start, talk to a fellow dog owner and ask for recommendations. You'll want someone who believes in positive training practices and is widely recommended by others. You're essentially trusting this person to do what's best for your dog, so you want the right trainer for the job. If the trainer is too focused on strange tactics and is very stern with dogs, they might be too harsh for a Cockapoo. But if the trainer uses positive-only or very gentle corrections, they're probably best suited to work with you as you train your dog.

Owner Behavior

Don't forget, your dog is constantly watching you and trying to make sense of your reactions to their behavior. They will soon understand when you're happy and when you're angry. This breed loves to see you happy. They're companion animals and will want to be by your side at all times. If you're angry with them while you train because you're frustrated by their behavior, they're not going to want to train anymore. However, when you're dealing with a little creature with a mind of its own, you're inevitably going to become frustrated.

To combat this frustration, remember that your dog is not a tiny human. They do not learn and understand things in the same way we do. To us, it's obvious that unwanted behaviors can be harmful. To a dog, they're just acting out of instinct and will continue to do so until they learn otherwise.

Also, remember that training doesn't happen overnight. If you work on a command for a day and your Cockapoo just isn't getting it, that's perfectly normal. You may have to practice the same command every day for months before they can do it on cue. Don't give up because things seem difficult. Instead, ask for some assistance from an expert and keep practicing.

If you can't hide your disappointment or frustration, take a break. It's not worth it to get so worked up that you end up lashing out at your dog. When you feel your emotions getting out of control, take a step back with the intention of picking things back up when everyone has had the chance to cool down. Training is important, but not as important as the close bond between you and your Cockapoo.

Dog training is no easy task. It takes knowledge, practice, and a good mindset. Especially if you're new to dog ownership, it takes a while to think like a dog. They've got their own ideas and quirks that are completely foreign to humans. But once you figure out what motivates them, you're on your way to having a well-trained dog. When training, be persistent, calm, and positive, and your Cockapoo will enjoy this time you spend together.

CHAPTER 11
Dealing with Unwanted Behaviors

"Cockapoos can nip at first, which is what they do with their litter-mates, and which can be perceived as biting. It might also be caused by teething. Channel the behavior. If they perceive long periods of "isolation" (not at night of course), they can view that as separation, which can lead to anxiety. Be consistent."

Jeanne Davis
Windhorse Offering

Everyone wants a well-behaved dog. When you're at home relaxing, you want your dog to be calm and cuddly. When you want to have some fun with your dog, you'll want them to play with you and go on walks. When you go in public, you want your dog to be friendly and listen to you. And at every time in between, you want your dog to behave himself and not destroy everything you own. Unfortunately, no dog is perfect, and you'll eventually run into issues with your dog's behavior. This chapter should help you start troubleshooting your dog's naughty or confusing behavior and figure out a plan to combat it.

What is Bad Behavior in Dogs?

It's hard to create a precise definition of bad behavior because it's largely relative to an owner's preference. One owner may be fine with their dog barking at all hours of the day, while others cannot tolerate it. As an owner, you must decide how you want your dog to behave, and then take the steps to ensure that behavior is taught.

A lot of bad behavior boils down to annoying habits, destructive tendencies, and dangerous behavior. There can be quite the range of behaviors, but even the smallest bad behavior can create discord in your home.

Annoying behaviors are those that aren't necessarily going to do any serious harm but are not polite behaviors. Barking, jumping on people, and crowding the front door are a few actions that drive dog owners insane. If your dog barks every time someone walks by your house, it's not really going

Photo Courtesy of Sue Walters

to hurt anyone. If it happens once, it's not even that big of a deal. But when it happens constantly, that's where the behavior becomes a problem. Left unchecked, your dog could be barking for hours every day. You'll never be able to make a quiet phone call or sleep through the entire night. If you live in an apartment, you're disturbing everyone else who lives in your building. It can be a serious problem if it isn't caught immediately and dealt with in the right way.

Destructive behaviors ruin your property and make it impossible to leave your dog unsupervised. We all have busy lives that require us to leave the house sometimes. If your dog insists on digging, chewing, and peeing on everything you own, you're going to have problems when you can't go to the grocery store without returning to destruction. If things get bad enough, you might wonder if you can even continue to care for your dog, especially if you live in rented property.

Finally, some owners have issues with aggressive dogs that threaten humans and other animals. This is by far the most serious of the bad behaviors. You might have a mischievous dog with a high prey drive that wants to hunt your cats. Or you may have a dog that plays too rough at the dog park and tries to fight other dogs. Or your dog may be great with you but bites at other people who want to pet him. In any case, these behaviors can cause a dog to be surrendered to a shelter or worse. Other behaviors may be handled by the owner with time, but any situation in which another living being is at risk by your dog, immediate, professional help is necessary.

Finding the Root of the Problem

Your dog doesn't misbehave because they are a bad dog. There are many reasons why dogs do the things that they do. It's your job to think like a dog and figure out their motivations.

Sometimes, your dog is just acting upon natural instincts. If your Cockapoo is chasing after smaller animals, it's probably because Poodles were originally bred to hunt rats and they're just trying to do their job. Or, maybe they're digging in your yard because it's hot outside and the burrow they're creating is helping them stay cool. Or your puppy is gnawing on your table legs because they're teething and their gums hurt. Before you scold your dog, make sure all of their canine needs are being met. There's a chance that they're doing something annoying because it's in their nature to do it.

Another reason dogs are naughty is because they're bored. Especially in intelligent breeds like the Cockapoo, dogs act out because they aren't getting enough entertainment or mental stimulation. These dogs love to play and be challenged. If no one is around to play with them, they might create their own games. These fun activities can include digging, chewing, and destroying anything within reach. If you have to be away from your dog for an extended period of time, try to make sure their needs are attended to before you leave. If possible, give them a puzzle toy before you leave the house to give them some entertainment while you're away. If that's not enough for your active Cockapoo, consider taking your dog to a doggy daycare or hiring a dog walker to spend a little time with your pup. It can be expensive, but not as expensive as replacing all of your furniture.

Or your dog might be destructive because he has separation anxiety. As mentioned in earlier chapters, some sensitive dogs suffer from separation anxiety to the point that they potty in the house or destroy your belongings. If your dog makes a mess when you're not home, this might be the root of the problem. If other methods of entertaining your pooch don't work, your veterinarian may be able to suggest supplements or medications that can help your dog relax.

If your dog is aggressive, make sure that they're not afraid of other people or animals. It sounds counterintuitive, but fear is what causes a lot of animals to lash out and harm others. One way to combat this aggression is to slowly socialize your dog with others. Do whatever you can to make your dog feel more comfortable around others, to the point where people or dogs can get near your dog without them showing any signs of aggression. In the meantime, make sure your dog doesn't get too close to anyone. You will have to be under constant supervision of your dog until you can trust him to behave. In the meantime, seek help from a professional dog behavioralist to nip the dangerous behaviors in the bud.

Bad Behavior Prevention

There are a few things you can do to prevent the generalized naughty behavior. For starters, make sure you're giving your dog enough physical and mental exercise. A tired dog is a good dog, so you'll want to keep your dog active so they don't have the extra energy to be bad. Try increasing the amount of daily exercise by at least a half hour. Take longer walks, try to move a little faster, and choose strenuous games to play in between walks.

Photo Courtesy of Julie Nicklin

Also, work on your training skills. Sometimes, it just takes your dog a little practice to get into "work mode". When you've been working really hard on your commands, your dog may feel as though they have a new responsibility to behave. The extra attention and activity may be enough to keep your dog out of trouble. Similarly, group classes are filled with different sights and sounds, so an hour walking around the ring might keep your dog calm for the rest of the night.

Finally, try to maintain some consistency with your dog. If you correct your dog when they bark on some occasions, make sure you aren't lenient at other times when you don't feel like training. Every time your dog misbehaves is a learning opportunity. Correct bad behavior, then praise good behavior. Don't forget that positive reinforcement goes a long way, even when your dog is doing something wrong.

How to Properly Correct Your Dog

Photo Courtesy of Jackie Massa

Correcting your dog is different from punishment. The goal is to catch unwanted behaviors and redirect their attention towards something more acceptable. Then, once your dog's behavior has changed, you need to reinforce the good behavior. This way, you can teach your dog how to behave within the context of their natural instincts or desires.

For example, let's say that your Cockapoo runs to the front door and barks incessantly at the sound of the doorbell. This is annoying behavior that may make the visitor fearful of your dog. Naturally, you're going to want to keep them from barking, but yelling at them doesn't seem to help. In fact, it only makes them bark more.

Instead of barking back at your dog, do something to catch their attention. A loud clap, a can of rocks, or a stern "no" should hopefully be enough to confuse them for a split second. In that time, give your dog a command. "On your bed" is a good one for this situation, but a "sit" or "down" will also suffice. Do something that will reroute their mind and give them a job to do. If they can accomplish this task with your help, give them lots of treats and love. You can practice this every time someone comes to the door. With enough work, you should get to the point where your dog hears the doorbell and automatically lies on their bed, without the use of rewards.

Of course, this is all easier said than done. It takes a lot of hard work to change your dog's behaviors. That's why it's so important to properly socialize and train your puppy from the start so you can remove the opportunity to pick up bad habits. However, if you're adopting a dog that's already had time to pick up bad habits, then you might spend half of your training time correcting these quirks.

When to Call a Professional

Sometimes, we just don't have the experience or expertise to deal with the issue. Your dog's problematic behavior might get to the point where you just don't know what to do anymore. When you're at the end of your rope, find a helpful resource. A trainer, vet, or breeder may be able to point you in the right direction. Otherwise, the behavior will spiral out of control to where you might not be able to keep your dog in your home. Of course, if your dog is a danger to others, you need immediate help. Some dog trainers will even come to your home so you don't have to worry about bringing your problem dog into public spaces. No matter how minuscule or insignificant the bad behavior seems, it's always worth it to work on positive ways to correct the behavior because it will make your relationship with your dog so much better!

It can be extremely frustrating if your dog is annoying, destructive, or downright dangerous. Everyone wants their dog to be a perfect canine citizen. However, good behavior takes a lot of work. Dogs aren't naturally polite. They like to make their own rules when they can get away with it. It's your job as an owner to keep an eye on your dog and stop bad behaviors before they become habits. It can be difficult to go against their strange ideas, but there are tons of resources to help you along the way.

CHAPTER 12
Basic Commands

"Cockapoos are usually pretty easy to train. I suggest that new owners find a basic puppy obedience class once the puppy is protected by the usual puppy vaccinations. The owners can benefit learning training techniques at the basic obedience class. It will enhance the experience of raising a puppy."

Linda S. Oberling
Cockapoos by Choice

Cockapoos are amazing, intelligent dogs that can do so many cool things. When you work hard on training, there's no limit to what your dog can learn. When you're just starting out with your new dog, it's good to master a few basics before moving on to the fun tricks. This chapter will cover a few of the most important basic commands to teach your dog and give a few tips and tricks to help you along the way.

Benefits of Proper Training

There are so many reasons to obedience train your dog. Well-trained dogs are generally safer, politer, and less hyperactive than dogs that are left to their own devices. Training is a good way to keep your dog's mind active, keeping them from getting bored and making trouble. Good obedience training can save your dog's life in certain situations.

For example, imagine a scenario where your dog gets loose and you need to get them back by your side before they get lost or hit by a car. In this situation, you want to be able to call their name and give the Come command to recall them. Then, you'll want them to sit or lie by your side until you can grab their collar or put their leash back on. But if your dog doesn't know any of these commands, they'll continue to wander around, making it difficult to retrieve them. Hopefully you'll never have to be in a scary situation with your dog, but good training could make a huge difference in your dog's safety.

In general, obedience training makes your dog much more pleasant to be around. Once you start working on commands, you'll find all sorts of practical applications for them. And all of these basic commands are prerequisites for more difficult commands. Once you master a few, you can start working on more challenging tricks.

Photo Courtesy of Sarah Spursettes

Places to Practice

Photo Courtesy of Diana Gregory

Starting out, you'll probably practice your commands at your house. The home is a good place to begin your practice because it's familiar and you can control the number of distractions around. A room with plenty of space to move is a good starting spot. That way, your dog's attention is on you and the awesome rewards you have to offer.

However, you'll want to move outside the home at some point. You want your commands to have practical, real-world applications, so you need your dog to be able to respond in unfamiliar places.

For example, your dog may be awesome at sitting when you're at home. In fact, you might not even need to bribe your Cockapoo with treats when you want them to sit. But perhaps you go for a walk in a new park and need your dog to sit for a second while you take a phone call or tie your shoe. If your dog has never needed to sit in a place with tons of distractions, they may not obey the first few times. For this reason, it's important to create some variation in location when you train.

Start off slow and work your way up to more challenging locations. Begin inside your home, then move to a familiar spot outside, like the backyard. Then, practice in familiar parks or at a friend's house. Finally, try to do a few commands at a farmer's market or somewhere unfamiliar with a ton of distractions. When your dog can obey you under slight stress, then you know that they've got the command down.

Clicker Training

As mentioned in the previous chapter, some trainers like to use clickers or verbal markers in conjunction with treats. This requires you to "click" or make an affirmative sound, like "Yes" every time your dog does the right thing. This allows for greater accuracy when rewarding your dog, it doesn't require you to carry treats everywhere you go, and you don't need to feed your dog as many rewards as you might if you didn't use a clicker.

When starting out with clicker training, use a click and a treat at once. This way, your dog connects the action with the reward and the sound. Use both the clicker and the treat for a while to make sure the connection is made. Eventually, you'll be able to use your clicker as a reward instead of a treat.

The reason this is more accurate than handing out treats is because the sound of the clicker is instantaneous. The second your dog's bottom touches the floor, you can give a click. When you're dealing with treats, you have to watch and wait for your dog to settle into the command before handing the treat over. If you're working on multiple commands at once, it's not easy to stop your progress to reward your dog. With a clicker, you can hand out as many rewards as you want with precision.

Another reason it's accurate is because your Cockapoo won't do the commands perfectly the first time. If you're using treats, you may accidentally give your dog the treat at the wrong time and reinforce the wrong action. A clicker can show your dog that they're on the right track with reinforcing the right movement. For example, maybe you're teaching your dog to roll over. To do this, you must first teach your dog the Down command. With clicker training, you might give your dog a click for hitting the down movement, even if he doesn't make the full roll. With this method, your dog understands that "Down" is an important part of the "Roll over" process, even if he hasn't figured out the whole command quite yet.

One downfall of the clicker method is that you always need your clicker on hand for training. For some owners, this isn't an issue. For others, it can be hard to remember to bring the little device wherever you go. For this reason, you may choose to use a verbal cue like "Yes" or "Good" or whatever affirmative noise you can think of that will let your dog know they are doing what you want them to do. However, once you pick a noise, stick to it. Otherwise, you're going to create confusion.

Basic Commands

There are so many commands to teach your Cockapoo, but some are definitely more important than others. There will be lots of time to work on fun tricks later, so stick to the basic commands to start. The following five commands are the building blocks on which you will obedience train your dog. Once you master all five, you'll find that life with your dog is so much easier because you finally have a little control over their wacky ideas. Once you master these commands, continue practicing them throughout your dog's life and build upon their knowledge with more advanced commands.

Sit

This is perhaps the first command you'll teach your dog because it's easy for Cockapoos to do and it's easy to teach. This command can be used in so many different scenarios. When you need your dog to wait or calm down for a moment, Sit is a good command to keep them quiet and still.

To teach this command, you'll want your dog in a standing position. Hold a treat in your hand and move it above and slightly past their nose. They should follow the treat with their nose, naturally causing them to sit. If this doesn't work, you can gently place your hand on their bottom and apply light pressure to show them what you want them to do. Once they are in the sitting position, give them a treat and lots of praise. After you've got the motion down, start adding the command "Sit" before they sit. When they do this command, the implication is that they will remain seated until you give them further commands, or release them by saying, "Okay."

Down

Once you teach Sit, you'll want to try Down. This is a bit trickier than the Sit command because your dog might not naturally want to lie on the ground on command. But it's useful for times where you want your dog to chill out for a little longer than you might put them in a sit. It also takes them a little bit longer to spring into action from a Down position, so when it's paired with a Stay it will give them more time to chill out.

To teach this, start with your dog in the Sit position. Hold the treat in front of their nose, then slowly move it towards the floor. They will follow the treat with their nose, but when it gets too close to the ground, they will naturally lower their body. You want your dog to go all the way to the floor. If they only go part way down, it's easy for them to spring back up. Once they are on the ground, give them their treat and praise.

If they have a hard time following the reward, you can try to gently nudge them into position with their leash. Try not to tug or force them down. Instead, gently apply downward pressure to the leash while moving the treat in front of their face to show them how to get into the Down position. Once you have them where you want them, give them treats and praise.

Photo Courtesy of Christine Kirby

Stay

This command can be tricky to teach, especially if you have an active puppy with a short attention span. However, it can come in handy if your pup loves to roam around and get into trouble. The Stay command is useful because when it's done right, your dog will freeze in place until they're given further instructions. If you find yourself in a situation where you need to leave your dog for a moment and don't want them to follow you, this command will be extremely useful.

To teach this, start with your dog in the Sit position. This gives them the hint that they're supposed to be performing a certain action. Place your hand in front of their face like a stop sign and say "Stay." Walk back a few steps while holding out your palm, pause a moment, then return. If they're still motionless when you return, give them their reward. If they break, put them back into a Sit and Stay and try again.

When you're starting out, don't take more than a few steps away. Naturally, they're going to want to follow you. Over time, build up the distance between you and your pup. You can also add challenging variables, like turning your back towards your dog, leaving the room, and even circling them. When you want to practice long distances in distracting environments, buy a 20-foot leash to give your dog some extra distance while still maintaining some control over them.

If your dog has a tough time staying still, practice this command on a leash. That way, you can drop the leash and put a foot on it when they start to get up. This should "self-correct" and make it harder for them to move. Or you might even want to start slower by putting them in a Stay and simply moving from their side to in front of them. Then, once they can stay still, face them and walk backward. At first, your Cockapoo will want to follow you and stay by your side. Over time, they'll understand that you're going to return and relax a little.

Come

Being able to recall your dog is so important. Occasionally, your dog will be doing something they shouldn't be doing, and you will need a way to get them close to your side. Or you may encounter a dangerous situation and you need to protect your dog or keep them out of the way. If your Cockapoo likes to wander, the Come command can save their life.

To teach this, put your dog in a Sit and Stay. When you're a few feet away, call your dog towards you. If you have a treat in your hand, your Cockapoo will likely hear your enthusiastic voice, see your open arms, and come barreling towards you. When your dog comes to you, put a hand on their collar so they don't run away and give them a treat.

If they don't run straight towards you, try nudging them along with the leash. When your dog is in the Sit and Stay, take the leash with you and call your dog. If they don't immediately come to you, give a gentle tug. This should redirect their attention to you, prompting them to approach you. Then, they'll be more inclined to come to you if you are waiting for them with treats and praise.

Because you want your dog to come to you every time, avoid calling them if you're only going to yell at them. Our dogs do things that frustrate us, but the Come command should not be used to call your dog for punishment. If your dog learns that responding to "Come" is not always a positive experience, they will not want to do it. If they have an unreliable recall, they may not respond to you when it really counts. For this reason, if your dog comes to you, make sure you give them tons of affection and praise so they will continue to do so.

Leash Training

Cockapoos love to go on walks with their humans. It's a great way to exercise while spending quality time together. However, if your dog doesn't walk very well on a leash, walks will become a tedious chore that will leave you frustrated. From the first moment you clip the leash onto your dog's collar, it's time to start practicing good walking habits. The more you leash train with your dog in the early days, the happier you'll be in the long run. It's not natural for dogs to walk right next to you on a leash, especially if they're curious and love to explore. Lots of quality practice is necessary for teaching your dog how to act polite on walks.

To start, your dog should be positioned on your left side. They should walk in line with you, not too far ahead nor lagging behind. There should not be any tension in the leash; it should hang loosely between you. When you stop, your dog should stop and sit by your side. When you turn, your dog should turn along with you, speeding up or slowing down to remain in position at your left side. Easier said than done, right?

It takes a ton of practice to get your dog to walk nicely. Sometimes, you'll feel like you're flying a kite because of the way your dog moves erratically around you. It's easy to give up on training and let your dog take control while he gets his exercise, but this behavior will get old very quickly. Good leash training will keep your dog in check and make walks much more pleasant.

Before you go on your walk, get your dog to sit on your left side. This is a nice way to say, "I'm in charge here, and we're going to do

Photo Courtesy of Michael Hibberd

things my way." Hold the end of the leash with your right hand and slide your left hand down your leash to keep your dog close. Also, keep a lot of treats on hand because you'll need to give out rewards every time your dog walks nicely.

Say, "Let's go" and take a few steps forward. If they walk alongside you without pulling, give them tons of praise and a treat. It helps to talk to your dog while you walk so that their focus is on you and not all the distractions around them. Tell them about how good they're being. If they start to pull or get distracted, give a quick tug on the leash to remind them what they need to do. Don't yank too hard or drag your dog. Instead, a quick pop will help keep them in line without hurting them. When there is slack on the leash again, praise and reward them.

Along with walking, practice changing your pace. Slow down and direct your dog to do the same. Or you can speed up and get your dog really moving. Work on right turns, left turns, and about-faces. Halt suddenly and have your dog sit beside you. Instruct your dog to wait at crosswalks or just in the middle of the sidewalk while you tie your shoe. Incorporate different events into your walk to practice real-life scenarios that may come up on your walk. All the while, your dog's shoulders should be in line (or very close) with your leg.

Sometimes, dogs have a really hard time walking on a leash. Pulling is a serious issue that can make walks a chore. If your dog is difficult, there are different harnesses and collars to try. If you choose a harness, pick one with the leash fastener on the front. This way, your dog is unable to pull without spinning them towards you. Avoid harnesses that clip on from the back, because this only makes it more comfortable for them to drag you down the street. Some trainers use pronged collars for serious cases because it allows your dog to self-correct without injuring themselves. However, it's important to use positive training alongside any kind of self-correction methods. Choke chains can injure a dog's throat if they pull too hard and should be avoided. Ideally, the flat collar should be used on all dogs, but sometimes other measures need to be taken to keep you and your dog safe on a walk. If you have serious issues with walks, talk to a trainer to help you with your difficult pooch.

When going on walks, remember to give frequent feedback to your dog. Let them know when they're doing a good job, and correct them when they're not doing so well. Bring lots of treats (and maybe some water) when you go on your daily walks to encourage your dog to explore new places and be on their best behavior. With lots of hard work, you'll love the special time of day when you and your buddy get to enjoy some time in nature together.

Once you master the basic commands, keep practicing! Even better, keep building upon their knowledge with new commands. When you get busy or have a hard time training, it's easy to give up and forget about obedience training. However, it's best to start good habits at an early age. That way, your dog doesn't have the time to make their own rules. Stick with it and remember that there are lots of experts out there who can help you train your dog to be the best Cockapoo ever!

CHAPTER 13
Advanced Commands

Once you have mastered the basic commands, it's time to move onto something a little more challenging! Some of these commands are very useful when it comes to having a safe and polite dog. Other commands serve no real purpose other than to have fun. There are countless commands to teach your Cockapoo, but here are a few that you might want to try with your furry friend.

Leave It

This command will come in handy with your curious pup. Your Cockapoo will want to stick their nose into anything that looks interesting. While it's nice to allow your dog to explore the world around you, sometimes you just know what's best for them. This command is useful if they are focused on something they shouldn't be, like a squirrel they want to chase or a dead animal they want to roll in.

To teach this, find a treat they'll really want. Set it on the ground with your foot nearby. Naturally, they're going to approach the treat so they can eat it. When they get close, cover the treat with your foot so it's unavailable. Show them that they can't just eat any treat on the ground.

Try it again, asking them to leave it. If they make a bee-line for the treat, tell them "No" and cover the treat. Repeat this until they appear uninterested or wait for the treat. If they successfully leave the treat, mark the behavior with a "Yes" and give them the treat. This command should teach them to break their concentration when you tell them to "Leave it." When your dog starts to get the hang of this command, you can command your dog to "Leave it," then teach them to "Take it."

Drop It

Drop It is another command that can save your dog's life. Dogs will put anything in their mouth. Sometimes, the things they find are easy to choke on or will make them sick. This command will ensure that if you catch them with something they shouldn't have, they'll drop it instantly.

This command can be taught during playtime. Throw a ball and have them fetch it. If your dog doesn't automatically hand it over, this is the time to teach the skill. Show your dog that you have a treat. They'll want to eat it but can't because there's already a ball in their mouth. If the treat is more rewarding than the ball, they'll drop the ball in favor of the treat. When they do this, say "Good drop it!" and praise them. After a few tries, start using the command when they come to you with the ball. If they drop it when you ask, give them the treat and praise, then throw the ball again for an added reward. Once your dog has the hang of this, move on to different objects until they drop everything on command.

*Photo Courtesy of
Liam Thompson*

Look at Me

Photo Courtesy of Joyce Wilson

This command is good for getting your dog to focus on you. This is extremely useful when you're going on walks because you want your dog to follow your lead. It's also useful when you want to break your dog's attention on something else, like a car they'd like to chase. Let's not forget that this is also a useful skill when you'd like your dog to look at the camera for an adorable photo.

Start with your dog in the sitting position. Hold a treat in each hand, close to their nose so they know what's at stake. Then, say, "Look at me" while slowly drawing both hands towards your nose. Naturally, their eyes will follow the treat and they'll look right at you. If they hold the gaze for even just a second, bring both hands forward, but only release one treat. The reason you want to use both hands is that it gets your dog to look at the center of your face, and not just follow one hand to the treat.

When your dog figures this out, try the command without leading your dog's gaze to your face with the treat. Instead, maybe just point at your nose for a hint. Then, give your dog the treats and praise. Eventually, you'll get to the point where your dog will stare at you when you give the command.

Shake

Shake is a fairly simple trick to teach that's fun to show off. Start by facing your dog in the sitting position. Hold a treat in your hand and place it where you would meet their paw if you were about to shake. For some dogs, this will cause them to put their paw on your hand in an attempt to knock the treat from your hand. If this happens, give them your hand and give their paw a shake. Afterward, give them the treat and lots of praise.

If this method doesn't work, you can always nudge your dog in the right direction by picking up their paw and putting it into the position you want. Add the verbal cue and reward, and your dog will be shaking on command in no time.

Sit Pretty

This command is all about the cute factor. Along with this trick being absolutely adorable, it will help with your dog's core strength, if that kind of thing is important to you. If your dog hasn't used these muscles a lot, then it's going to take some time to get used to sitting like a person. Your dog will probably be a little wobbly at first. Keep practicing until they can hold the position.

To teach this command, have your dog start in the sitting position. Hold a treat in front of their nose, then slowly move it up and back behind their head. If they're following the treat with their nose, they'll naturally lift their body so they don't tip over. Reward them if they lift off of their front paws. Keep practicing until your dog can sit on their hind legs with their paws in front of their belly.

Roll Over/Play Dead

Especially when paired with fun hand actions and sound effects, Play Dead is a crowd-pleaser of a trick. Be forewarned, if your dog does not like to expose their belly to people, this is going to be a challenge. It's not natural for every dog to feel comfortable in that position.

Start with a sitting dog. Use the treat to guide your dog into the following positions. Lower the treat to the floor to get them lying down. Then, slowly rotate the treat around their head, until they lie on their side. Praise them and give the reward if your dog hits the desired "dead" position. Some owners like to make a gun with their hand and say "Bang!" as the command word. Others like to say "Dead dog" or "Play dead." Your dog will respond to whatever cues you teach him, so feel free to get creative.

A Play Dead is halfway to a Roll Over. Instead of stopping the rolling motion when your dog gets to their side, continue rotating the treat for an entire roll. It may take some time until your dog is able to make a full revolution. But when he does, make sure to give your dog a ton of praise because it's a fairly challenging trick.

Crawl

Photo Courtesy of Susie Thomas

This is another fun trick that's easy to teach if your dog already knows basic commands. You'll have so much fun watching your dog wiggle around on the ground.

To teach this command, start with your dog in the down position. Hold the treat between their paws, then slowly move it towards you. If you move the treat too quickly, your dog will probably pop back up to standing. As your dog moves towards you, you'll have to back up a little so there's enough room for your dog to move. If your dog crawls a foot or two, give them their reward. Keep practicing while increasing the distance, and then try getting them to crawl without the use of the treat.

Competitions for Cockapoos

If you find that your Cockapoo really enjoys obedience training and performing tricks, there are fun competitions out there where your dog can show off their skills. Your dog doesn't need to be a champion to be able to participate in such events. Consider joining a local dog club to get training help and information about events in your area.

Obedience competitions are a fun way to test your dog's ability and your training skills. These competitions will take you and your dog through a series of challenges. Your dog will be expected to walk nicely on a leash and to sit and stay with a bunch of other dogs around him. Some dogs really love to get into the ring and strut their stuff, so if your dog is great at obedience training, it might be a fun activity for the two of you.

Nose work is another fun class you can take that can lead to competitions. This activity is kind of like drug or explosive sniffing, but without the drugs or explosives! Instead, you'll use little containers with essential oil scents to teach your dog how to sniff out and identify different con-

Photo Courtesy of
Harriet Draper

tainers. This is a great way to burn some mental energy, especially when the weather doesn't permit you to spend a lot of time outside.

Agility competitions can also be a lot of fun for a Cockapoo. Competitions are divided into classes based on dog size, so your little dog won't have to go up against a big, fast dog. The easily trained and energetic Cockapoo can do well in this event because it requires them to follow their owner's direction and race through a series of obstacles. It might take a few classes for your dog to figure out how to do the activity, but once your Cockapoo has aced the course, you can compete against other dogs and owners to complete the course the fastest and take home the prize.

If you can master these advanced commands with no problem, then don't stop here! Once you've figured out the basics of how to teach commands, you can use your creativity to come up with cool tricks that you won't find in the competition ring. You might be able to teach your Cockapoo how to open doors or even fetch a drink from the fridge. When it comes to positive reinforcement, you can teach your dog just about anything!

CHAPTER 14
Traveling with Cockapoos

"Most Cockapoos travel very well. There are exceptions and a few may get motion sickness. However, I often hear reports that the owners take them camping, fishing, beach walking, trail walking, swimming, etc."

Linda S. Oberling
Cockapoos by Choice

There's going to be a day where you'll need to leave home with your Cockapoo. Whether you're moving halfway across the country or just visiting the vet, your dog will need to be transported away from their familiar home. For some dogs, this can be a very stressful time. For others, it's a ton of fun. The difference is mostly in preparation and your attitude towards traveling with your pup. This chapter will cover some information that will hopefully make your dog happy and safe when it comes to going on adventures with you!

Photo Courtesy of Angela McCartney Prentice

Photo Courtesy of Nicola Welch

Dog Carriers and Restraints

If you insist that your car passengers wear seatbelts, then your dog should be no exception. In the event of a car crash, your dog will become a projectile and can become seriously injured. It doesn't take a lot of speed or impact for your dog to be launched forward or knocked off balance. You would be absolutely devastated if your dog was injured when many auto accident injuries are preventable.

Similarly, if you wanted to transport your furry passenger safely, you would try to minimize any distractions that would impair your driving. This includes said furry passenger running all over the car, or even hopping onto your lap. It doesn't take a lot of activity to momentarily become distracted and disaster can strike quickly. Your dog should be in the backseat and unable to move freely around the car.

This is why safety restraints are so important for dogs. There are many different types of products on the market, so it's not hard to find one to suit your dog's needs.

If you are crate training, the crate can keep your dog safe and secure in case of a crash. When secured in your car, the crate keeps your dog from being thrown around in a crash. Plus, it adds another layer of protection to keep your dog safe from flying debris. If you have one of the smaller varieties of Cockapoo, there are soft traveling cases to transport your dog in. These are often used for air travel and can keep your dog contained in the event of a crash. The soft sides of the carrier aren't as resistant to impact, but it can keep your dog safer than if they were not restrained at all.

There are also seatbelts available for dogs that don't like to be in tight spaces. These are affordable safety belts that can be attached to a dog's collar and buckled into a car's existing seatbelts. When using these, you may choose to put your dog in a harness, then attach the seatbelt to the harness clip. Otherwise, a car crash may cause neck injury if your dog is restrained by the collar around their neck. With a harness, your dog will be pulled around their shoulders, reducing trauma to the head and neck.

Whichever method you choose, it's important to regularly use some form of restraint to keep your dog safe. It will give you some peace of mind to know that your Cockapoo is a little bit safer in your car. Plus, all of your passengers are safer when your dog isn't able to run amok in the car!

Photo Courtesy of
Harriet Draper

Photo Courtesy of
@cockapoograham on Instagram

Preparing Your Dog for Car Rides

Sometimes dogs get nervous in the car. When you look at it from their perspective, it makes sense. You're asking your dog to jump into a strange box that moves very fast. There are so many strange sights and sensations that it can be downright overwhelming. Some dogs love nothing more than to ride in a car, but for other dogs, car rides are a great source of anxiety. This anxiety can also lead to car sickness, which will make your dog absolutely miserable. The best way to make your dog enjoy car rides is to slowly prepare them for your vehicle.

To start, let your dog explore your car while it's in park. Let your dog sniff around the back seat and give them treats if they're staying calm. You might even shut the door and take your place in the driver's seat as if you were going on a drive. Then, try out your dog's restraint and reward them if they can handle being restrained in the car.

Next, it's time to start driving. Take short drives around the block, talking to your dog in a soothing voice and praising them for staying calm. Give your dog a reward before getting out of the car. Increase the time spent in the car, gradually increasing the drive duration until your dog is no longer fearful.

For extreme cases of car-related anxiety and car sickness, talk to your vet about other things you can do to help your dog. For situational anxiety, a vet may decide to prescribe medication to give your dog in the event that they need to be in the car.

Not every dog will have this aversion to the car. You may find that your Cockapoo puppy jumps into your car with no problem and never wants to leave. But if your dog is nervous in your car, you'll want to address this fear before it becomes necessary to transport your dog somewhere.

If you're going on a long car trip, make sure to take frequent stops. While humans can go for hours without needing to stop, your dog will get antsy if they're cooped up for too long. Find rest stops along the way that have plenty of space for your dog to stretch their legs. Also, make sure that water is readily available for your thirsty pooch. Try making a stop in a city with a dog park, if possible. Being able to let your dog play freely in a safe place will make them so much happier than if they're only allowed a quick potty break at an interstate rest stop.

Flying and Hotel Stays

Sometimes the adventures you go on with your pooch require air travel or hotel stays. A completely new environment can confuse your dog, so you definitely need to take some extra precautions. The first thing you need to decide is if it's worth the hassle to take such a long trip with your dog. If you're making a big move or there's no one to watch your dog, then airplanes and hotel stays may be unavoidable. But if you think your travels will stress you and your dog too much, then you might decide to leave your Cockapoo at home with a trusted person.

Air travel can be especially stressful for a dog. For this reason, it's best if you only fly in extreme circumstances. Unfortunately, it's too common that an airline loses precious cargo or a dog suffers a medical emergency in the air. If you're not willing to deal with that risk, it might be better to drive.

If that's just not possible, there are some things you can do to ease your mind while flying with your dog. If you have a small Cockapoo that can fit in an airline-approved carrier, find an airline that allows small dogs in the cabin. You won't necessarily be able to have your dog on your lap, but it will make both you and your dog feel better to be close.

If your Cockapoo is too big for the cabin, they'll have to ride in the cargo hold in a crate. Make sure they have plenty of access to water because the high altitude can be dehydrating. Make sure their crate is com-

Photo Courtesy of Diana Gregory

fortable and maybe throw in a familiar toy to ease their worries. The cargo area can be loud and frightening to a dog, so talk to your vet to see if there's anything you can give your dog to keep them calm on the flight. It's a good idea to take your dog to the vet for a checkup before a flight to make sure they're in good health before putting them in a potentially dangerous situation.

You'll also want to take special care to ensure that your dog cannot be lost. Before your trip, look up important phone numbers for your airline and save them in your cell phone. Put a tag or label on your dog's crate with all of your contact information. Make sure you know where you need to be to pick up your dog and who to contact if there are issues.

Once you get to your destination, you'll have to stay in an unfamiliar place. When booking a hotel, make sure they allow pets and you pay whatever deposit is needed. Even the most well-behaved dog will leave behind traces and you don't want to face heavy fines for breaking the rules. Also, try to find a hotel that is located somewhere you can walk your Cockapoo. If you find yourself surrounded by cement, it might take some extra effort to find a spot to let your dog use the bathroom. Also, lots of exercise can make your stay more enjoyable. If your dog isn't bouncing off the walls or nervously destructive, then you'll be much more likely to have a good time.

If you can, try to bring some familiar items to make your dog feel more at home. A favorite blanket and a few toys can make your dog feel more at ease.

Kenneling vs. Dog Sitters

Sometimes it's just not worth it to take your dog on a trip with you. If you're flying, going on a long drive, or too busy to spend lots of quality time with your dog in a strange place, it might be best to leave them at home. When you leave your dog with a trusted person, your choices are to board your dog in a kennel or hire a dog sitter to visit your dog in your home. Both options have their pros and cons, so it's best to decide based on what is best for you and your dog.

A good doggy daycare will keep your pooch supervised and entertained all day. These boarding facilities have a small kennel for your dog to sleep in alone but also allow for your dog to play with others. These facilities keep people on staff to tend to your dog's needs at any time throughout the day (as well as overnight). You'll feel at peace to know that if something goes wrong with your dog, there will be someone

Photo Courtesy of David Thomas

around to check in on your pup. During the day, your dog will never be bored with the endless playtime with other dogs.

However, this set up isn't best for all dogs. If your dog is especially submissive around other dogs or has had issues with other dogs in the past, you might not feel comfortable leaving your dog to play with others without your supervision. It's more expensive to hire one person to take care of your dog, but it might be worth it if your dog becomes stressed around other dogs.

Look for a pet sitter who can make frequent visits to your house. You want to maintain your dog's normal schedule if possible. Make sure your sitter can stop by briefly to let your dog out and hang around longer a few times a day for exercise and attention. Ideally, your sitter will be there as much, if not more, than you are normally home so your dog doesn't feel neglected. It might be hard on your Cockapoo to be away from their favorite person, so a good pet sitter is important.

In any case, make sure to properly vet anyone who will be taking care of your dog. There are tons of websites and apps to help you find someone to watch your dog, but personal recommendations will take you much further. If a friend or coworker can trust their dog with someone, chances are that you can, too. Meet with your sitter or kennel and talk about your dog's needs. Have your dog meet their new caretaker before you leave on your trip. When you're on vacation, the last thing you want to worry about is how your dog is doing. With any luck, you'll return from your trip and go home to a happy puppy.

Traveling can be stressful for a dog. There are so many new sights, sounds, and smells that can be overwhelming to a young pup. The best thing you can do for your dog is to slowly prepare them for new experiences. And when you're planning your trip, keep your dog's temperament in mind. If you know your dog will struggle with all the change, find a good caretaker for the duration of your trip. If you decide your Cockapoo can handle the journey, take measures to make sure they're comfortable and happy. Traveling is stressful enough, so don't add any extra stress by bringing along an ill-prepared Cockapoo.

Photo Courtesy of
Tracey Thompson

CHAPTER 15
Grooming Your Cockapoo

"Don't be afraid to learn grooming procedures that you can do at home. Keep their bangs short so they stay out of their eyes. Groom them often and start it young so that they are used to it. Get them used to having their paws handled, their nails trimmed, and the sounds of a clipper at a young age so that their first grooming isn't traumatic."

Jamie

Cute Cockapoos

Cockapoos are beautiful dogs with soft, fluffy coats. Cockapoos love to be the center of attention, so you'll want them looking nice. Grooming is also necessary in maintaining your dog's health. Whether you choose to do your dog's grooming on your own or hire a professional, you'll have to spend some time making sure your dog's hygienic needs are met. Sometimes, dogs don't totally enjoy being groomed, especially when it's more fun to roll around in stinky things; but if you start early, grooming will become a normal part of your dog's routine.

Coat Basics

The Cockapoo coat allows for some variation, depending on how your dog was bred. A straight-coated Cockapoo is possible but very uncommon. A curly or wavy coat is the norm with this breed. Perhaps the best thing about the coat is how little it sheds. This is due to the Poodle's curly coat genes. The coat does not grow excessively long, either.

Like with many other dog breeds, regular brushing is necessary to keep your dog's coat shiny and tangle-free. Brushing helps redistribute natural oils throughout the length of the hair and brushes away dead skin. If a Cockapoo's fur gets tangled and matted, you may have to cut the patch of fur to get rid of the problem. A regular pin brush should be enough to do the trick. If your dog has problems with mats, a slicker brush may also help get down to the root of the problem.

Professional Grooming

This breed can get a little shaggy around the face, so you might decide you want to take your dog to a professional groomer for a quick trim. What the groomer does is up to your preference. Some Cockapoo owners like their dog's coat to be long and full. Others like it to be trimmed and neat, especially during the summer. You can keep your dog as fluffy as you like, but pay special attention to the fur around their eyes and mouth. You may find that this fur gets too long and in the way. Long hairs can fall into the eyes, irritating them. Dirt and germs from outside can make their way from their fur into their sensitive eyes, leading to infection. At the very least, the extra fur might be annoying and make it hard for your dog to see. When this happens, take your pooch in for a trim. As far as breeds that need grooming go, the Cockapoo is fairly low-maintenance.

*Photo Courtesy of
Irene Blackhaw*

Bathing

Eventually, your dog will get so dirty that they will require a bath. When this happens, you'll want to have a few things on hand. First, you'll want a good dog shampoo. Choose one specially formulated for dogs. A gentle solution is best, as to not strip too many natural oils from the skin and hair. It's not absolutely necessary, but a detachable shower hose can make your dog's bath so much easier than filling up a tub and rinsing with a cup. If your dog doesn't take to the water, keep a few treats on hand use as positive reinforcement.

Fill the tub with a few inches of warm water. Give your Cockapoo a quick rinse and then work their fur into a lather with the shampoo. Pay special attention to their face to ensure that no soap or water gets into sensitive areas. It's best to use a damp rag on the face and save the scrubbing for the rest of the body. Give your dog a thorough rinse when you're done. Any excess soap will dry out their skin and make their fur brittle and dull. Once finished, towel dry your Cockapoo and give them a treat to remind them that bath time doesn't have to be a bad time.

Photo Courtesy of Jackie Meredith

If your dog fights you during every bath, try to smear a little peanut butter on the back of the bathtub or shower wall. This will keep them busy for a few minutes while you give them a wash. Also, make sure that the water isn't too hot or too cold. Remember, dogs only need a bath once every few months, unless they're particularly dirty. Otherwise, you'll take away the natural oils that protect their skin and coat.

Trimming Nails

Long claws on a dog are not ideal. Not only do they click and clack on the floor, but they scratch people and furniture. And if toenails grow too long, they can cause foot pain. Nail trimming is something that can be done at home. However, dogs don't always sit patiently and wait for you to cut their nails. Before you even begin to cut nails, practice touching your dog's paws. If they tolerate you touching their paws and nails, give them a treat. This will create a positive association between touching paws and rewards.

When it comes time to trim the nails, clip the nails with tiny snips instead of taking off big chunks. Some dog nail clippers have guards on them so that you don't take too much off. If you cut too much, you might nick the blood supply, or quick. This can be extremely painful and will make your dog hesitant to let you clip them again. If your Cockapoo is too squirmy, this is a service that a groomer can help with. They have lots of experience with a variety of dogs and can get the job done quickly.

Brushing Teeth

Brushing your dog's teeth is about more than keeping them shiny. It also reduces doggy breath and removes harmful plaque from teeth. The condition of a dog's teeth makes a big difference in their overall health. When the teeth begin to decay, it makes it painful for your dog to eat. The bacteria from the decay can wreak havoc on your dog's overall well-being. Bad teeth have been linked to heart disease and can even take years off of an otherwise healthy dog's life.

It may seem like a lot of work but brushing a dog's teeth is not so hard. Before you begin, practice touching your dog's mouth to get them used to the strange feeling. Gently pull their lips back and poke at their teeth. This is also good practice for visiting the vet.

When they're comfortable with you poking around their mouth, it's time to brush! Use a toothbrush and toothpaste made for dogs. Dogs can't spit out toothpaste, so they need a special formula just for them. These kinds of toothpaste come in a variety of dog-friendly flavors. You can decide which type of brush to use, depending on the size of your dog's mouth and your comfort. There are traditional-handled toothbrushes in a variety of sizes or rubber-bristled brushes that slip on over your finger.

When brushing, focus on the outsides of the back teeth. When your dog eats crunchy foods, the kibble scrapes plaque away from the inside parts of the mouth. The outsides tend to collect more of that nasty build-up that leads to disease. Gently brush their teeth, taking care not to injure the gums with rigorous brushing.

The more you brush, the better your dog's teeth will be in the long run. Some owners are great about brushing every night before bed, while others get around to it once a week. Prevention is key when it comes to your dog's teeth. If you can keep your pup's pearly whites clean, then they'll be less likely to need professional cleaning in the future.

Cleaning Ears

Photo Courtesy of Nataliya Ratosh

Cockapoos have floppy ears that can become fected much more easily than in other breeds. Moisture and bacteria get trapped inside and become a breeding ground for nasty infections. When left untreated, this can cause a lot of pain and potential hearing loss in your dog. For this reason, Cockapoo owners need to pay special attention to their dog's ears.

First, take special care to keep water out of your dog's ears. In the bath, don't rinse their face with the shower hose. You might even want to place cotton balls in the opening of the ear to prevent water from going in. If your dog gets water in their ears when they slurp from their water dish, consider buying a platform to elevate their bowl to keep their head up and their ears away from the splashing water.

If you notice that there's a lot of waxy buildup in your dog's ears and they're scratching and shaking their head a lot, it might be a good time to clean their ears. Pet stores sell ear cleaning solution that's safe for your dog. To use it, squirt the solution directly into the ear. Then, massage the outside of the ear, working the solution down into the ear canal. This liquid will work to break up the wax in the ear. Let your dog shake the extra moisture out and you're good to go! If there's a lot of wax on the ear flap, you may use a moistened cotton ball to gently wipe the residue away. Never use Q-tips or any other small instrument to clean deep inside the ear, as this can damage your dog's delicate inner ear.

Of course, if your dog appears to be itchy or in pain after cleaning, see a vet. They can diagnose infection and prescribe medication to help with your Cockapoo's floppy ears. They will also clean their ears if this is too big of a task for you. Many dogs dislike the sensation of something cold and wet squirted in their ear. Sometimes, it's best to leave the important tasks to the professionals!

Home Grooming vs. Professional Grooming

Photo Courtesy of Kerry Lyon

While it's not absolutely necessary to pay another person to perform these tasks, sometimes it's worth it. If you have a squirmy dog, you risk injuring your pooch with sharp objects like scissors and nail clippers. Professional groomers have a lot of experience and can handle anything that comes their way. They also have an eye for how certain breeds are meant to be trimmed, so they can make your dog look neat and tidy if you're not exactly sure what kind of cut to give.

On the other hand, grooming can be expensive, and it may be hard to find the time to take your dog in for an appointment if you just need to trim a few long nails. Keep grooming equipment on hand in case you ever need it. But if you truly feel uncomfortable doing these tasks, leave it to the groomer. It's not worth injuring or traumatizing your dog if you're not able to do something yourself.

There is much more to dog grooming than just looking pretty. Though your dog loves to eat and roll in all sorts of gross things, cleanliness is very important to their health. Trimmed nails, clean ears, and brushed teeth can improve your dog's quality of life, and maybe even their overall life expectancy. It takes some time and effort, but it's absolutely worth it when your dog looks and feels good.

CHAPTER 16
Nutrition and Healthcare

"I feed my dogs a grain free diet, usually chicken based. Occasionally the fat from a base like duck will upset their gastrointestinal system. Keep it simple. Do not feed a kibble that is devoid of meat (like a pea or lentil based kibble). Dogs are innately carnivores."

Jeanne Davis
Windhorse Offering

There's nothing more important than your dog's health. Unfortunately, our dogs aren't on this earth for long, so every owner wants to make sure they get as many years with their furry friend as possible. And the quality of those years matters, too. Luckily, there are a few things you can do to keep your dog's health top-notch. Along with good hygiene, good nutrition and regular checkups will go a long way to keep your dog happy and healthy.

Photo Courtesy of Lee Carpenter

Importance of a Good Diet

Just like with humans, what you feed your dog matters. If you feed your dog nutritious food, they'll have lots of energy and their body will work efficiently. If they eat junk, their bodies will not get the important things they need. Extra fat will accumulate around organs, causing them to work harder to function.

Because there is a lot of variation in Cockapoo sizes, the food you give your dog may depend on their size. Large breed formulas are for medium- to large-sized dogs, while small breed foods are suited for the mini and toy sized breeds. Different dogs need slightly different nutrients.

A big dog can stand to have more carbohydrates in their diet because they burn more energy. Smaller dogs tend to need foods higher in protein. Any sized dog should be eating foods with good sources of proteins and carbohydrates. When it comes to protein, multiple meat sources can provide a better range of amino and fatty acids. When it comes to carbohydrates, complex carbs are good at keeping your dog energized and full for longer. Ingredients like oatmeal, brown rice, and barley will keep your dog's stomach from growling between meals.

Also, don't be afraid of fats in your dog's diet. Fats and oils are what keeps your dog's skin moisturized and their coat smooth. Look for foods that have omega fatty acids, like from fish oil. These nutrients are great for the skin and also promote healthy brain activity.

We all know that fruits and vegetables are good for people, but many don't consider all of the vitamins and minerals dogs need in their food. There should be a wide variety of vitamins and minerals at appropriate levels for your Cockapoo's size. Virtually all foods will contain some sort of multivitamin mix, but some contain the actual produce it comes from. Produce contains antioxidants that fight the aging process and keep the immune system healthy. These fruits and vegetables also contain fiber, which keeps your dog regular.

When it comes to feeding your dog, use the feeding guide on the bag to figure out how much they need per meal. The guide will tell you how much food a dog needs by weight. So, it's helpful to have an accurate weight for your dog; otherwise, they might get too much or too little food.

Weight issues aren't very common in this breed because they like to get their exercise and are not prone to overeating. However, if your vet notices that your dog is overweight, it's important to address this concern immediately. Too much weight can be hard on their joints and internal organs. The first thing you will want to do is reduce their daily calories and increase their exercise. Find the right balance of food and exercise to keep them at a stable, healthy weight. Remember that treats add to this calorie count. If you don't see results after a few months, consult your vet to make sure that there aren't other underlying health issues at play.

How to Choose Your Dog's Food

Photo Courtesy of Sandra Mcglynn

Once you know what nutrients your Cockapoo needs to be healthy, it's time to choose a food. This can be a daunting task when you go to the pet store because there are countless options for your furry friend. Each brand boasts different qualities and comes in a wide variety of flavors. So, how do you choose?

If you're buying a dog from a breeder, ask your breeder what they use. This will give you a good idea of the quality of food a Cockapoo enthusiast swears by, and also tell you what your new puppy is used to. Sometimes, dogs can be picky when it comes to flavors. If you don't know what kind of food gets your dog's mouth watering, many stores will offer free samples of kibble to try.

You'll also notice that food comes in wet and dry varieties. The wet foods contain moisture, which makes the food more aromatic and appetizing to a dog. However, it sticks to the teeth. It's easy to eat if your dog has mouth issues, but it is not necessary for a healthy dog. Crunchy food, on the other hand, scrapes the plaque off of teeth every time your dog eats. For this reason, it's best for dogs to eat dry food, as to limit the amount of plaque that develops on your dog's teeth.

Another thing you'll notice is that there's a wide variety of prices in dog food. Cheap dog foods can keep their prices down by using lower quality ingredients. Expensive dog foods often use ingredients that are closer to what people might eat, yet they're not technically human-grade foods. Also, a high price may signal to dog owners that it's a superior product, which may not always be the case. When in doubt, start by examining food labels in the middle of the price range. If the nutrient levels and ingredients look good to you, then it's probably a good dog food.

Homemade Food

Some dog owners make their own dog foods instead of buying commercial brands. While this is unconventional, it's sometimes beneficial for dogs. Occasionally, dogs will have food allergies and intolerances to certain ingredients, making it hard to find a food for their pup. Other times, owners don't like the idea of their dog eating anything lower quality than what they would feed their human family. In any case, making homemade dog food should be done under the supervision of a veterinarian or pet nutritionist to ensure that a dog is not missing any vital nutrients. These experts can recommend recipes and calculate caloric needs. There are tons of websites out there with owner-created recipes for inspiration, but be cautious in who you trust.

People Food

Whether you give your dog people food or prohibit it is controversial amongst dog owners. It's no surprise that dogs love to eat table scraps and any other tasty treat they can get their paws on, but it's not necessarily good for their bodies. When it comes to people food, it's best to err on the side of caution. First of all, you don't want to make your dog sick because the food contained something toxic to dogs. Onions, grapes, avocados, and chocolate are just a few things that humans can eat that make dogs very ill. Some foods, like dairy products, are not necessarily toxic, but your dog may not be able to digest them well, leading to tummy aches and diarrhea. Second, if your dog is eating a balanced diet with their dog food, adding high-calorie globs of fat from your steak trimmings is going to pack on the pounds over time. Finally, if you teach your dog that they can have the occasional scrap from your dinner table, they're going to sit under the table and beg every time you eat. This will become extremely annoying and it's hard to break that habit once it begins.

On the other hand, some owners like to use people food as training treats because they can be nutritious and can be a special treat when used sparingly. Some dogs go crazy for leafy greens, berries, and cooked pumpkin. These are great for dogs because they are low calorie and packed with nutrients. As long as you use these as special treats, it's fine to feed these to your dog on special occasions.

Checkups and Preventative Healthcare

When it comes to the health of your dog, it's best to prevent any issues before they cause harm. One way to do this is to take your dog to the vet for an annual checkup. During this time, they'll ask you if you've noticed any changes in your dog's health or ask if you have any concerns. Even if your concerns turn out to be nothing, it's still a good time to ask any questions you might have.

Your vet will do a quick, but thorough examination of your dog. They'll check the eyes, ears, and mouth for any abnormalities. They'll listen to your dog's heart, lungs, and belly to make sure everything sounds normal. Your dog will have their temperature taken to check for any infection. Finally, the vet will run their hands along your dog to make sure everything is fine with their legs, back, and belly.

The reason it's so important to go every year is that a vet can quickly diagnose an issue you might not even notice. And if you go regularly, they can track changes from year to year, pinpointing issues to keep an eye on. If you only go to the vet when your dog is sick, there's no benchmark when your dog is in healthy state to compare to.

Photo Courtesy of Linda Jones

Fleas, Ticks, and Worms

Part of preventative care is taking precautions to keep parasites off your dog. Dogs are like magnets for these awful creatures because dogs eat things they shouldn't and wander around areas with lots of vegetation. And once the parasites latch on, it may be hard to tell that your dog has an infestation.

Intestinal worms are fairly common in puppies. If you notice your dog's eating habits have changed, their bowel movements are irregular, or they're lethargic or vomiting, it's a good idea to have a vet check them out. A stool sample can quickly reveal if there are any worms in their gut and medicine can be prescribed to take care of the issue. Heartworms are another parasite that travels through the bloodstream. Infected mosquitoes bite your dog, which releases the heartworm into the bloodstream, eventually making its way to the heart. This parasite can be deadly if not treated immediately. Luckily, there's a monthly preventative medicine that can keep your dog protected against heartworm. After a quick blood test, your vet will prescribe a medication to give to your dog monthly. As long as you give this medicine to your dog on a regular basis, you won't have to worry about heartworm.

Fleas and ticks are other nuisances that can easily latch onto your dog. These creatures suck the blood from your dog and can possibly pass on dangerous diseases. Plus, fleas cause extreme itchiness and are hard to kill once an infestation starts. To prevent your dog from bringing these pests home, choose a preventative that works best for your pup. Topical preventatives can be applied to your dog's coat once a month, or there are oral preventatives that cause fleas and ticks to die when they bite your dog. If fleas and ticks cannot survive on your pooch, then there's less of a chance of these pests reproducing and causing your dog harm.

Vaccinations

Vaccinations are another big part of preventative care and are even required by law. There are a handful of contagious diseases that veterinarians can vaccinate against, starting when your dog is a puppy. At many places, your dog must be up to date on their recommended vaccinations in order to take training classes or go to dog parks. The rabies vaccine is required to license your dog because an unvaccinated dog can become a public health risk.

While vaccinations have become a hot topic in recent years, there is no reason not to vaccinate your dog. By keeping your dog free of contagious diseases, you're doing your part in eliminating terrible viruses that kill lots of dogs. You're not only protecting your dog, but also other dogs who might not be up to date on their vaccines. When you get your puppy's first round of shots, your vet will put your dog on a vaccination schedule. The clinic will then notify you every time your dog needs to get booster shots to maintain their immunity.

Genetic Illnesses

"Cockapoos can carry genetic health concerns found in the Cocker Spaniel or Poodle breeds. It's imperative to ask about any testing before buying a Cockapoo. Cocker Spaniels are known for cardiac and eye diseases. Poodles give the longevity genes, but should be tested for hip dysphasia and deformity in elbows. Many breeders use OFA testing or Paw Print Genetics to verify their health."

Luann Woodard

Cockapoo Cottage

Because the Cockapoo is half Cocker Spaniel and half Poodle, common genetic ailments come from both breeds. The good thing about crossbreeds is that they're less likely to suffer from deadly genetic diseases because there's less in-breeding between dogs. Also, if you're buying from a reputable breeder, their practices limit the number of genetic ailments by choosing only healthy dogs to use in breeding. However, there are some ailments that are more common in certain breeds, so it's a good idea to know what to look for.

There are a few conditions of the skeletal system that you'll want to look out for if your dog starts suddenly limping. Luxating patella is a condition in which the kneecap slides around and "catches" in certain circumstances. The simple act of running and jumping can cause the knee to slide out of place, which can be extremely painful. Hip dysplasia is another condition that's generally found in larger breeds where the hip joint doesn't fit in the socket very well, causing pain and issues with mobility. Both conditions need to be treated with surgery if serious enough.

This breed is also more likely to suffer from retinal atrophy and other eye issues. Retinal atrophy can lead to blindness over time. Of course, this is one of those conditions that should be eliminated in the breeding process. However, if you adopt a dog from an unknown origin, you may want to have your dog's eyes tested if they have trouble seeing in the dark. This is a sign that their overall eyesight is deteriorating. Poodle crossbreeds are also at a higher risk for thyroid issues. Talk to your vet if your dog is suddenly lethargic or has patchy fur. They can prescribe medications that can return their hormone levels to normal in no time.

Senior Dog Care

Cockapoos have a relatively long lifespan compared to other breeds, but one day, they will be considered a senior dog. Senior dogs still love to play and explore, but they will slow down a little, especially compared to the energy levels they had as a puppy.

You may find that your senior dog has joint pain when they try to walk or play. This is often noticeable when they first get up in the morning or

Photo Courtesy of Kelly Cunningham

try to walk around after a nap. There are a few things you can do to ease this stiffness and pain. For starters, make sure that your dog has a soft and supportive bed to rest on. If they're used to hopping up on the couch, they may have a harder time doing that as they age. There are also joint supplements that you can give your dog that will help repair some of the damage that occurs to leg joints over time. If your dog seems to be in a considerable amount of pain, talk to your vet about anti-inflammatory medication. This may be a good remedy for joint pain.

Your Cockapoo may also gain weight if they're not exercising as much as they used to. Older dogs require fewer calories than their younger counterparts. If your senior dog is gaining weight, consider reducing their daily food intake. If they have trouble eating crunchy kibble due to reduced smell or painful teeth, try mixing dry and wet food together to make it easier to chew. Or pour a little water or broth on top of the crunchy food to soften it up.

You may also have to change your exercise routine. While you may have been able to go on runs before, you will reach a time where that's just too much exertion for your old dog. Exercise is still important, but you may decide that an easy walk will lead to less pain and stiffness in your dog's legs. Continuing to test your dog's mental fitness with puzzles and other games is still important as they get older. It can keep their mind sharp, which will lead to less confusion and agitation.

Most of all, it's important to spend quality time with your Cockapoo. These dogs are companion animals and want to snuggle up to you. You may find that as your Cockapoo ages, he's less interested in playing fetch and more interested in nestling up to you while you read a book. Cherish these moments with your dog because they won't last forever. Also, remember that dogs are considered "senior" around age eight. With proper care, it's entirely possible for your dog to live another decade beyond that.

Eventually, there will come a time where you have to say goodbye. If your dog is in a lot of pain, can no longer use the bathroom on their own, or is suffering from a lot of different age-related ailments, you may decide that euthanasia is the best option. This can be extremely difficult to decide for your pet, but you'll know when your dog's condition will only get worse and their quality of life is suffering. When you're reaching this conclusion, talk to a vet for guidance. An examination can tell you if there's anything they can do for your dog. If not, they will take you through the euthanasia process.

Once you bring your dog home, you'll come to realize that there's nothing more important than ensuring your pup lives the best life he possibly can. The decisions that you make along the way have a lot to do with his health and happiness. Exercise, food, hygiene, and preventative care can extend your dog's lifespan by years and give them lots of quality time with you. Remember that your veterinarian is a great resource, and you should work together to give your dog the healthcare they deserve.

Cockapoos are great companions for a first-time dog owner or an experienced owner of a whole crew! They are adorable, peppy, sweet dogs that love to spend time with their people. Their intelligence makes them easy to train, and their goofiness makes them easy to love. There's a reason that this crossbreed has been popular for so long—they're the total package when it comes to awesome dog breeds!

*Photo Courtesy of
Michelle Clark*

Infant Massage:
The definitive guide for teaching parents

PAULINE CARPENTER
ANITA EPPLE

Ditto
International

Published and distributed in Great Britain by Ditto International Ltd, 7 Regent's Hall, St Mary's Avenue, Stony Stratford, Buckinghamshire. MK11 1EB

Printed in Great Britain by Veldonn Printers Ltd., Worcestershire.

Ditto
International

Acknowledgments

We would like to offer many thanks to Suzy Sherratt for her significant contribution to the Anatomy and Physiology chapter.

We are also extremely grateful to David Thomas, Jim Carpenter, Cathy Guibouret, Louise Cooper-Bevan, Stéphane Carpenter and Sue Brough for their support and input.

Appreciation must also go to our trainers and students, as a wider acknowledgement, for their continued evaluation and support that has helped to inform and guide us as we wrote the Definitive Guide.

Thank you
Pauline and Anita

3

Foreword

From the very beginning, healthy infants actively seek interaction with others and, through everyday routines, their unique personalities become increasingly apparent to carers who are able to 'tune in' to their individual likes and dislikes, sensitivities and strengths. Research from a range of disciplines has indicated that the earliest years of life are a crucial period when young children are making emotional attachments and forming the first relationships which lay many of the foundations for future mental health.

Touching another person is a powerful way of establishing physical and emotional connections and an intrinsic part of caring for an infant. In many areas of the world, especially in the African and Asian continents, indigenous South Pacific cultures and the Soviet Union, infant massage is a traditional practice. Recently in the UK there has been increasing interest from parents wanting to attend a programme to learn the art of massage with their babies.

Infant massage is increasingly being taught in the community and a recent systematic review (Underdown et al 2006) found that infant massage has beneficial effects in terms of reducing and balancing stress hormones, promoting sleep and encouraging positive interactions especially where mothers have been experiencing post-natal depression.

I have also been involved in primary research into infant massage and have had the great privilege of acting as a student with my 'model baby' as I have video taped and observed the classes. I would like to pay tribute to all the parents and teachers who have welcomed me into their classes and taught me so much. I quickly became aware of how skilful the group leaders must be, not only to teach the massage strokes but to facilitate interactions between all participants – parents and babies, parents and parents and, something I found particularly fascinating, the infants' interest and pleasure in watching one other. Many of the leaders I observed, from a range of different trainings, had the skills to lead a group, teach massage, be warm and welcoming to both infants and parents, help people share any worries and concerns all while creating a relaxed and fun atmosphere!

Leading an effective infant massage group is highly skilled work and it is crucial that leaders receive the level of training to support them in this important role. The way in which infant massage is taught is crucial and it is with great pleasure that I write the foreword for this manual which documents good practice in the teaching of infant massage. Pauline and Anita have written a comprehensive manual which will be an invaluable reference tool for Infant Massage Practitioners. Their writing is underpinned by a deep respect for the parents and infants as they show how learning infant massage can be an important medium for helping parents to tune into to their baby's individual likes and dislikes, strengths and sensitivities.

Tuning into a baby's cues and signals has implications far beyond massage and parents often report that there has been a positive impact on sleeping and feeding routines. Research too has shown that being massaged reduces stress hormones and promotes sleep. More research is still needed into infant massage and the useful section on writing for publication will hopefully encourage some practitioners to share their learning from working with parents and babies. The wealth of information in this book will give Infant Massage Practitioners knowledge and confidence as they provide a fun and a sensitive forum in which parents and babies can enjoy the communication through touch.

Angela Underdown
Associate Professor of Public Health in the Early Years.
Deputy Director Warwick Infant and Family Wellbeing Unit
University of Warwick Medical School.

Table of contents

Teaching infant massage 41

7

9

12

13

14 Anatomy and Physiology · 165

Research, References and Further Reading 186

15

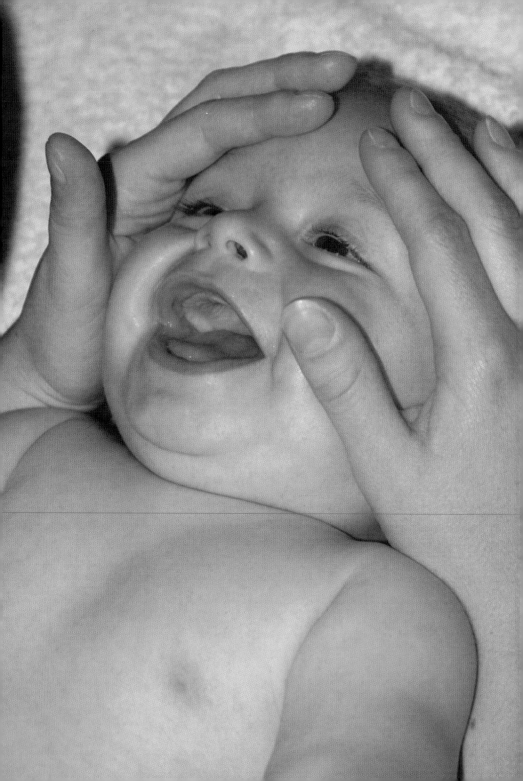

Infant
Massage

Introduction

In-utero, a baby experiences constant massage because of their mother's gentle movements. Once born, babies need to be touched in order to thrive and parents can use the powers of positive touch, such as massage, to satisfy this need and help them communicate with their child.

Touch is one of the first senses to develop in-utero

18

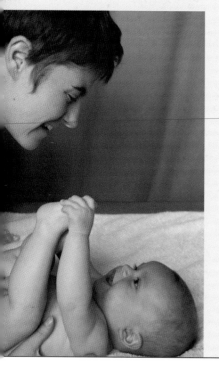

Parents, particularly new mothers who are returning to work after the birth of their baby, often like to find activities that give them quality time with their children. infant massage is simple and free and can be done almost anywhere; which fits in well with parents who juggle a host of responsibilities and have hectic lifestyles.

Massage gives parents the opportunity to use positive touch, have special hugs and holds, use nursery rhymes and music, spend special time, learn about, and play with their baby. Furthermore, a parent's ability to understand their baby's cues can be greatly enhanced through massage, allowing the parent to comfort and reassure their baby through positive touch.

Above all, massage enables parents and babies to relax and have fun together!

Historical and cultural origins

The use of massage as a tool for healing and for relaxation is centuries old and is still a regular practice for many cultures, including western society. Infant massage however, though an intrinsic part of the heritage of some cultures, is a comparatively new concept to the west.

It came to Western Society in the 1970's and has become increasingly popular since the turn of the 21st century and is now taught to parents by many health professionals and complementary therapists, who recognise its wonderful benefits.

History

It is possible to establish just how important infant massage has been throughout history for different cultures, as the physiological benefits have often been documented, or are a part of the tacit knowledge passed down from generation to generation. For example, the use of massage for babies is known to have been used:

- During the Qing dynasty in China (1644-1911)
- In Ayurvedic medicine in India, from 1800BC

19

Cultural differences

Families from many cultures, such as those of Nepal, Tibet, Malaysia and India, recognise the value of massage to promote health and a sense of well-being for the mother and child, before and after birth.

In India the art of infant massage started in Kerala; where babies are still massaged morning and evening for 10-20 minutes. In the Gujurat region it is commonplace for babies to be massaged daily until they are 12 days old and in the Punjab area until they are 30 days old.

> Cross-cultural studies support the idea that infants should be held, massaged and carried much more than they are in present-day western cultures

Regular massage for babies is also a part of their daily life, for varying lengths of time after birth, in Malaysia, Mexico, Thailand, Tahiti, China, The Philippines, Vietnam, Ceylon and Indonesia.

Different cultures have different reasons for massaging their off-spring.

Most consider the physiological benefits only, but the emotional ones are intrinsic, whether considered important or not, as long as the baby finds the experience a positive one.

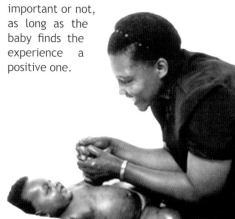

And for Mums...

In the Gujurat and Punjab regions mothers are massaged daily before and after childbirth, as well as the baby!

Benefits for different cultures

Africa	Used to calm and relax
India	Used to keep joints and muscles supple and enhance facial beauty
Russia	Used to develop the central nervous system
Ibo of Nigeria and Kwakiutls of North America	Used from birth to stimulate survival mechanisms and help resist disease
South America	Used to promote energy, health and happiness

The importance of touch

Why we need touch?

Touch is a fundamental human need and is vitally important for both emotional and physical health. Therefore, all children should be held and receive loving touch well beyond infancy to enable them to reach their full potential.

Touch is considered to be a form of communication and helps a person connect with another. Parents can use the power of positive touch, such as holding, containment and massage to help their baby feel secure and to enhance the communication and bond they have with them.

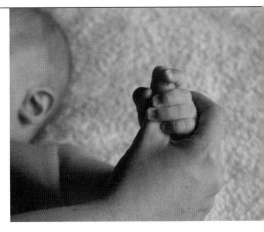

Sensory Homunculus

The importance of touch as a sensory stimulation is graphically depicted by the model of the sensory homunculus. This clearly indicates what a man's body would look like if each body part grew in proportion to the area of the cortex of the brain concerned with its sensory perception.

Notice that the hands especially, as well as the mouth and the feet are much larger than other parts of the body. This helps to explain why babies naturally put the objects they are holding into their mouths for it to be a full sensory experience from which they can learn.

This may also be a reason why babies find their feet so interesting.

Touch can be so much :

Loving	Sexual	Supportive
Healing	Therapeutic	Directive
Stimulating	Diagnostic	Calming
Responsive	Comforting	

Babies benefit from and respond to loving, stimulating, comforting, supportive, calming, responsive and, when necessary, healing touch.

Categories of touch

TYPE OF TOUCH	WHAT THIS MEANS	EXAMPLES
Instrumental	Deliberate physical contact	Holding a child's hand to cross the road
Expressive	Loving and spontaneous	Giving someone a hug or a kiss
Therapeutic	Healing	Rubbing a child's 'hurt' better
Systemic	Aimed at improving holistic health	Shiatsu/reflexology

The significance of receiving 'expressive' touch

Loving and spontaneous expressive touch will indicate to a child how important they are. To be shown this kind of love can help to raise their self-esteem and social skills. As Montagu states:

"For a child to develop into a content, balanced, well rounded individual it is important that they receive regular loving touch. A lack of caring touch may affect the holistic well-being of the child, which may negatively impact on their ability to relate to others throughout their childhood and into adulthood." (Montagu, 1986. Page 97).

The significance of receiving 'therapeutic' touch

Touch is considered to be a form of therapy in many parts of the world. Even in the UK, "Rub it better" is a phrase very much used to reassure a child that has been hurt. It is a natural reaction to stroke the area of the skin that has been affected. The affects of this type of massage encourages the natural processes of our body to start the repair process, because:

- Blood and oxygen are brought to the damaged area and swelling and inflammation is reduced by the body producing its own corticosteroids
- The pressure on the skin interacts with receptor corpuscles under the skin, triggering a supply of natural opiates, which are stronger than most commercial analgesia

How the categories of touch are integral to infant massage :

TYPE OF TOUCH	WHAT THIS MEANS	EXAMPLES
Instrumental	Deliberate physical contact	The parent makes the time to massage their child
Expressive	Loving and spontaneous	Massage is a loving act to share with their baby and shows respect
Therapeutic	Healing	Many of the physical and emotional benefits indicate how therapeutic massage is
Systemic	Aimed at improving holistic health	Infant massage improves overall good health

When loving touch is missing

The majority of research into the effects of receiving little or no touch has been carried out on young rats and monkeys. Time after time it is shown that the withdrawal of touch, or removal from their mothers, results in immune suppression and behavioural problems.

Our need for touch is not often considered until we see the profound effects that little or no touch has on a child. Because there are several unfortunate cases of sensory deprivation, there is now a sufficient body of evidence to indicate clearly that parallels can be drawn between the research carried out on animals and the impact that lack of touch can have on humans. The effects

on babies and children, who were deprived of touch in orphanages around the world, show us how important positive touch is, particularly for the developing child.

Emotionally disturbed children from neglectful home environments are more likely to:

- Suffer from growth defects
- Be inclined to be small for their age

(indicating an Adrenocorticotropic hormone deficiency (ACTH) and deficiencies in the growth hormone)

- Suffer with learning difficulties

Furthermore, when these children experience a more nurturing environment, where loving touch becomes a part of their lives, they show a significant increase in development and growth.

Skin-to-skin for neonates

Throughout life, no matter what the age of the person, to be held and comforted is the most loving act one human being can give to another. The need for touch is essential for everybody, but 'skin-to-skin' contact is very important for a newborn baby. It can help with:

- Temperature control
- Stabilising breathing and pulse rate
- Preserving energy
- Accelerating metabolic adaptation
- Increasing the well-being of the baby

If the need for skin-to-skin contact between the mother and baby is ignored, it can potentially affect the mother's ability to recognise her baby's non-verbal cues; through which the baby tries to communicate. Maternal sensitivity and the infant-parent attachment process also improve if skin-to-skin contact is initiated at birth.

Holding and containment

Not only is the need to be touched often disregarded once the baby has left the confines of the uterus, but also their desire to be contained can be overlooked.

Babies in-utero are able to float effortlessly in the amniotic fluid; moving, kicking and stretching, whilst protected by the uterine wall. By the end of the nine month period these confines are at their greatest, limiting a baby's movement considerably. The baby's next experience is that of the open world with open space and gravity to deal with. For the newborn there is nothing more reassuring than to be placed immediately into their mother's arms; so that they feel a sense of containment again.

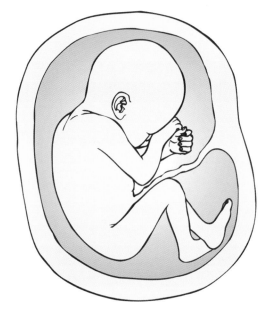

Newborn babies have limited control of the neuro-muscular activity of their limbs, which can be startling for them when their arms and legs are moving around on, what seems to be, their own accord. This can be upsetting for the baby, who may not be calmed by their parents' voice alone. At these times they are more likely to respond to being picked up and hugged, which reduces the disorganised movement of their limbs and calms them. When a newborn baby is held they are able to maintain a natural position; their legs are bent at the knee and held towards their trunk with their arms much the same, giving them the sense of security they once had in the uterus. This position is lost when the baby is placed in a cot, or car seat, or on a changing mat, and with it the sense of containment is lost too.

Benefits for babies

There are a host of benefits to be gained from receiving a massage, no matter what your age. The physiological effects are particularly well documented; but infant massage goes far beyond these, as it can have a positive influence on the emotional and cognitive development of the baby as well.

The physiological benefits of infant massage

The many physiological benefits of regular massage include:

- Increasing and improving circulation - especially venous and lymphatic flow
- Maintaining muscle tone and improving flexibility and function
- Improving skin condition
  (Particularly when the skin is dry and flaky, such as cradle cap. When massaged with a vegetable oil, the positive effects are even greater)
- Improving the general functioning of the immune system
- Regulating and supporting the respiratory system
  (Particularly useful in helping to loosen mucus and alleviate the symptoms of colds and snuffles)
- Regulating and strengthening the digestive system
  (Which may reduce the discomfort of colic, wind and constipation)

- Stimulating and balancing the nervous system
- Stimulating the senses
  (Remote senses: visual and auditory. Mechanical : kinaesthetic. Chemical senses: olfaction)
- Stimulates the production of Oxytocin;
  (The hormone responsible for love and bonding and associated with the ability to maintain healthy interpersonal relationships and healthy psychological boundaries with other people)
- Pain reduction; because of the production of endorphins
  (Such as soothing teething pains)
- Prevention of fibrosis/adhesion in muscles and decreasing the tendency toward muscular atrophy and/or contractures
- Reduction of certain types of oedema
  (Although massage is contra-indicated in cardiac and kidney failure)

Massage can also:

- Be soothing and calming, which can reduce heart rate and lead to a better sleep pattern
- Help with general growth and development
- Enhance body awareness
- Encourage parents to let their baby 'play' on their front when they have their back massaged. *This may help to prevent plagiocephaly and/or brachycephaly (flat head syndrome)*

Reducing the incidence of colic

Colic often draws parents to infant massage classes – in desperation! But they soon find out there is a lot more on offer once they have come along to the first class.

It can be a most upsetting experience for a parent to watch a young baby screaming in agony with, what appears to be, severe abdominal pains. It often lasts for many hours and usually starts around the same time each day. The condition is harmless, although it can be distressing for a baby to experience and for the parents to observe. This distressing condition often creates stress and anxiety within the home, particularly as parents often feel frustrated and upset because they feel powerless to help their baby.

What is colic?

Colic presents as uncontrollable, extended crying in a baby who is otherwise healthy and well-fed. Every baby cries, but babies who cry for more than three hours a day, three to four days a week, may have colic. It can start when a baby is around two to four weeks of age and may last for three months, or possibly longer. There is a school of thought that believes colic does not exist; but for those parents that experience the early evening bouts of screaming and obvious distress with their babies it is definitely real enough. However, colic is not a serious medical condition.

What causes colic?

The cause of colic is not really known. It is often thought to be related to the digestive system. Another possible cause is a combination of the baby's temperament and an immature nervous system. The baby's temperament may make him highly sensitive, and he may react to normal stimulation, changes to the environment or parental stress by crying. The baby is unable to regulate crying once it starts because of its immature nervous system.

The Vagus Nerve and the digestive system

The Vagus Nerve starts at the brain stem and travels through the neck into the chest and then into the abdomen. It innervates the lungs and stomach and is responsible for heart-rate and peristalsis.

The digestive system is closely linked to emotions and state of mind and this connection is largely due to the Vagus Nerve.

What are the symptoms of colic?

The main symptom is continuous crying for long periods of time. The baby may:

- Look uncomfortable
- Appear to be in pain
- May lift their head
- Draw their legs up to their abdomen
- Become red in the face and pass wind
- Refuse to eat *(though many babies with colic continue to eat and gain weight normally, despite the crying)*

Although this crying can occur at any time, it usually worsens between 4pm and 8pm in the evening. This is often a time when there are a lot of external sources of stimulation in the home; perhaps older siblings are arriving home from school, the television goes on, the telephone may ring, other family members are arriving home from work, the evening meal is being prepared and the baby, very often, is in the middle of this commotion. Some babies will love this hustle and bustle, but others may hate it, especially those that are sensitive and inclined to suffer with colic.

Using massage to help alleviate colic

Abdominal massage can help regulate and strengthen the digestive system and alleviate wind, constipation and colic. Furthermore, as massage can be relaxing, the more stressed baby may become less anxious if they have a regular massage.

The best way to alleviate the problem is to catch it early before the baby is in real pain. Parents with a colicky baby will know the signs and the usual time that their baby will begin to suffer with colic, so should be encouraged to massage two or three times a day, but particularly within the hour of their usual time of on-set.

! Caution

It is extremely important to encourage parents not to do the massage whilst their baby is crying during a bout of colic. As crying is a negative cue, it would not be appropriate. Furthermore, massaging a tight, tense abdomen is unlikely to impact on the bowel below and therefore would not be very helpful.

The key is to try to alleviate the problem before it takes hold and encourage parents to massage regularly and most definitely about an hour before it is inclined to present.

Suggested exercise for parents (Early evening when colic often presents)

Encourage parents in your classes to think about the external sources of stimulation. This will give them the opportunity to think about how they could reduce some of these in order to help their baby.

(It might not actually be possible for parents to reduce many of the over-stimulating factors in the environment. However, teaching them massage, particularly a routine to directly help alleviate colic, may make a difference.)

The emotional and psychological benefits of massage

The physiological benefits of massage are only one aspect of the overall benefits that can be associated with infant massage. What also need to be considered are the emotional and psychological benefits for the baby, of which there are many. If parents understand how important it is to honour their child's wishes, and only massage them if they say 'yes', they will help the developing child realise that they are entitled to be heard and that their feelings are understood and, more importantly, honoured.

Massage can potentially help:

- A baby adapt to his new environment and become generally more settled
- Enhance a baby's feeling of being loved, respected and secure
- To promote relaxation which can improve quality of sleep
- A baby cope with stressful situations *(by regulating Cortisol levels)*
- A baby associate touch with positive handling *(particularly important for babies who have experienced intrusive medical intervention)*
- A baby learn to interact and play with others

The physiological, psychological and emotional benefits, although seemingly separate, are indeed entwined. Therefore, infant massage necessarily offers the parents the opportunity to holistically nurture their developing child. Furthermore, as Infant Massage is a wonderful communication tool, which strengthens the bond between the parent and child, it will also enhance their developing relationship.

Benefits for the older child

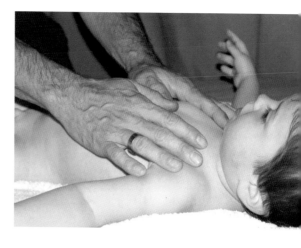

Many of the benefits experienced by babies can also be experienced by the older child. Furthermore, it helps them to feel loved and secure as they experience the challenges of growing up.

Helping to alleviate sibling rivalry

When a new baby arrives into a family that already has one or more children, the family dynamics can change dramatically. Older siblings can feel alienated, neglected and just down-right jealous of the new arrival. Parents who are sensitive to this know the importance of helping the older children come to terms with, and accept the new baby. infant massage can be extremely useful in this process.

Suggested exercise for parents to try at home

When teaching, you could suggest to parents, who have older children and a new baby, that they involve the older sibling/s in the routine.

Older siblings can get involved by:

- Helping to prepare the room
- Choosing the music and the nursery rhymes
- Holding the bottle of oil
- Watching for the baby's cues
- Singing the nursery rhymes with their parent

A fun idea is for the older child to copy the massage strokes their parent is doing with their new brother or sister, using their favourite doll or teddy as their 'baby'.

(This can really help make a difference to the way the older child feels about the new baby; and it shows them that they are still just as important to their parents. Not only that, they may enjoy the new found responsibility as 'older' brother or sister.)

Benefits for parents

For a parent, learning to massage their baby is a wonderful experience, which may help to enhance their knowledge of their baby, as they steadily gain an understanding of what their baby is 'telling' them during the massage.

If a parent is able to understand whether a baby is saying 'yes' or 'no' to massage, they are subsequently more likely to be able to understand what their baby is trying to 'tell' them during their day-to-day activities as well. Infant massage is therefore a very empowering tool for parents. It may help to improve their self-esteem and confidence in their parenting skills; and help to develop a sense of security within the whole family unit.

Infant massage can help parents:

- Have confidence when handling their baby
- To understand their baby's non-verbal cues
- To relax with their baby
- Develop a feeling of closeness with their baby
- It may also:
  + Encourage lactation through the stimulation of Prolactin
  + Encourage the nurturing instinct through the stimulation of Oxytocin

Infant massage classes can:

- Empower and support parents
- Give parents the opportunity to join a group where they meet and share their experiences in a non-stigmatising environment
- Give parents the opportunity to learn by demonstration and practice

Benefits for health professionals

Teaching infant massage has been identified as being particularly well-suited to support professionals in their preventative and health promotion work with parents and infants.

And for infant massage teachers

The calming effects of massage can benefit the Infant Massage Teacher too! No matter how busy the rest of the week is, the teaching sessions can bring welcome, light relief to help recharge everyone's batteries.

This skill may:

- Enhance the role of the health professional, as it gives the opportunity for the development of a working partnership between the professionals, parents and infants

- Allow for the development of a sensitive service that refocuses the needs of the infant and parent in terms of well-being and encourages life skills development and education

Benefits for society ?

Anti-social behaviour, over-crowded prisons, an increase in young teenage pregnancies, epidemic levels of bullying, etc all indicate that new ideas and methods to bring stability to society need to be explored and implemented.

As onfant massage encourages respect and understanding; and enhances relationships within a family, there must ultimately be long term benefits for society as a whole (should classes became available to all parents with babies).

Parallels can be drawn between the relationship in the family unit with the wider community, particularly as societies that closely nurture their infants produce less aggressive adults.

Contraindications
and precautions

Precautions for infant massage

The age of the baby

Over-stimulation

When babies are born their life experiences take on a whole new dimension and they need time to adjust. Positive touch, holding and containment are wonderful tools for parents to use at this early stage in their baby's life. However, a full massage routine may be far too stimulating in the first few weeks after birth.

Consider not only the new environment that a baby has to adjust to, but certain aspects of the anatomy and physiology of the newborn that will amplify the sensory experience of massage.

Synaesthesia Senses are experienced more intensely by the infant due to the fact that their early experiences are multi-sensory, or 'synaesthetic'	There are connections between the auditory and visual cortices, which means that a baby 'sees' sounds and 'hears' colour	As the cortex develops the sensory information becomes categorised and the senses are experienced in a singular fashion
The Skin The Meissner Corpuscles, the main touch receptors, are tightly packed in the skin of a newborn, but slowly disperse with age	There are 80 Meissner Corpuscles per square millimetre in a three year old, and 20 per square millimetre in a young adult	As the Meissner Corpuscles disperse over a larger area, over-stimulation is less likely to occur

34

The Meissner Corpuscles may not have dispersed significantly by the time a baby is six or eight weeks old and synaesthesia may still by present. However, by this stage a baby is at least becoming familiar with its surroundings and is more likely to be able to cope with the massage routine.

Enjoyment for parents?

During 'one-to-one' teaching sessions, an Infant Massage Teacher can develop an individualised programme that suits both parent and baby. However, when teaching a varying number of parents in a group, over four to six weeks, the Infant Massage Teacher will have to offer a more standardised programme.

A parent of a very young baby may become frustrated if they find that not only does their baby not want massage during each class (sometimes the case with babies of all ages, because it is not the right time for them) but that they will not tolerate much massage between classes either. When they return to each class and listen to the other parents enthusing about how much their babies have enjoyed the massage, they may feel that:

a) They are missing out
b) It is their fault that their baby does not like it

The classes are just the beginning of their experience and it is necessary to try and encourage the parents to continue after the course has finished. However, it is much more likely that a parent who had the opportunity to massage their baby either during the classes or at home will continue to do so regularly, long after the course has finished. Whereas the parent who has not is less likely to continue, especially if they feel they lack practice.

Health check

As massage has a physiological affect on the body, it is important to practise safely at all times. Parents are invited to take their baby for a health check at about six to eight weeks old. Waiting until a baby has had this check-up reduces any potential risk associated with massage vis-à-vis conditions that may present at this time.

You may be wondering if this is a little unnecessary, but when you consider that:

- 1 in every 100 babies are born with clinically unstable hips (approximately 1 in 800 develop a dislocation)
- The prevalence of congenital heart disease in the UK is about 8 in 1000

Any potential hip dysplasia and heart problems can be picked up at the six to eight week health check. (This may not prevent the baby from experiencing massage, but the parent should be advised to check with their baby's medical practitioner before commencing classes.)
It is necessary to consider the legal implications for you as a professional (as well as the health of the baby), if teaching massage to parents with babies who have not had a health check and who have not signed a disclaimer.

Disclaimers

This is not to say that parents with babies that are less than six weeks old must not be taught. If approached by a parent who wishes to attend classes before the baby's health check, ask them to sign a disclaimer.

This simply states that they take full responsibility. Another occasion that a disclaimer may be useful is for parents who do not feel it necessary to take their baby for a check-up. As an Infant Massage Teacher, it is important to empower parents and if they do not believe it necessary to take their child for a check-up, that is their choice. By asking the parent to sign a disclaimer, you are supporting them in their decision, but protecting yourself as a professional.

Colic

Colic often presents much earlier than six weeks, and a regular massage routine for colic may help a parent alleviate their baby's suffering. This is a wonderful tool for parents to use, but should only be applied if it has been established that there are no other reasons for the abdominal pain. For a health professional, such as a health visitor, it may be suitable for them to show a colic routine to parents during a home visit or at the clinic. For private teachers it is advisable that they suggest that the parent checks with the baby's medical practitioner to confirm that it is colic and nothing more serious, before teaching a massage routine for colic. Again, the disclaimer is an option if the parent does not want to take this route.

> **! CAUTION**
>
> It is necessary to consider the legal implications for you as a professional (as well as the health of the baby), if teaching massage to parents with babies who have not had a health check and who have not signed a disclaimer.

Summary

Consider the following when teaching parents with very young babies :
- It can be very over-stimulating
- There may be limited enjoyment for parents and babies
- There may be health implications for babies who have not had a health check
- There may be legal implications for the Infant Massage Teacher

However, the use of disclaimers means that you can :
- Empower parents by giving them the choice to join your classes
- Teach parents the colic routine that may give relief to their baby and encourage them to join a class at a later date

Fitting in with feeds

The baby's comfort is the main consideration at all times. A delay after feeding is advisable, because massage encourages the blood to flow more readily to the peripheries, away from the major organs – including the stomach and small intestine that are involved with digesting the recently ingested food.

Particular regard must be given to the baby's comfort during the abdomen and back sequence, because within 45 minutes to an hour after a feed, the direct pressure on the abdomen from the massage or the pressure from the floor when lying prone may cause discomfort, or reflux.

It is important to offer this precaution as a suggestion to parents, but they are the best judge of when their baby is comfortable, so it is important to leave the decision to them.

Contraindications to massage

Massage should be avoided when a baby:

 Is asleep, tired, hungry, crying or fretful. These are all 'no' cues

 Is unwell, or has a raised temperature. Their immune system needs to be left to deal with the problem and not be over-stimulated by massage

 Is suffering from fever

 Has undergone recent surgery. Refrain from massaging the affected area for at least eight weeks to allow scars to heal after surgery, but unaffected areas can be massaged if this will not cause discomfort. *(Though it is advisable for parents to check with the baby's GP or consultant)*

 Has an infectious skin condition. This may aggravate the infected area and there is the risk of cross-infection *(The most common skin infections in children are impetigo and ringworm)*

 Is suffering from bruising, sprains or a fracture. It is advisable to refrain from massage until the injuries have healed completely and swelling has reduced. It may be possible for the unaffected areas to be massaged

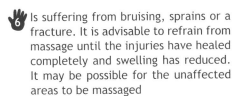 Has open, weeping wounds and rashes. Breaks in the skin may become infected if massaged

 Has an unhealed navel

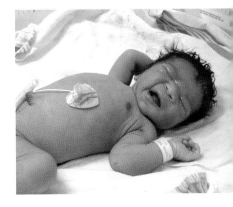

37

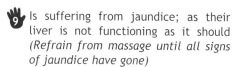 Is suffering from jaundice; as their liver is not functioning as it should *(Refrain from massage until all signs of jaundice have gone)*

Has suffered haemorrhaging. *(Massage increases the blood flow in the body and there may be a risk of further bleeding)*

Is diagnosed with brittle bone disease *(The bones in children suffering from this disease can be so brittle that they break with normal handling)*

If the baby has been vaccinated within the previous three days

Why not massage after vaccination ?

Vaccinations necessarily have an impact on the immune system, as vaccines trigger the production of antibodies in a similar manner to that of the actual disease. Massage is stimulating and has a direct effect on all body systems, including the immune system. It is therefore necessary to have a break from massage, so that the baby's body is not overloaded/over stimulated whilst it is trying to deal with the vaccinations given.

Until quite recently the 'killed' vaccines for diphtheria, tetanus, whooping cough, Hib were administered via an injection and the 'live' polio vaccine was give orally at the same time. However this has now changed and there is a new 'five in one' injection that incorporates a 'killed' polio vaccine as well. Although the potential of a reaction to a 'live' vaccine is a much longer period of time, there is still the potential for a reaction to a 'killed' vaccine to occur within a 72 hour period after it has been administered.

Therefore it is advisable to suggest to parents that they avoid massage for at least three days after the injection has been given. After all, if there is the potential of a reaction then the baby's immune system must necessarily still be dealing with the effects of the vaccination. After three days massage may recommence as long as the injection site is avoided until all bruising has subsided.

39

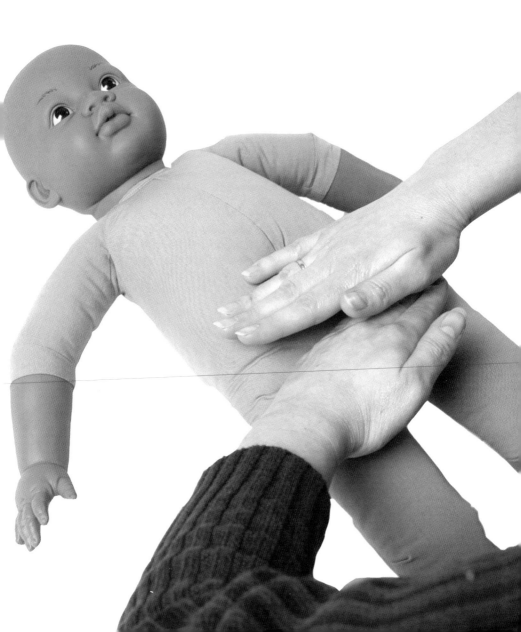

Teaching Infant Massage

Introducing touch
to parents and babies

Massage can be fun and is a great way for parents and babies to spend time together, but sometimes it can be a little too stimulating, particularly for the newborn. However, a baby's need to be touched and feel secure should not be overlooked, so when teaching infant massage it is useful to discuss containment holds, swaddling and each individual baby's methods of self-calming. This helps parents find ways of supporting their baby through positive touch techniques other than massage itself.

Containment holds

Babies live the first nine months of their life cocooned, completely protected and safe. By the end of this period the uterine space has become so restrictive and confining, limiting the baby's movement considerably and giving them the greatest sense of containment. Once born, however, the baby will cease to have this natural containment.

When a newborn baby is held in someone's arms they are able to maintain a more natural foetal position, giving them the sense of security they experienced before birth, to which they became accustomed and still desire. Containing a baby, so that they feel safe and secure can be all they need, particularly in the early days and weeks after birth, when the world is so stimulating and anything more would be too much.

Swaddling

Swaddling, though common practice for many cultures, is viewed with some scepticism by western society. Current trends tend to imply that swaddling may be unsafe because a baby's airway might be compromised and their physical development may be impaired. But, using a swaddling technique that allows the baby's hands to be free from the covers not only gives them access to their hands, but also prevents the covers from riding up over their face.

Research shows that babies born to cultures that regularly swaddle their young for up to a year, reach the same physical developmental milestones as those who have not been swaddled.

Swaddling can be very beneficial, as it can:

- Give baby a sense of containment
- Be relaxing
- Prevent baby being startled
- Reduce crying
- Calm a fractious baby

Not all babies want to be swaddled, but many do. The steady pressure and the boundaries created by swaddling are akin to the sensations a baby experiences in the uterus; which is so unlike the undefined boundary of a cot or a pram, where tactile stimulation is at its lowest.

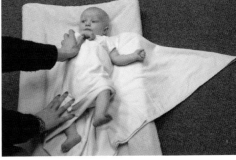

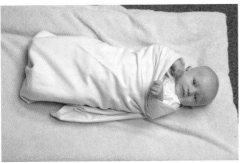

Self-calming

Young babies who are fractious are less able to calm themselves and manage the state they are in without the support of their parents. They need help to deal with their distress, so that they are able to return to a more balanced place. By encouraging parents to watch their baby, they will learn ways to support them when they are trying to 'self-calm'.

SOME EXAMPLES OF SELF-CALMING

SELF-CALM TECHNIQUE

REASON WHY

Thumb/finger sucking

Babies are born with the intrinsic need to receive tactile stimulation; the hands and mouth have more sensory nerve endings than any other part of the body

Eye rubbing

Stimulates an ocular-cardio reflex, which causes a response in the vagus nerve. This stimulation lowers the heart rate which helps prepare baby for sleep

Pushing themselves into the corner of their cot

By finding boundaries babies are replicating the sense of containment they once experienced in the uterus

44

Suggested exercise for parents to try at home

- Ask your parents to observe their baby to see how they self-calm and to record their observations in preparation for discussion in future classes.

(Parents will begin to see what their baby does and how they can support them to self-calm)

Practical massage techniques for babies

There are essentially only a limited number of strokes that are likely to be used for any form of massage with babies. Regardless of the name given to a particular stroke, in order to help parents remember it, the routine will undoubtedly be a combination of the following types of strokes:

Effleurage

This is one of the main strokes used in the baby massage routine and massage for the growing child. The effleurage stroke is used to:

- Introduce touch to the child
- Put the child at ease
- Warm the tissues prior to the deeper massage strokes
- Increase the circulation
- Stimulate peripheral nerves
- Relax muscles

Effleurage is a soothing, gliding and long-stroking movement using the palms of both hands on larger body areas, or thumbs and fingers on small areas. It generally moves relatively firmly in an upwards direction towards the heart, and uses light pressure on the return. It is an excellent stroke to indicate to the child which area is to be massaged and perfect for applying the massage oil. Effleurage massage strokes are generally relaxing, increase circulation, and warm up soft tissues. This stroke is also used as a linking move between the different strokes and movements and should be light with very young babies and firmer once the child is older.

45

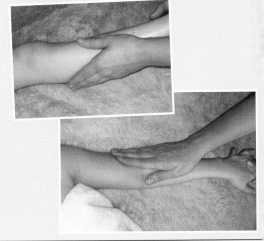

Kneading

This massage movement is designed to work the more fleshy areas of the body and is more focused than the effleurage stroke. Kneading is the rhythmical, alternately grasping and releasing, rolling and squeezing of soft tissue, using the whole of the hand, pads of the fingers and thumbs. The pressure should be firm then relaxed and then repeated on another area.

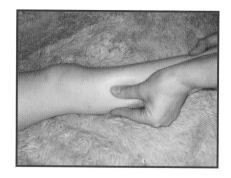

Kneading is used to:

- Release tension in the child's muscles
- Help eliminate waste
- Help with emotional stress

Frictions

Frictions are small circular movements made by the pads of the thumbs or fingers over a small area. In adults this would be deep, but for a baby these frictions should be applied lightly.

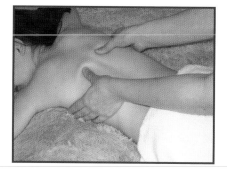

The friction movement is used to:

- Release tension in the child's muscles
- Increase circulation
- Help eliminate waste

Reflexology

Reflexology is a touch-therapy which works on the principle that all organs and parts of the body are represented energetically on the feet. When stimulating reflex points on the feet, the energy flow will correspond

to specific areas of the body. Massaging the whole of the foot may induce an holistically beneficial effect on the whole body, allowing for areas of congestion to be released, contributing to relaxation and pain relief.

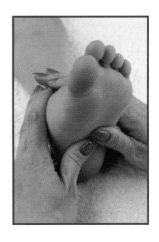

Reflex points for the teeth are situated on the top of the toes, so massaging these may help with teething pains.

For the sinuses, eyes and ears the specific points are situated on the underside of the toes, so stimulating these may help with nasal and ear congestion.

Massaging the feet may help to alleviate colic too; as the bowel is also represented within the feet.

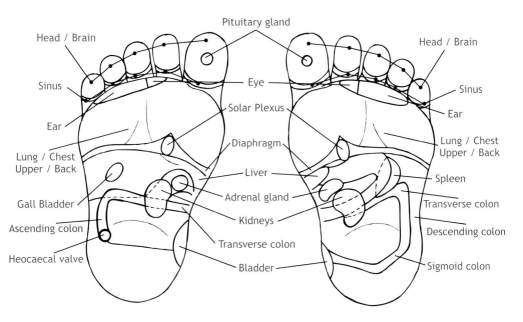

Head / Brain
Pituitary gland
Head / Brain
Sinus
Eye
Sinus
Solar Plexus
Ear
Ear
Diaphragm
Lung / Chest
Upper / Back
Lung / Chest
Upper / Back
Liver
Spleen
Gall Bladder
Adrenal gland
Transverse colon
Ascending colon
Kidneys
Descending colon
Heocaecal valve
Transverse colon
Sigmoid colon
Bladder

Venue, resources and equipment

Setting the scene and preparing the venue is very important when running Infant Massage classes. Having the venue well prepared with all the necessary resources and equipment ready to hand will help your classes run smoothly. The room you decide to use should ideally have a relaxing atmosphere about it. Soothing music, playing in the background, as the parents arrive can create a calming ambience.

The ideal venue

The ideal venue should have:

- A warm room which is light and airy, spacious and carpeted
- Adequate parking, or close to public transport
- Toilet and hand-washing facilities
- Space for pushchairs and car seats
- Access to kitchen facilities and, in particular, drinking water

As well as being:

- Risk assessed for health and safety
- Free from strong odours
- Clean

Equipment required

- CD player and music
- Demonstration doll
- Cushions for comfort and positioning
- Spare hand towels

Optional:

- Spare demonstration doll(s) *(for parents with sleeping babies)*
- Change mats

  (if not provided, remind parents to bring one with them)
- Flip chart, paper and pens

  (this may not be suitable

for the groups you teach and a more informal method might be expedient)

- Nail file

  (a useful extra if a parent has a snagged nail!)
  - Hair band

    (a useful extra if a parent has long hair which impedes their vision whilst leaning forward to engage with their baby during the massage; or if it is irritating and tickling the baby).

Consumable equipment

- Vegetable oils for the massage
- Roll of paper towelling or large tissues to clean up spillages, etc
- Baby wipes
- Drinks and refreshments
- Waste bags for rubbish and soiled nappies

Optional:

- Spare nappies

If practical the room, ideally, should be ready when the parents arrive. The more you can provide, the less the parents have to carry, which will always be appreciated.

49

Teaching resources

You will also need to remember each week:

- Class register
- Lesson plans
  - Completed health check records
    - Infant Massage books/handouts
- Pictures and visual aids, such as cue cards
- Parental evaluation forms *(for the last class)*

Optional:

- Name cards
- Certificate of attendance

Facilitating successful classes

Following a code of practice

If the following code of practice is implemented your parents will be guaranteed an enjoyable, empowering, respectful, safe, relaxing, and supportive learning environment.

WHEN TEACHING IT IS IMPORTANT TO REMEMBER :

Advise all parents to do a patch test with the chosen oil on themselves and their baby. This should be done at least 15 minutes before the massage is to commence – if this is not possible at the beginning of the class, encourage the parents to massage over the clothes without the oil and do the patch test at home

Remind parents to remove any jewellery which may be sharp

Ask parents to turn off (or put onto silent) mobile phones

Remind parents to ask for their babies' permission to massage them.
(By encouraging parents to observe their babies' non-verbal cues and signals they will soon learn whether the answer is 'yes' or 'no')

Always address the group as a whole when reiterating a point.
NEVER single out an individual parent in any circumstance or situation

Regularly remind parents that it is perfectly alright to stop the massage to adapt the baby's position, or adapt the strokes if their baby is responding to the massage with negative cues

Demonstrate clearly at a calm, steady pace and repeat each stroke many times to support parents

Be supportive, reassure and listen to the parents and the babies

Helping a baby feel secure during massage

It may be a little disturbing for the baby when their parents undress them in a bright, airy, possibly noisy room with strong smells. Even if the baby had already said "yes" to massage whilst their clothes were on, they might change their mind rather rapidly when their clothes are taken off, simply because they are feeling vulnerable and insecure. So, it is important to suggest to the parents ways to help their baby feel safe at all times during the massage. Once a baby is comfortable with the massage routine they will, in the main, be happy to be completely undressed, whilst lying on a mat.

Helpful suggestions:

- If the baby is unhappy about being completely undressed, suggest to parents that they expose only the area of the body that is being massaged
- Some babies like the feeling of boundaries around them

  + During massage a boundary can be created by rolling up a bath towel, length ways (like a sausage) and placing it around the baby

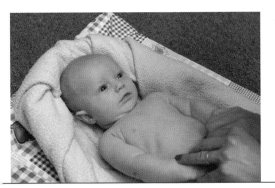

+ By leaning against a wall, or solid object, a parent might feel comfortable cocooning the baby between their legs, creating the boundary the baby requires

+ It is possible to buy change mats that have inflatable sides, which allow the baby to feel secure whilst on the mat because of the boundaries they can feel around them

- Some babies need to be held close to feel secure. It is possible to massage a baby whilst they are in the parent's arms. This requires a certain amount of adaptation, so that the massage can be carried out one handed (whilst the other arm/hand is occupied with supporting the baby) but is a lovely way to do massage - having a cuddle at the same time, which makes the baby feel safe and secure

- Simply chatting to a baby can help reassure them that they are alright; particularly if the voice is soft and gentle. Babies also find lullabies and nursery rhymes quite soothing and these encourage them to respond to sounds and rhythm

Using music to enhance infant massage classes

Once born, most babies love to listen to music. They will find certain types of rhythm soothing and comforting, particularly music that reminds them of the sound of a resting heartbeat. This is because, long before birth, babies continually feel the rhythm and hear the sounds from their mother's body. Also a couple of months before birth, they can hear the sounds from the outside world; especially the tone of their mother's voice.

Without necessarily realising it, music can affect us in many ways. So often, a piece of music or a particular song will conjure up an image, or remind us of a particular time or event that has happened in the past. With the image or memory, we often have a particular feeling come over us, which may make us feel excited or calm; happy or sometimes sad. Music can even affect our breathing and heart rate. The effect music can have on an individual is related to the key in which it is arranged. The keys F and C are considered to be particularly peaceful and can have a calming affect on babies, children and adults.

Music is actually very similar to language, as they are both processed in the same areas of the brain, and can contribute to overall brain development. For both music and language to be understood, they require an element of organisation, structure, rhythm and a sense of timing; and both have a variety of sound frequencies that make them interesting and give them intonation and melody.

Using nursery rhymes with massage

It is the rhythmical aspect of both music and speech that babies may find soothing and comforting. This is why babies enjoy listening to rhymes that are sung, or spoken in a voice that is softer, slower and a higher than normal. Some parents struggle with 'chatting' to their baby, but find that talking can be replaced with nursery rhymes that they feel more comfortable using. Babies seem ready to tune into rhymes sung by their parents and tend to respond enthusiastically to this form of communication. They are able to follow simple rhythms long before they are able to speak.

When parents have the opportunity to recite rhymes, their baby will be listening to the sounds and the words. When singing is coupled with an interesting and enjoyable activity, such

Suggested exercise in your class

∶ You could try playing some ∶
∶ soothing music during your ∶
∶ classes and see how it works ∶
∶ with your groups. ∶

as massage, babies are more likely to start to understand the meaning behind the words. For example, a baby will not understand the question *'Would you like a massage today?'* However, when accompanied with the same opening massage stroke, they will, if massaged regularly, soon come to associate the words with this action and understand that massage is being offered.

> Nursery rhymes are a part of a society's linguistic heritage. Introducing babies to these enables their continuation from generation to generation. How great it is to be able to pass on the songs that are so much a part of our culture, that have survived for hundreds of years and hold such historical stories within them?

A brief guide to working with diverse cultures

When teaching in a multicultural society such as Britain, it is important to work towards developing a genuine understanding of cultural diversity; and to avoid stereotyping. Always try to accommodate individual needs as far as possible; and try to be aware of the cultural traditions that may help to inform your teaching and to further empower and respect the parents you are working with.

Non-verbal communication

Many non-verbal conventions are culture-based, acquired in childhood and often used unconsciously. What might be quite acceptable for one cultural group, may in fact be offensive to another; so consider eye contact, posture, touch, physical distance. For example, in South Asian culture, direct eye contact is generally regarded as aggressive and disrespectful, whereas in the British culture eye contact is acceptable, but too much can be uncomfortable.

Dress code

In the summer, when working with people from different cultures, consider your clothes. It may be more appropriate to wear long sleeves, because bare arms and shoulders are sometimes considered disrespectful and, if you see a row of shoes as you enter the door, consider the possibility that you may need to remove yours.

Points to remember

When working with diverse cultures, endeavour to:

- Respect cultural traditions
- Avoid booking classes on holy days and religious festivals
- Pronounce names correctly

Remember that:

- Communicating across a language barrier can be very tiring for teachers and parents alike - don't make the agenda too taxing
- Following migration, women may suffer from isolation and lack of traditional support because their families have been fragmented after their migration
- Some may misinterpret or not understand words *(such as depression, which may not be recognised as a concept in some cultures)*

Teaching
practice

Learning styles
and teaching strategies

There are many teaching strategies that can be employed when teaching infant massage. Some will be appropriate for one group/individual, but not all methods will suit everyone's needs. When teaching it is therefore important to consider different learning styles.

Learning styles

The Visual, Auditory and Kinaesthetic (VAK) learning styles of the parents in your classes will all need to be supported in all classes so that you successfully engage with the whole group; which will ensure an effective learning experience.

STYLE	EXPLANATION	EXAMPLES RELATED TO TEACHING INFANT MASSAGE
Visual	Occurs through images, demonstrations and body language	• Cue cards will enhance learning • The demonstration must be clear and pronounced • Role modelling with the demonstration doll is vital
Auditory	Occurs through hearing the spoken word	• Clear and concise explanations of massage strokes and underpinning knowledge and safe practice is essential
Kinaesthetic	Occurs through doing, touching and interacting	• Parents need to practise massage. So, if their baby is asleep, offer parents a spare demonstration doll to aid their learning • If possible, allow parents to experience themselves, eg a small hand massage

Teaching strategies

Consider carefully the strategies that are going to be implemented. Remember, what might be suitable for adults may not work when babies (who have their own agenda) are present. Babies are necessarily in attendance with their parents, unless you are working with an antenatal group, who are all using dolls to practise on. Appropriate strategies for teaching infant massage to parents include:

- Demonstration with group participation
- Discussion
- Brainstorming

- Lecture *(may only be necessary when imparting information about the oils and precautions at the beginning of the first class)*

The parents' expectations, motivations, abilities and interests have to be taken into consideration when planning the course, particularly:

- method of teaching
- content
- pace of delivery

This can be very different for each group depending on size, participants, age and social background, etc.

OTHER ASPECTS YOU MAY WISH TO CONSIDER TO HELP YOU TO ENGAGE WITH YOUR PARENTS:

How will you interact with the group?	Ensure you are an active listener
How do you address the group?	Consider the terminology you use
How will you introduce discussions?	Consider the audience you have. For example, would it be appropriate to use a flipchart, or would that be too intimidating?
What resources will you use?	For example, would it be appropriate to use a 60 cm doll if the parent you are teaching has a premature baby? To relate to the parent, it may be more expedient to use a 'premature' size doll
How will you ensure parents feel confident to carry on massaging at home, after the class?	By observing that they are massaging correctly and confidently before they leave the class

Do you need teaching aids?	Often there is some confusion with the strokes, such as which direction to massage the bowel. Do you need to consider producing a visual aid that will make it absolutely clear which direction the abdomen should be massaged? For example:
	  o A poster
	  o A hand-out
	  o A vest for your doll with a diagram depicting the bowel and the direction for massage

Engaging parents

Just as it is important to encourage parents in the group to engage with their baby, so that they can ascertain whether their baby is enjoying the massage or not; so too is it important that the Infant Massage Teacher engages with the group. This will allow you to ensure that the parents are finding it enjoyable, understanding what is being taught and are learning from the experience. If they are not, they may lack confidence to continue with what they have learnt during the week between classes and may not return to the class at all.

Effective communication skills

Adults often have preconceived ideas of what to expect from the 'learning environment'. In the main, parents are aware that their baby often has a different agenda; because of their unease they may arrive at the first class a little apprehensive about how it is going to go. They are likely to be wondering whether their baby will 'be good' and have a massage. It is important therefore to set the scene early and make parents feel welcome and at ease on arrival to a class. You will be able to help the parents feel more comfortable, for example, if you explain to them that:

- The massage routine will be taught gradually and each section will be covered several times, over the whole course
- You will be supplying them with

massage sequence handouts each week as a guide for them to use at home

- You have spare dolls for them to practise on in the class, if their baby is asleep

They will probably need reassuring that just because the massage class is booked for a particular time, it may not be the right time for their baby. By taking time to explain about infant behavioural states (sleep/awake states), and which is the most suitable state in which to introduce massage, you will be offering reassurance and support. So you can confidently, at the beginning of the class, put everyone's minds at rest and inform parents that it is no problem if their baby is:

- Crying
- Needs to be fed *(breast or bottle)*
- Asleep
- In need of a cuddle
- Saying 'no' to massage
- Needs cleaning if their baby has opened their bowels or emptied their bladder

Gauging time

With any teaching situation there is the potential of saying too much. This is very much the case with an infant massage demonstration. Very often the parents (particularly during the first class) have assumed the aim of the class is to get in, massage their baby and then get out. As there are certain matters that need to be discussed first (patch test, etc.), it is often difficult to get a balance between giving the pertinent information, or saying too much and missing the moment. It could be very frustrating for all if you miss the window of opportunity when both parent and baby are ready to progress with the massage sequence because the baby has passed their 'active alert stage'. So, remember to keep to the point and only discuss essential information that the parents need at the beginning of each class.

Structuring classes

Your own personal time constraints and those of the parents you are teaching will inform your decision as to how many classes you will include in a course. Four weeks is manageable, but six is optimal. Running classes for six weeks allows time for the group members to get to know each other and you. It is really beneficial to provide refreshments in the interval so that the opportunity is there for parents to talk, gel as a group and offer each other continued support. This is where friendships can blossom and sharing experiences can empower and develop the confidence of the parents.

Scheme of work

A scheme of work establishes the framework for how the Infant Massage Teacher delivers the course content and over what period of time, by working out a sequence of sessions for the massage strokes, discussion topics, safety aspects and homework that need to be included in each class.

As with all planning, you still need to be flexible and prepared to adjust if needs be, especially when working with parents and their babies. Consider that your scheme of work is not cast in stone, but a working document. It is also a useful tool to help guide you when making changes that you feel are needed for the next course.

Week-to-week continuity

If you teach a course of infant massage over a period of weeks, it is important to ensure that there is continuity from week-to-week; both for the discussion topics and massage strokes covered.

This is helpful as it is easier for parents to learn new information when it relates in some way to what has been previously taught.

For example:

	INTRODUCING SOMETHING NEW	KEEPING A FLOW
Massage strokes	Deliver new massage strokes each class	Cover strokes from the week before to consolidate learning
Underpinning knowledge	Explaining the importance of understanding when a baby is saying 'yes' or 'no' to massage	Setting homework that guides parents to understanding their baby's cues
Practising safely	Bring safety aspects to the parents attention when teaching new strokes	Upon consolidation of strokes in subsequent weeks, reiterate the respective safety aspects
Discussion topics	Use one of the 'Suggested Exercises For Parents' as homework	Ask parents to feedback the following week
Preparing for the following week	Putting baby in the prone position to prepare them for the back massage	Ask for feedback the following week, then show alternative positions if baby is unhappy in the prone position

Suggested sequence for each class

There are a number of standard elements that can be included in each class. The following is an example of a tried and tested successful format:

- Introduction
- Feedback on the previous weeks' massage practise (week two onwards)
- Relaxation and breathing exercises (week two or three onwards)
- The massage
- Break for a chat and refreshments
- Discussion topics and feedback from the previous week's homework
- Homework

Lesson plan

Once you have decided upon the complete course content and the overall aims and objectives, you will then need to plan how this information is going to be delivered to the parents to enable them to meet their learning outcomes.

Once the scheme of work has been designed, each individual class requires a lesson plan, which is a more detailed document depicting what will be delivered in that particular session. Each individual lesson plan should ideally include the:

- Aims and objectives
- Time it will take for each activity
- Topics
- Activities
- Resources

Preparation is essential and a lesson plan helps to keep the teacher focused whilst they deal with the practicalities of running a class, as it supports and guides them through the session in hand.

Whilst, more often than not, the lesson plan will be followed as originally designed, occasionally group dynamics or circumstances will require that the teacher adjusts that particular week's lesson plan accordingly.
For example:

- Allowing 10 or 15 minutes for late-comers or
- Move the discussion prior to the massage, if most or all of the babies are displaying negative cues at the beginning of the session and teaching the strokes would be inappropriate or disrupted

Sample Lesson Plan

Date: 00/00/0000	Class 1	Time: 10.00 - 12.00		

Aims
- o Teach leg strokes
- o Introduce parents to oils
- o Introduce parents to infant massage
- o Discuss benefits of massage and baby non-verbal cues

Objectives: at the end of the lesson, parents will:
- o Have an understanding of different types of oils
- o Have an understanding of the benefits of massage
- o Have an understanding of non verbal cues
- o Be able to confidently massage their baby's legs

TIME	TOPIC	TEACHER ACTIVITY	PARENT ACTIVITY	RESOURCES
10 mins	Patch test oil (allowing adequate time for a potential reaction to occur) Introduction Ice-breaker	Distribute oil for test Introduce yourself and your doll Explanation of whole course and specifically the current class	Parents to apply oil to themselves and their baby Introduction of parent and baby Questions Participation	Oil Name cards Depends on ice-breaker
10 mins	Discussion about suitable oils	Explanation of range of types of oils	Question Check patch test area	Selection of oils
20 mins	Massage sequence for legs	Demonstration Encourage and support parents	Follow demonstration Check baby's cues	Demonstration doll Oil CD and player
Etc...				

61

SUGGESTED ACTIVITIES AND TOPICS SCHEDULE FOR THE COURSE

ACTIVITY	TIPS AND EXAMPLES
Introduction	Week 1 Include introduction of yourself and your doll Introduction of parents and babies Structure of course Discussions topics during patch-test time: ○ Non-verbal cues ○ Contraindications ○ Sleep/awake states ○ Suitable oils to use ○ Benefits
Housekeeping and ground rules	Switch off mobile telephones Confidentiality Health and safety, e.g. fire drill Lavatory facilities
Patch test	Week 1 (or prior to first class) Patch test for baby and parent
Ice-breaker	Week 1 helps with group dynamics
Asking permission	Reinforcing the need to respond to non-verbal cues
Relaxation and stretches	Introduce this preferably after week one or two when parents are more comfortable with their group
The massage routine	Introducing new strokes first whilst concentrations levels are at their highest Recapping previously learnt strokes can enhance learning, so think about scheduling enough time for this as well
Rhymes and stories	Encouraging parents to sing during the class encourages eye contact between baby and parent
Refreshment time	Think about health and safety issues
Homework activities for parents to try in the week	Supply handouts and leaflets to support learning
Feedback on 'homework'	Consolidates prior learning and understanding
Discussion topics	Allows time for parents to share experiences and knowledge
Parent evaluation	Supports your own reflections on your teaching practice

- To help the parents gel, it is useful to include 'ice-breakers' at the beginning of the first class. For example:

  - Teach a hand massage for the parents to try on each other either during the 'patch test' time or instead of a discussion after the baby massage
  - During the introductions, ask them to tell the group why they chose their baby's name

SUGGESTED HOMEWORK AND CLASS DISCUSSION TOPICS

TOPIC	HOMEWORK/DISCUSSION	REASON
Colic 	When does the colic occur? What is happening in the home at this time? Observe what is going on in the house between 5 pm and 7 pm	Helps parents think about ways they might be able to alleviate periods of stress or over-stimulation that might exacerbate colic
Cues	What does your baby do before they cry? Observe your baby's different awake/asleep states – see how many times they are in the alert awake state on a daily basis and try to introduce the massage during one of these times	Gives parents some ideas about what their baby's negative cues are and subsequently may help them recognise the positive ones as well. Guides parents to suitable times when baby is more receptive to massage
Self-calming 	What does your baby do to try and self-calm?	Guides parents to think about ways their baby tries to self-calm and how they might be able to help them with this

TOPIC	HOMEWORK/DISCUSSION	REASON
Sleep issues	Discussion	Gives the opportunities for parents to share sleep issue stories. They can gain support from each other and help them realise they are not the only ones suffering with sleep deprivation!
Birth experiences	What was your birth experience?	Gives mothers the space to share their experiences and 'get things off their chest'
Parental stress	What do parents find stressful ? What do parents do to cope ? What helps to relax them ?	Gives the opportunity for parents to receive peer support and suggested coping strategies
Adapting massage for the growing child	Discuss adaptations	To encourage parents to continue massaging throughout their child's life

Suggested reading for parents

- Teach Yourself Baby Massage And Yoga
- The Pocket Guide to Baby Massage
- Rhythm Kids: Rhymes and Fun-time Exercises For Babies
- The Social Baby
- Why Love Matters
- The Power of Touch
- Parent Handouts

Suggested music

- Music For Dreaming range of CDs
- Rhythm Kids: Rhymes and Fun-time Exercises For Babies Book and CD
- Playsongs range of CDs and Books
- Songs to Sing With Your Baby CD

All available from www.touchneeds.com

Enhancing your teaching

Once you have considered how to structure your classes and your scheme of work and lesson plans have been designed, you will need to put them into practice. There will be a great deal to remember and manage during the sessions you run, particularly as babies tend to have different agendas and do not appreciate the structure of a carefully devised lesson plan! To help your classes run smoothly, to make the experience as positive for the parents and the babies and to help you teach, you may find the following tips useful.

TIP	REASON
Use an oil bottle as a prop *(Pretend to 'oil your baby' so that the parents follow suit)*	Reminds you to guide the parents to use oil for the massage.
Sing nursery rhymes	To enhance the massage experience, to encourage greater interaction between parent and baby and help language development
Demonstrate alternative holding positions for back massage	If a baby is unhappy in the prone position offering alternatives does not preclude the baby from having a back massage
Try to ensure when demonstrating the abdominal sequence that your hands are clearly below where the rib cage is	If the stroke includes the lower ribs there will be no benefit for the digestive system
Try to ensure when demonstrating the chest sequence that your hands are clearly above where the diaphragm is	Any upward stroke that puts pressure on the digestive tract will work against the clock-wise, downward direction required for the abdomen

TIP	REASON
Role-model 'checking-in' with your demonstration doll	Parents will follow suit and check-in with their baby
Check-in with the parents so that they regularly ensure that their babies are happy	Helps parents to re-focus on their baby if they are only focusing on your teaching
Reaffirm cues during the massage session	Serves as a reminder whilst parents are concentrating on learning new strokes
Avoid jargon wherever possible *(eg use 'tummy' instead of 'abdomen')*	Helps parents to feel comfortable in the teaching environment and supports an informal learning experience
Include some benefits of the strokes whilst teaching the massage	Offering the information about the benefits at the relevant points during massages as this helps to conceptualise the theory
Encourage parents to try to maintain contact with their baby, once undressed and role model this with your demonstration doll *(Make a point of telling parents you are 'letting go' of your doll if your teaching requires you to do so.)*	When contact is maintained it allows for continuity between strokes, reduces startling and enhances the babies' sense of security

 ### Checking-in with the parents

When teaching a group of parents you may find that you are often the only person in the room getting any eye contact from the parents, even from the babies too! Parents tend to be listening and watching you and, because you are the only one talking, the babies are drawn to your voice as well. By asking the group as a whole if their babies are enjoying their massage, you will encourage them to focus on their baby, and thus watch for cues and give more attention to them.

Think carefully about how you phrase this. 'Are your babies enjoying their massage?' should prompt the parents to turn towards their baby, in order to ascertain whether they are or not. However, try to avoid stating 'Your babies are enjoying the massage!' This negates the need for them to check-in with their baby themselves, as you have already told them they are fine. This also suggests that you are the 'expert' on their babies and not them.

Working as a caring professional

Every group of parents you teach will be different and the mix of the group will be diverse in their needs. Parents will come with their own agendas and will respond to the environment and interact with other group members in many ways.

When teaching infant massage, you may well find that initially some parents are shy, may not interact much with other members of the group and may lack confidence when handling their baby. The early months of parenthood can be extremely stressful and trying to fulfil their own and others' expectations can affect a parent's confidence and self-esteem. Being listened to in an accepting, non-judgemental way can encourage the parents to believe in themselves, feel empowered and more confident about their parenting skills.

Role modelling - using a realistic demonstration doll

The demonstration doll should be a useful and influential tool when teaching infant massage; it can help the parents feel that what they experience and learn during a class is positive and memorable. As the demonstration doll is the Infant Massage Teacher's 'baby', it is important that the doll is handled and treated realistically at all times during each class. The use of a realistic doll allows the Infant Massage Teacher to engage successfully with parents when:

- Demonstrating the strokes correctly
- Demonstrating safe practice
- Encouraging parents to observe and respond to their baby's cues in a non-judgemental manner

To enhance teaching and to role-model effectively, it is important to:

- Use your doll to support your teaching at all times
- Give your doll a realistic name
- Handle your doll as you would a baby

during the whole of the teaching session
- Endeavour to keep your doll clean
- Dress your doll in seasonal baby clothes
- Wash the clothes regularly, so that they do not appear soiled and unkempt
- Dress and undress your doll as you would a baby *(keeping pace with the parents in your class, so that they do not feel rushed; and re-dress the doll at the end of the massage)*
- Always use your doll to highlight important points

Offering support during classes

Infant massage is a practical skill, but it needs to be taught by a professional who will support and empower parents. An Infant Massage Teacher should not try to be a professional counsellor (unless qualified in this field). However, you may need to develop skills to deal with vulnerable parents who may come to your classes.

When working with parents in a one-to-one situation, you may find that a parent, particularly when they are in their own home, is more likely to express their personal fears and worries. When working with a group this may not be the case. However, as the group gels, each person may gain confidence and become more trusting and feel that this is the place to disclose personal feelings. Sharing of experiences can be cathartic and beneficial for everyone present, however, at these times, group confidentiality is of paramount importance so that parents feel secure when displaying personal emotion and discussing their hopes and fears. Sharing experiences without being devalued and criticised and in an atmosphere of confidentiality and respect can promote feelings of self-esteem.

When facilitating a group discussion that is emotionally charged, it is important to:

- Smile, show warmth, be kind and considerate
- Show respect
- Be aware of confidentiality and encourage trust
- Listen attentively
- Suppress your own opinions and views
- Show sympathy and where possible, empathy
- Encourage parents to speak but also allow quiet periods for them to collect their thoughts or even cry
- Reflect back what is being said to you, so parents feel they are being heard and understood
- Accept and validate
- Be aware of your own posture, facial expressions and how you may react

Offering support after the course has finished

The support gained from being a part of a group should never be underestimated and you may wish to offer other parenting classes, such as Rhythm Kids™ or Baby Yoga, so that the group can maintain contact on a regular basis. Or you may wish to promote other parenting activities in the community. It is useful to gather and keep information about what is available locally, such as library activities, crèches, postnatal groups, toddler gym classes, singing groups, etc.

You could ask parents if they want to share telephone numbers, so that friendships can be encouraged and fostered. If parents are agreeable, perhaps you could photocopy the class list and give it to each parent on the last week.

69

Managing interruptions in your class

There will be occasions when you may have to deal with interruption to the flow of your teaching. The table below outlines some of the most common that Infant Massage Teachers experience and gives advice for dealing with them.

SITUATION	GUIDANCE
Late arrivals *(Parents can be embarrassed if they are late but sometimes this is outside of their control)*	It is important not to be judgmental. Welcome parents with a smile, ask them to join in when they are ready and remind them to ask permission before they start. If they missed the massage session, reassure them that they can catch up in the next session
A baby is massaged whilst it is crying	• Initially check-in with the whole group and ask the parents if their babies are enjoying the massage so they focus on their baby • If they continue to massage reiterate to the group the importance of listening to their baby • Remind parents it is alright to stop at any time as strokes will be recapped the following session • If all else fails check-in with your doll and suggest the whole group has a cuddle with their baby **Never single out the individual**
Mobile telephone rings during the massage session and parent answers the telephone	• Do not make the individual feel uncomfortable or embarrassed whilst they are taking the call (Maybe they were expecting an urgent call) • At the end of the session remind the whole group of the 'ground rules' you set at the onset of the course • At the beginning of the next session reiterate the ground rules

SITUATION	GUIDANCE
Someone massages their baby's abdomen in an anti-clockwise direction	There are a number of strategies that will help you teach safe abdominal massage. Addressing the whole group : • Ask your parents to imagine a clock-face on their baby's 'tummy'. Start with '12 pm' above the 'belly button' and stroke round to 3 pm etc until the clock-face is complete • If using pictorial cue cards, show these to the group • Hold your doll up facing the group so they can see your demonstration more clearly • Use a vest on your doll with a diagram of the bowels with arrows in a clock-wise direction • In subsequent weeks surreptitiously place the name card of the parent next to you so they can see your demonstration more clearly **Never single out the individual**
A parent needs boiling water/ jug for a feed	Always ensure there is a boiled kettle or a flask of boiled water available
A parent massaging too roughly or too gently *(massaging too gently is more common place)*	• Initially check-in with the whole group and ask the parents if their babies are enjoying the massage • Remind parents to watch for cues • If they continue to massage too roughly/lightly reiterate to the group the importance of watching how their baby is responding to the pressure • If all else fails suggest to the whole group that they take a moment to experience the pressure they are using on themselves **Never single out the individual**
All babies are either asleep or feeding	• If this is the case revisit your lesson plan to see if is more expedient to have the break and group discussion first • If they are still sleeping or feeding or have only just finished their feed, demonstrate the strokes so the parents can observe, reassure the group that they will have the opportunity to practise at home and that there will be a re-cap in the following session. (Handouts and aide memoirs are useful revision tools for parents to use at home)

71

SITUATION	GUIDANCE
Persistent chatting between two or more parents which interrupts the massage session	• Firstly, introduce a nursery rhyme to refocus the parents attention on their babies • Simply stop teaching, rest your hands on your doll and look down and wait for the conversation to finish. This generally results in the rest of the group looking at the chatting parents, who become aware that they are disturbing everyone, so they usually stop
Tearful parent/s	• Be supportive and sympathetic to help the parent feel at ease • Do not worry about disrupting the massage session, as other parents are generally very accommodating and supportive • Be available for the parent, if they so wish, during the break
Crying babies	• Set the scene early on in session one. Let parents know it's alright if babies need consoling or need your attention • Revisit your lesson to see if is more expedient to have the break sooner • If your teaching would not be disturbed and the other babies are quite happy to be massaged, continue with your demonstration • Reassure the parents that they will have the opportunity to practise at home and that there will be a re-cap in the following session (Handouts and aide memoirs are useful revision tools for parents to use at home)

Fussy, disorganised and hyper-sensitive babies

Most babies from about the age of six weeks old will normally enjoy a full massage. Though for some babies, on occasion, it may not be the appropriate time; by encouraging parents to be sensitive to their baby's needs this will help them to overcome these barriers so that their baby can soon enjoy a full massage.

However, some babies are not able to respond positively to a full massage routine; particularly if they are inclined to be a little fussy, disorganised or hyper-sensitive. With all babies it is important that they receive only the amount of massage that they are happy with, but with more sensitive babies it may be necessary to give greater guidance to parents as to how the routine may be adapted to suit their baby's particular needs.

The fussy baby

When a baby is inclined to be fussy, the parents often feel that they have a particularly 'difficult' or 'demanding' child. A fussy baby is in fact desperate to be heard. The fussiness is an indication of a baby who is crying out to be calmed. They want to be able to feel safe and secure and are desperately seeking the level of care that is required so that they feel as if their needs are being met.

Suggestions below are purely a guide to help you advise parents on how to adapt the massage if they indicate that their baby is displaying any of the characteristics considered to be 'fussy', 'disorganised' or 'hyper-sensitive'.

! Caution
Teaching sensitively

An Infant Massage Teacher can make suggestions so that a baby might be more accepting of massage, which will help parents decide the best way to adapt the massage routine for their baby. It is advisable to avoid labelling a baby by using the terms 'fussy', 'disorganised' or 'hyper-sensitive'. When parents indicate that their baby tends to display certain characteristics typical of these 'types' of babies, it is important to remember that all babies are individuals. The best way for parents to really understand what their baby is 'saying' is to try to become familiar with their non-verbal cues.

Characteristics of a 'fussy' baby:

- Only content when in contact with a parent and cries when put down
- Extra-sensitive to disturbing noise, or to being disturbed
- Does not adapt well to changes in their routine

Tips for massage

Before teaching massage it is important to suggest that parents:

- Always be sensitive to their baby's cues
- Approach positive touch carefully and gradually - starting with the gentle stroking and the containment holds
- Try massaging over their baby's clothes, until they feel more secure about being undressed
- Choose a time in the day when their baby tends to be less fussy
- Maintain close contact when massaging by holding their baby across their lap

The disorganised baby

'Disorganised' characteristics are often seen in babies who have had a stressful delivery. A disorganised baby needs help in order to become calm and to find an inner peace. Gentle rocking and soothing sounds may help the baby to become calm. Swaddling may help them feel contained, as it can be relaxing and may prevent startling.

Characteristics of a 'disorganised' baby:

- Unable to maintain eye contact
- Moves arms and legs in a fast, uncontrolled manner
- Distressed crying
- Holds hands in front of face
- Prone to having hiccups

Tips for massage

Before teaching massage it is important to suggest that parents:

- Introduce the massage routine whilst the baby is still dressed
- Start with containment holds and introduce massage slowly
- Gradually increase the baby's exposure to full massage
- Position their baby on their side, during massage, which may reduce the over-stimulation of face-to-face contact

The hyper-sensitive baby

Premature babies, babies with special needs and those that have experienced medical intervention at birth may be hyper-sensitive. Hyper-sensitive babies struggle to cope with over-stimulation and are inclined to tire quickly.

Characteristics of a 'hyper-sensitive' baby:

- Does not enjoy being cuddled and often gives the impression that they would prefer to be left alone. They may even become distressed when someone tries to offer comfort
- Avoids eye contact and often displays a fretful facial expression
- Easily disturbed and frightened
- Cries hysterically, often during the evening

Tips for massage

Before teaching massage it is important to suggest that parents:

- Ensure that the environment is calm and quiet
- Dim the lighting
- Start with containment holds
- When their babies are accustomed to containment holds, introduce long, gentle effleurage strokes (keeping their baby clothed). All other strokes are likely to be too stimulating at this stage
- Only expose the immediate area that is being massaged, so that their baby continues to feel contained and secure, and is able to cope with skin contact
- Return to the containment holds to reassure their baby, if the massage is too much
- Only use one form of stimulation at a time. For example, avoid eye contact when massaging
- Handle their baby slowly and carefully with no quick or sudden movements

suggested exercise
containment hold for
hyper-sensitive babies

Some babies may not cope with even the gentlest of strokes, so before introducing the massage, start with a containment hold, which is calming and contains their positive energy.

Suggest to a parent that. Either with their baby lying on its back (on a change mat) or the parent's lap. Gently rest a hand close to or on top of the baby's head. Rest the other hand underneath their feet. Remain still and quiet in this position for 2 or 3 minutes

Premature babies

Premature babies usually experience a lot of invasive, investigative procedures and live in a highly technical environment in the early days and/or weeks of their lives. Those babies who are not physiologically stable can find tactile stimuli far too overwhelming, so great caution must be taken when introducing any type of positive touch. These premature babies are generally far too sensitive to receive a full massage from their parents and even light stroking can be extremely irritating and stressful.

If parents are encouraged to try containment holding for their premature baby, as well as very gentle touch, then this can be extremely positive for the baby and the parent. Some premature babies, who receive positive touch from their parents in hospital show improvement in physical and cognitive development. For example they often gain weight more rapidly.

Often parents can experience feelings of helplessness, disempowerment and alienation from their baby who is attached to wires and machines; so getting involved in using positive touch and containment holds for their baby is extremely beneficial in helping parents feel as if like they are helping their vulnerable neonate. Crucially, this is also helping the parents and baby to bond.

On the neonatal unit, where babies are monitored closely, not only will the parent have the opportunity to start to learn what their baby is 'telling' them, by trying to understand their individual cues – they will also be monitored closely via the medical equipment they are connected to. Negative changes in the baby's vital signs need to be observed closely (e.g oxygen saturation levels), along with the baby's cues.

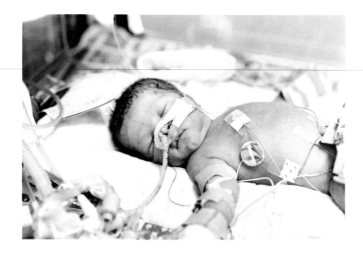

Introducing touch to premature babies

It may be necessary to introduce 'touch' in stages, so that the parent can be assured that they are understanding their babies needs and not over-stimulating them with too much, too early.

- **Skin-to-skin contact,** sometimes known as 'Kangaroo Care' is often a good first step to introducing positive touch to the premature baby. This involves the parent tucking the baby inside their top so that the baby's skin is in contact with their parent's skin

- **Containing positive energy -** in some cases actual physical touch may be far too stimulating for the premature baby. Parents should be encouraged to simply hold their hands about 8 – 10 cm from their baby's body, just so their presence can be felt by the baby

- **Containment holds** to the head; chest; head and buttock; head and back can be very beneficial, which can:
  - ✦ Help to centre and calm both the baby and parent
  - ✦ Allow for gentle touch
  - ✦ Give comfort and 'contain' babies during procedures
  - ✦ Settle distressed babies

Introducing massage to premature babies

- **Stroking** is often the first step to introducing massage to the premature baby. Once the baby is a little more robust and more accustomed to their environment, they may be ready to experience the benefits of receiving some massage; particularly long, slow, gentle effleurage strokes along the limbs

- **After feeding,** leave at least half an hour before carrying out any massage (in many units premature babies are fed hourly as they need to eat little, but often)

- **Once massage is introduced,** subdued lighting, gentle music and a minimum number of strokes may be tolerated and enjoyed by the baby
- **Being sensitive to invasive procedures.** For example, many babies have to endure the presence of cannulae in their feet. Because of this, these babies often do not like their feet being massaged. Simply hold the feet gently until the baby feels more comfortable and understands that the touch being offered is positive

Babies with special needs

The rewards of working with parents and babies/children with special needs can be great, although we accept there are also challenges. Teaching infant massage gives the professional a valuable tool to offer to parents who are coming to accept a child that has special needs.

Parents have great expectations during the pregnancy, so coming to terms with the birth of a baby with special needs may be very challenging and difficult for them. The condition may affect not only the child's life forever, but it may also impact on the whole family. The baby may not respond to many of the usual signals that parents use to communicate with them (eye contact, smiling, speech and body movements) because of their particular condition.

With the bonding and attachment process potentially hindered because of the condition, and the challenges the parent and baby may have communicating with each other, the parents may feel disconnected from their baby and unable to help. Infant massage can help overcome this.

For all babies, massage strokes generally need to be simple and the pressure less intense than that given to an adult. The general rule is that the person giving the massage must always be mindful of the baby's non-verbal cues. However, for babies and children with special needs, the cues may be different, or more challenging to understand. Through massage, parents can learn more about what their baby is trying to 'tell' them, even when a baby's cues are subtle. Massage is a highly interactive experience and may help parents gain confidence when they are communicating with their baby.

Through massage parents can 'tune-in' to their baby, giving them time to do something special 'with' their baby; particularly as a parent with a child with special needs may find much of the time they spend with their baby taken up with medical procedures. Therefore, the massage experience can play an important role in enhancing the relationship between parents and babies/children with special needs.

As well as the emotional benefits to be gained from introducing massage to a baby with special needs, the physical benefits of massage may also have a positive affect which offers the parents a useful tool to enhance their child's potential physical ability and ultimately their enjoyment of life.

Babies with hypotonicity

Babies that are hypotonic have poor muscle tone and can appear floppy.

Tips for massage

- Massage strokes should be brisk and stimulating to help improve muscle tone
- Massaging the chin and cheeks can help support the tongue and help with speech

Babies with hypertonicity

Babies that are hypertonic have very tense muscle tone and can appear stiff and lack flexibility.

Tips for massage

- Massage strokes should be slow to help relax the muscles
- Encourage parents to massage the unaffected areas of the body first, so that the baby learns to appreciate how good massage can feel on the affected areas of the body; tense muscles can be tender when pressure is applied to them
- Encourage parents to continually reassure the baby, particularly whilst the affected body areas are being massaged

Babies with visual or auditory impairment

Tactile experiences are of great importance for the visually and hearing impaired baby as they help them define the world. Massage can offer them a positive tactile experience.

Visual impairment

Tips for massage

Encourage parents to:

- Talk gently and to sing to their baby during the massage
- Describe the area of the body that is being massaged which may promote body awareness
- Hold and cuddle their baby frequently which gives reassurance and makes their baby feel secure
- Give their baby boundaries by putting a towel rolled up like a sausage around them, for an added sense of security
- Reduce the noises in the immediate area to a minimum
  - So that their baby is more likely to stay focused on them and will not be distracted
  - So that their baby feels secure

Auditory impairment

Tips for massage

- Lots of eye contact is very important so suggests to parents that they avoid strokes that impede eye contact, such as the back massage, until the baby is used to the massage and feels secure
- Talking and singing rhymes is still important because
  - The baby may still focus on the parents lips moving and may feel the vibrations from the singing
  - This helps the parent focus on the baby

Congenital malformation

A baby with a congenital malformation may benefit from receiving massage in infancy as well as throughout their childhood, as it may help them develop a positive self-image. This may help parents to overcome their fears and to accept their child's body shape more readily.

> Some children with special needs also have the added challenge of medical illnesses to contend with too. For example, many children with Down's Syndrome also have a heart or circulatory condition. Massage increases blood flow, which potentially increases the volume of blood flow through the heart, arteries and veins. Therefore, it is important that the Infant Massage Teacher advises the parents to consult the baby's specialist to confirm that massage can be introduced.

Infants affected by alcohol and drug abuse

These infants are often difficult to console, not easy to cuddle and can be passive in terms of alertness and responsiveness. They may be premature, low in birth weight, have poor feeding habits, be irritable, cry, be disorganised, have delayed development and have poor interactive skills.

Tips for massage

- Massage should be slow and gentle
- Where possible the routine should be done at the same time each day
- A tranquil environment may help them accept massage more readily
- Boundaries around the infant may give security
- Wrapping the infant in a thin blanket or sheet gives a sense of containment. Suggest to parents/carers they try effleurage through the blanket
- Prone, or a side-lying position (to avoid further stimulation) may make the massage experience more acceptable

The abused child

Massage can help children who have been abused recognise the value of positive, loving touch. A trusting relationship is likely to take time to develop and it might take some time before permission from the child is granted.

> **Tips for massage**
>
> Encourage parents to:
>
> - Offer massage for feet and hands first. This may help to build trust before massage to other body parts is introduced - whatever the child feels is safe and non-threatening
> - Offer massage over clothes, as this may help the child feel relaxed
> - Suggest the child may feel more comfortable sitting rather than lying down
> - Remember massage over a bruise or a fracture, or open wounds must be avoided

Massage gives parents something that they can have control over; such as the care and general wellbeing of their child and helps them feel that they are able to do something positive for their child. This empowerment will help these anxieties start to dissipate.

> **Tips for massage**
>
> - It is so important for parents to maintain communication with their child whilst they are in hospital so talking, smiling and singing nursery rhymes should be encouraged during massage
> - If the child is too unwell to be touched, parents can be offered the choice of learning the strokes on a demonstration doll so that when their child is well enough they can then start to massage them. This also helps parents feel like they are doing something valuable for their critically ill baby and focus on something positive

Terminal illness

Massaging a child with a terminal illness can be of huge benefit for the child as well as the parent. Always advise parents to seek permission from the specialist to ensure that any symptoms are not exacerbated by massage. Massage can be used to comfort the child and perhaps even ease the pain.

Loving touch can reassure and give peace and relaxation to this child; and allows parents quality time with their child.

Relaxation techniques can be beneficial depending on the age of the child.

Tips for massage

- If the child is too unwell to be touched, parents could be offered the choice of learning the moves on a doll so that when the child is more stable the parent will already have the skills to massage their child
- Be sensitive to parent's needs as much as the child

Childhood ailments

Colds and snuffles

A blocked nose or 'snuffle' is common in babies under six months old. It is usually due to normal mucus that collects in the nose which is difficult for the baby to clear.   Massage can help alleviate some of the symptoms.

83

Tips for massage

Encourage parents to:

- Use chest massage strokes and upper back strokes to help loosen mucus
- Use face massage strokes to help loosen and drain mucus from the sinuses. (If the baby is old enough to sit up and support its own head then parents can try the face massage with them sitting up to avoid the mucus blocking their airways)
- Massage the toes, which works on the reflexology areas that correspond to the head, sinuses and teeth so may help to ease the congestion

Colic, wind and constipation

Stomach discomfort from colic and wind can be very distressing for a baby, not to mention the parents.

Abdominal massage and relaxation holds can be very beneficial for a baby suffering from and wind.

Tips for massage

- Suggest parents follow a colic routine for a number of weeks as it will continue to alleviate this ongoing ailment

- Suggest to parents that they massage their baby's abdomen and follow the colic routine about an hour before the usual onset of the colic

- Reduce as many of the external stimuli as possible around the time of the colic attack

Cradle cap

Cradle cap is flaky, dry skin that looks like dandruff, or thick, oily, yellowish or brown scaling or crusting patches. Although at its worst it may not look very pleasant, it is actually quite harmless. Most often it appears in the first few months of life, and it usually clears up on its own in about six to 12 months (although some children have it for several years).

Tips for massage

For stubborn cases, parents may wish to try:

- Using small circular movements (with only gentle strokes over the fontanelles) rub a small amount of pure, natural oil, such as olive oil, on to baby's scalp and leave it for about 15 minutes. (The oil helps to loosen dry flakes.) Take care when using olive oil as it can stain clothing

- Gently comb out the flakes with a fine-toothed comb or brush them out with a soft brush

- Wash baby's scalp with a gentle baby shampoo afterwards and leave the shampoo on for a minute longer before rinsing, to help neutralize the oil. Washing ensures that the oil does not clog the pores and cause the flakes to stick, which might exacerbate the situation

Eczema and psoriasis

Dry skin is a common complaint and is one of the key symptoms of conditions such as eczema and psoriasis. Babies suffering from mild eczema or psoriasis may benefit from regular massage with a natural vegetable oil, which will help to moisturise their skin. It will also help soothe and relax baby, which in turn may improve their condition.

In severe cases, where the skin is broken, sore and inflamed, parents should refrain from massaging the affected area. However, unaffected areas can be massaged as it keeps the rest of the skin moisturised and will help to calm an agitated baby.

! CAUTION

Massaging safely

Skin consultants recommend that emollient creams that are supplied to ease the itching and dryness of eczema should be applied in a light downward sweeping movement, following the direction of the hair growth (rather like applying butter to toast). This is so that the cream does not clog the follicles and so minimizes the risk of inflammation of the hair follicles.

It is advisable that you suggest parents follow guidelines for the application of the emollient and refrain from using it as a massage medium, to eliminate any risk of infection.

When massaging, firm strokes should be applied in an upwards direction, towards the heart. This supports venous (blood flow) return and works with the valves in the veins. In the main, upward strokes would be working against the direction of hair growth.

85

Multiple births

Trying to incorporate infant massage into an already hectic daily routine for parents of twins or multiple births can be challenging. However, as it is such a wonderful activity, it may give parents the chance to have some individual fun-time with each of their babies. Also, if a parent has bonded with one baby more than the other(s), massage can help to overcome this.

Tips for massage

- If possible, it may be a good idea to involve both parents, a willing grandparent or older sibling, should the babies be ready for a massage at the same time
- Even identical babies will be completely different in their needs and may display different cues, have different self-calming techniques and may enjoy different strokes
- The babies may wish to be massaged at different times of the day, for instance one may prefer to be massaged in the morning whilst another prefers a massage after a bath and before bed time

Adoption and fostering

As massage communicates love, respect, safety and acceptance; all essential for a healthy parent-child relationship, there is no reason for adoptive or foster parents not to participate in this too. As touch is a universal language, it does not matter if the parents adopt from abroad or locally, they can express their feelings for their adopted child through touch.

Whether for a newborn baby or a slightly older baby, massage can really play an important part in successful adoption and fostering. The age of the child and each individual case needs to be considered carefully, but massage can help to form trusting relationships and offer adoptive or foster parents a way to make up for lost time through quality contact time that promotes closeness, security and love. As bonding involves all the senses, but primarily touch, Infant Massage can really help in the bonding process and help parents and their adopted child to become accus-

tomed to one another and help the baby feel nurtured and loved at a most unsettling time.

Positive touch, especially skin-to-skin contact and containment holding, can help bring a new baby closer to its adoptive parents, especially when the baby will be grieving for the familiar touch, sounds, and smells of their birth mother. Involving siblings in the massage can help the new arrival to become accustomed to all members of their new family.

When fostering, a gentle, loving massage after visits to the birth mother in the very early days after separation can help with anxiety for both the baby and the foster parents. Also, when there may be the possibility of the baby being returned to the birth mother, massage can help with the developing relationship if it is taught during contact visits with the baby.

Suggestions for adapting massage for the growing child

Once the massage has been introduced and enjoyed by both the parent and the baby, it would be a pity for massage time to stop just because the growing baby is more interested in discovering all the new things in their environment and can not sit still long enough to have a full massage. However, as an Infant Massage Teacher you can introduce the idea of adapting the massage the parents have learnt, so that they can continue with this wonderful experience; particularly as it is important that positive touch is maintained throughout the child's life to help them feel loved, respected and increase their self-esteem.

When 'asking permission' is introduced to the baby, they learn very quickly that they can say 'no' if they wish and that they will be heard and their wishes respected. Asking permission to touch a child should never cease as the child is growing older. They will be empowered to say what happens with their body, which is a very valuable life skill. This may seem a little hard to imagine when a parent is looking at their four month old baby lying on the changing mat eager for a massage!

Keeping a growing baby interested

As baby is growing they naturally become more and more fascinated with their environment and what is going on around them. This is quite natural and parents should not feel despondent as the original massage can be adapted somewhat to keep a baby interested.

Possible adaptations:

- Introduce more up-tempo rhymes into the massage

- Give the older, more inquisitive baby something to hold and look at whilst massage is taking place, such as a brightly coloured rattle or finger puppet

- When massaging the back, suggest the parents lay the baby across their lap (taking care to support their back) and lay a mirror on the floor just beneath their face. Babies love to look at themselves and this will keep them amused whilst their back is being massaged

- Offer the massage in bite size pieces; eg offer a massage for the legs, feet or tummy after a nappy change
- Stroke the face or the head during feeding if it does not irritate or distract the baby

The crawling stage

Parents should not feel disheartened when their baby regularly refuses massage during the crawling stage, because the world around them is just far too interesting and they are becoming rather more independent. In the middle of the massage their attention may shift to something new and exciting and they may turn over and crawl away!

Parents can adapt to this stage, as follows:

- If baby is still happy to be massaged, parents should massage the areas that they can see or gain access to such as their back, legs, feet or head
- Make the massage more stimulating and maintain interest by introducing new nursery rhymes and music
  - Do not give up on massage entirely, at about 18 months old they usually become more amenable to receiving a longer massage again

Toddlers

Toddlers are growing in confidence and are very much more independent and not all toddlers want to receive a full massage. Their attention span is much shorter and they can become easily frustrated and tense if they have to stay still for any length of time. They will fiercely exert their independence, even turning to tantrums as their self-awareness increases; and by now can verbally communicate whether they wish to receive a massage or not.

Adapting the massage will introduce the toddler to new sensations and stimulate their very active imaginations. The key to keeping youngsters interested is to make massage as fun and enjoyable as possible. Parents should be reminded that they should still be very mindful of their child's non-verbal and verbal cues.

The following tips can enhance the massage for the toddler:

- Introduce their favourite nursery rhymes and songs into the massage
- Mention parts of the body being massaged, which helps with body awareness
- Introduce props such as finger puppets and chiffon scarves to enhance sensations
- Adapt the massage routine to include only the strokes they prefer, thus empowering them to make their own decisions and boosting their self-esteem

Pre-school children and beyond

The attention span of a three or four year old child is now much longer and they can now enjoy interactive games with parents, siblings and other children. Massage can really help stretch their imagination by introducing fun massage games. Children may prefer not to have their clothes removed; however massage games can still give some benefits not least maintaining the closeness between parent and child.

- The inquisitive toddler may want to copy their parents and massage a teddy or dolly after receiving massage; this is great fun and helps them come to terms with thinking about others at this developmental stage of their life

The following tips can enhance the massage routines for the pre-school and slightly older child:

- Ask the child to choose where they want to be massaged, i.e. on a bed or a favourite, cosy spot in the house
- Let the child say which massage strokes they would prefer each time, thereby empowering them and boosting self-esteem
- Use massage strokes to ease aching muscles and 'growing pains'
- Children may wish to keep clothes on as they get older; massaging over clothes is still beneficial
- Story telling whilst massaging can be great fun. Encourage parents to ask their child to use their imagination and come up with new stories, such as 'weather stories',

'planting a garden', 'grooming a horse'. Use the child's hobby to inspire a massage game too - the list is endless and can really help with imagination and speech

- Introduce props to help with cognitive development, such as a basket of food when performing the pizza massage. Smelling and touching slices of pepper, onion, mushroom, ham, etc can enhance the physical massage game and turn it into a fun learning experience

- Children at this age often want to 'give' as much as they 'receive'. So encourage the child to massage their parent, sibling or friends when they want to – this can enhance relationships and friendships and respect for others

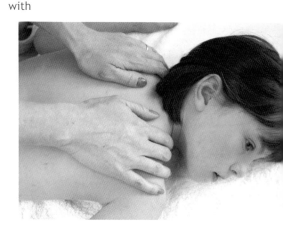

The teenager

If the teenager has received regular massage since birth, they will have developed a special relationship with their parents and may still be amenable to receiving, and indeed giving a massage. However, this is a time when many children are body-conscious and may prefer to cover up when having a massage or they will only be prepared for certain areas to be massaged that they are comfortable with exposing, such as feet, hands, head, neck and shoulders. Again, respect is the key to an enjoyable experience for both teenager and parent.

The massage, of course, will no longer be called infant massage and the strokes will need to be changed somewhat to accommodate larger limbs. Parents can rename the routine to suit the child, for example, a strapping son who plays football or rugby, may be more receptive to massage if it were called 'the post match rub down' or girls may prefer something like 'hockey match warm up'. Encourage parents to adapt the massage to their needs.

Many teenagers are dealing with surges in hormones and changes in body shape, and may become less communicative as they are approaching and going through puberty. Massage is an excellent way of finding some space in a busy day to help them relax and feel more comfortable with themselves. Also, it is often the case, when children feel more relaxed during the massage they are more inclined to open up to parents and off-load any worries and anxieties they have. Massage is a wonderful communication tool.

The following tips may enhance the massage routines for teenagers:

- Preparing the environment to suit the teenage child's preferences. For example, they may prefer a scented oil in the room
- Asking the child to select their favourite relaxing music will make them feel in control of the experience. *(Be prepared for this to be different to what one might expect; they may prefer rock music to a melodic tune or classical music)*

- The teenage child may wish to have an essential oil mixed with the massage medium, which may help them relax.

! CAUTION _____
Even for teenagers, it is important to do a patch test and this is particularly important if an essential oil is being used.

91

Benefits of continuing massage with the growing child

- A back massage can be very effective for reducing stress, helping with relaxation and shoulder tension, insomnia, general aches and pains, breathing difficulties, skin problems and poor circulation (when combined with hands and/or feet massage)

- Leg massage helps with poor circulation, 'growing pains', hyperactivity, minor sports and play injuries, muscle fatigue, general stress and tension
- Arm massage is good for easing aches and pains, skin conditions, cramp and tension

Teaching safely
and professionally

Professional practice

It is important for all Infant Massage Teachers to practice in a safe and professional manner. The most important step is to gain a qualification from a reputable training company so that you are assured of a high standard of training, with excellent supporting material, assessment tools and tutorial support (and hopefully on-going support, long after qualification).

After qualifying it is advisable that you obtain adequate insurance before you commence teaching parents. Becoming a member of a relevant organisation, which sets high professional standards, is also prudent. The Guild of Infant and Child Massage (GICM) is the regulatory body for Infant Massage Teachers and positive touch training organisations in the UK; and you are strongly advised to join the GICM, either as a student or when qualified. Information is available at *www.gicm.org.uk*

Good practice

As an Infant Massage Teacher, it is advisable to practice safely, ethically and professionally. By adhering to the following key points your practice will be deemed to be within safe, legal and professional parameters; whilst allowing you to successfully facilitate groups and empower the parents you work with:

1	Only practise infant massage when qualified (or during teaching practice sessions prior to qualification)
2	Remember that facilitating infant massage classes is about supporting, teaching and empowering parents. It is not a 'hands on' qualification
3	Never disclose information about a parent or baby without the prior written permission of the parent; except when required to do so by Law
4	Keep accurate and confidential records of all clients
5	Keep a professional portfolio containing certificates of qualification and insurance

6	Ensure that the working environment complies with all current health and safety legislation
7	Refer parents with issues outside your skill range or therapeutic knowledge to those with relevant qualifications (see Working Within The Scope Of Your Practice)
8	Remain up-to-date and informed through continuing professional development, attendance at relevant study days and membership of the GICM
9	Respect the religious, spiritual, social and political views of parents, irrespective of creed, race, colour, age and sex
10	Ensure that all marketing material represents your practice/business professionally
11	Explain what you offer and discuss fees with the parents before class/sessions commence

Keeping records of your clients

It is important for all Infant Massage Teachers to keep records of at least:

- The name and address of the parent and baby
- The baby's date of birth
- The oil supplied for the massage classes
- The dates of the classes attended - i.e. a register

It is also useful to know:

What type of birth the baby had	This allows you to be better prepared when teaching. For example, a Caesarean birth will alert you to the fact that the parent might still be affected by the major surgery she has had; and extra thought about her comfort (e.g. extra cushions, the space to brace against a wall) would be required. A baby that has had a Vontouse or forceps delivery might be particularly sensitive about having their head massaged
Whether the baby has had, or is in the midst of a series of vaccinations	This will allow you to pre-empt the situation and let parents know that it is best to avoid massage for at least three days after the vaccinations have been given. However, it also allows the opportunity to assure parents that they are still quite welcome to come along to the classes to watch, learn and possibly have the opportunity to practise on a spare doll

93

Whether the baby suffers with colic	This will help to inform the structure of your lesson plans and when you introduce a colic routine. If you know that the only reason a parent has come to your class is because they have heard massage alleviates colic – you might decide that it is pertinent to include a colic routine in the first class. However, if no parent has indicated that their baby has this condition, you may decide to impart this information after the abdominal sequence at a later stage

Data protection registration

It may be necessary to register with the Data Protection Agency. For further information visit *www.ico.gov.uk*.

Working within the scope of your practice

The unwell child is a test of parenting skills and can certainly cause real anxiety for first-time parents. When dealing with an unwell child good parenting skills are required, along with the recognition of illness and minor ailments and using basic common sense. Generally parents will rely on their own experiences from their childhood, family networks, education and general life experience.

It is the parent who needs to make the decision whether or not to seek further help. The Health Visitor/Midwife/ Paediatric Nurse practitioner may be in a position to take off their 'Infant Massage hat' at the end of a teaching session and deal with parents' health queries. Other teachers, without this professional background, may wish to offer guidance on where to seek further help.

It is important to remember that the Infant Massage Teacher is a facilitator, not a therapist/ practitioner. However, when teaching infant massage classes you may be asked questions about minor ailments. Many parents know what to do, but underestimate their abilities. If a parent asks you 'what should I do', find ways to reflect the question back to them, so that you help them draw out the answer themselves.

> Always remember to stay within the framework of your own expertise. Be professional and accountable.

Reflection and evaluation of your teaching practice

Maintaining a reflective journal is an excellent way to record your teaching experiences and is an invaluable aspect of ongoing professional development and self-evaluation. Clearly identifying a specific situation, reflecting on this and keeping a record of the experience will help you to focus and recognise what has made your massage classes go well and what you feel needs to be changed to improve them.

When you take the opportunity to write down your thoughts and observations after each session, you will be able to reflect on what is happening on a weekly basis; which will help you recognise your own good practice.

Parental evaluation
As well as your own reflections on your teaching, evaluation from the parents is invaluable and will help you to make adaptations and subtle changes to the way you teach and give you some good ideas to enhance your practice.

95

How to reflect on your teaching practice

Reflective cycle

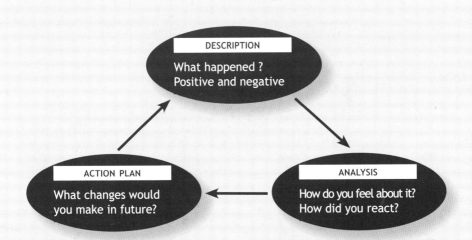

DESCRIPTION
What happened ?
Positive and negative

ANALYSIS
How do you feel about it?
How did you react?

ACTION PLAN
What changes would you make in future?

THE PROCESS	ANALYSING YOUR TEACHING	EXAMPLES
Description	What happened in the class that caused you to reflect on how you taught? What was negative about the situation or what was positive?	A parent massaged the abdomen in the wrong direction despite you teaching correctly, using the demonstration doll and addressing the whole group. The other parents were massaging the correct way.
Analysis	How did you feel about the situation? How did you react?	You are concerned about the discomfort and potentiel health risk for the baby. You introduced different methods of teaching (eg asking parents to visualise a clock face on their baby's abdomen), to help the parent.
Action plan	What changes you have decided you will make for future classes.	You will take props to help parents to understand the direction of the bowels. E.g. posters, diagrams, handouts You will always start the demonstration with your doll facing forwards, so that there is no confusion for those sitting opposite you, for whom the direction appears to be the other way (mirror image).

Oils - safety advice and usage

For massage to be enjoyable for a baby it is best to use a massage medium, such as oil; which enables the strokes to be carried out without causing friction. Without oil, massage can be irritating and uncomfortable, especially for a sensitive newborn.

Plant-based oils are ideal mediums for infant massage; however care needs to be taken as oils have the potential to cause an allergic reaction. It is recommended, where possible, that an organic or cold-pressed vegetable oil is used because they are generally the most natural and contain little or no preservatives or additives. This is especially important as babies may ingest some of the oil during the massage. Natural vegetable oils:

- Allow the skin to breathe
- Nourish and moisturise the skin
- Are easily absorbed by the skin
- Are unscented
- Are natural and safe

Patch test

As a precaution, it is advisable to ask all parents to carry out a patch test on themselves and their baby in order to avoid any allergic reactions. A small amount of the oil should be rubbed on the inside of their wrists.

The patch test should ideally be carried out 10-15 minutes prior to using the oil for the first time so that if there is an allergy to the product, a reaction will occur before it is applied to a larger area.

If the oil you supplied (or is brought by the parents) does cause a reaction, immediately advise the parent that the area should be washed thoroughly with lukewarm water and patted dry.

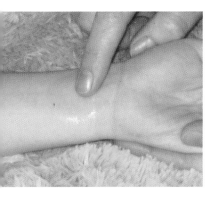

! CAUTION

If a baby or parent has a reaction to the oil you normally supply, suggest they try one that has hypoallergenic properties. However, it will be necessary for them to patch test with any new oil they try - even the hypoallergenic ones.

It is strongly advised that you keep a record of the oil you supply for each class; and for each parent/baby (note any reactions).

Vegetable oils

Organic oil

Oil that is truly organic will have been grown in strict organic conditions; starting with the seed, nuts or fruits, the condition of soil, no use of pesticides and the oil extraction process needs to be free of chemicals. These oils may be difficult to find and can be expensive.

Cold pressed oil

Cold pressed oil is produced by using high pressure to squeeze out the oil from soft, oily seeds such as sunflower and olive. For harder seeds, more pressure is used to crush the seed, which generates some heat (and may alter the oil). After crushing, the shells are removed by filters and the oil is natural. (Some oils may be further refined after cold-pressing).

Refined oils

The vegetable pulp that remains after cold-pressing still contains some oil and is refined either by high temperatures, high pressures or may be treated with steam or solvents. This process alters the oil somewhat to remove allergens and impurities, which can help to make it hypoallergenic and safer to use with babies that are prone to allergic reactions or who have weaker immune systems.

Sunflower oil (Helianthus annuus)

Sunflower oil is excellent for infant massage, in particular, the organic and cold-pressed varieties. It has a light texture and does not leave the skin feeling greasy. The oil is made from the seed of the plant and closely resembles sebum (the oil that is already present in the human skin) and therefore the sunflower oil is easily absorbed by the uppermost layers of the skin. As the oil is rather light it can be used to dilute a heavier oil, such as olive oil. This oil produces few allergic reactions, but those people that are allergic to sunflower seeds

should avoid cold-pressed and refined sunflower oils.

Olive oil (Olea europaea)

This oil, produced from the flesh of the olive, is rather heavy and viscous and may stain clothing, so therefore is not a suitable oil to supply to parents, unless it has been diluted with a lighter oil, such as sunflower. Some varieties of olive oil can have quite a strong, possibly over-stimulating odour too. It is said to have anti-inflammatory properties and can help with sensitive chapped skin, burns, stings and even nettle rashes! Olive oil is an all round general emollient. Again, it is recommended that organic, cold- pressed oil is used.

As a caution, it is advisable to suggest to parents that they gently wipe off any residue of oil to avoid staining the baby's clothes; even when diluted with lighter oils.

Grape seed oil (Vitis vinifera)

This oil is made from the hard stone of the grape and is highly refined due to the manufacturing process and has little odour, keeps well, is good for slippage and isn't too greasy when applied to the skin. Depending upon the type of refinement process this oil is said to have hypoallergenic properties and therefore good for babies who are prone to allergic reactions and have weak immune systems.

This particular oil is suitable if storing the oil in a cool, dark place is a problem, or not possible. Grapeseed oil does not change its chemical composition until heated to 220 degrees centigrade – therefore it is likely to remain more stable than other types for longer.

Coconut oil (Cocos nucifera)

Coconut oil is made from the flesh of the coconut and in its raw state is a solid, thick fat and very good for skin. (Coconut is not a 'nut' and does not have the same properties as nut oils.)

Fractionated coconut oil

Fractionated coconut oil is refined oil that has been produced from the original solid fat coconut oil through heat treatment. The fractionation of the oil removes all potential allergens, mould spores and impurities leaving pure, perfume-free oil that remains as a liquid. This oil will not oxidise as quickly as other oils and is excellent for slippage in infant massage.

Nut oils

Nut oils such as almond and peanut (the Anaphylaxis Campaign suggests that peanut is a high allergy risk in the UK) are generally not recommended for infant massage and most particularly for a baby with a suppressed immune system and/or a nut allergy problem.

Supplying oil and advising parents

When supplying parents with suitable oil, or advising them what to use after they run out of the oil you have supplied to them, you may wish to consider the following points about each oil:

SUITABLE OIL	CONSIDERATION
Sunflower	• Beneficial for dry skin • Enhances skin barrier function for neonates • Closest oil to human sebum
Fractionated coconut	• Greatly reduces the risk of allergic reaction • Suitable for babies with suppressed immune systems
Grape seed	• Does not change its chemical composition until heated to 220° C • Has hypoallergenic properties
Olive oil	• Best mixed with a lighter oil, such as Sunflower • Has anti-inflammatory properties

Parents will be swayed by availability of specific oil, the skin type of their baby, if their baby is particularly sensitive and is more inclined to have allergic reactions, as well as how the oil will be stored.

Buying, storing and using oils

For both the oil you supply as an Infant Massage Teacher and the advice you give parents, it is important to:

- Buy from a reputable supplier (www.touchneeds.com)
- Buy organic and cold-pressed vegetable oils in small quantities, as the shelf-life is limited (a 50ml bottle per parent should last several massage sessions)
- Store oils in a cool, dark place such as a larder
- Leave the oil to warm to room temperature before massage
- Discard oil that has gone rancid

(Rancid oil has a rather unpleasant odour)

- Discard oil that has been left for a long period of time as the air in the bottle will oxidise the oil and it may become rancid
- Discard any oil that has been decanted into a dish for a massage session. Do not return unused oil back into the original bottle as this could potentially contaminate the oil with bacteria

Although not ideal, it may be necessary for parents to buy food grade oils from a supermarket. Advise parents to only use organic cold-pressed varieties.

Oils to avoid

The following oils are not suitable for infant massage because of the potential health risks to the developing child.

Nut based oils   STOP

Where possible suggest that parents avoid nut-based and wheat-based oils such as sweet almond, peanut and wheat germ oil as these may contribute to or cause an allergic reaction. Nut oils are commonly known to contain more potential allergens than any other oil.

! CAUTION

If parents do feel they want to use nut based oil, advise them to patch test as usual before the first application, but also before the second application because if there is a potential of an allergy developing, it may note present itself until this stage.

An allergic response is caused by exposure to a foreign substance, such as nut oil, to which the individual has previously been exposed. The substance acts as an antigen, provoking a preliminary immune response during the first exposure that results in a sudden reaction during secondary exposure, called an immediate hypersensitivity reaction. A full-blown attack resulting in an Anaphylactic shock would require emergency treatment.

Mustard oils STOP

There is a strong indication that it is unwise for mustard oil to be used for infant massage. Application of linoleate-enriched oil such as sunflower oil may enhance skin barrier function in neonates. Mustard oil, however, has toxic effects on the epidermal barrier particularly with babies with poor skin barrier function.

Furthermore, due to the high erucic acid content which renders the oil quite toxic to young babies it is not recommended for infant massage as there is the potential that a baby may ingest some during massage as they regularly put their hands in their mouths.

Mineral oils STOP

There are a number of mineral oils and commercially available oils or gels for massage on the market, but it is strongly recommended that these are not used for infant massage – even the ones that state that they are for babies. Mineral oil/gel is a highly processed by-product of petroleum and contains potentially harmful chemicals and preservatives. Some oil may be ingested by the baby during massage as it may be on their hands and mineral oil is best avoided as it is not broken down by the body's digestive system.

Unlike vegetable oil, mineral oil is not absorbed into the outer layers of the skin (the epidermis), therefore it creates a barrier of film on the surface of the baby's skin. This locks in moisture

containing toxins and waste and can block pores as it impedes the natural functions of the skin, such as excretion and heat regulation. Mineral oil also prevents the skin from absorbing oxygen, to keep it healthy.

For massage purposes this oil is used purely for slippage and does not really offer any benefit to the skin. Indeed, as this type of oil sits on the skin it can be dangerous when lifting a child whose body may be particularly slippery. Also, long-term use of such oil can actually have a drying effect of the skin.

Mineral oil's only appeal is that it is usually cheap and does not oxidise and become rancid.

Artificially scented STOP

Some commercial infant massage oils and gels often contain artificial perfumes and preservatives. It is important to avoid these particular oils be cause they will contain chemi-

cals that may be harmful when ingested. As the artificial scents are often quite strong the baby may find them overpowering and over stimulating for the senses. Furthermore, the scent prevents the baby from smelling their parent's natural scent. Also, it may mask a rancid base oil.

Emollients STOP

Dry skin is a common complaint and is one of the key symptoms in relation to conditions such as eczema and psoriasis; emollients are considered effective therapeutic agents for managing these conditions. Broadly speaking emollients work by smoothing, soothing and re-hydrating the skin. However, as they are a treatment it is important to follow the guidelines for application.

> Emollients should only be applied to the skin following the direction of the hair growth.

Guidelines for application of emollient creams suggest that they should be applied in a light downward sweeping movement, following the direction of the hair growth (rather like applying butter to toast), so that the cream does not clog the follicles and so minimizes the risk of folliculitis.

It is not generally recommended to use emollient creams, such as those used for eczema and other skin conditions, during infant massage as it is neither safe nor advantageous. For massage, firm effleurage strokes should be applied in an upward direction working with venous flow, which is generally against the direction of hair growth. To err on the side of caution we would suggest that parents follow guidelines for the application of the emollient and refrain from using it with nfant massage to eliminate any risk of infection.

Essential oils STOP

As the popularity of Aromatherapy has gained momentum, many products containing various essential oils are appearing on the market. Essential oils work in very subtle ways, in very small amounts to give therapeutic effects; some of the stronger oils being the antidote to homeopathic remedies.

Indeed, some of the stronger essential oils are so potent when blended that they are capable of eradicating the life-threatening bug MRSA!

The chemical content of an essential oil enters the body via the olfactory system and can have a direct influence on brain chemistry. Also, as the molecular structure of essential oils is much smaller than vegetable oils, they are able to penetrate through the top layers of the skin. About 60% of an essential oil, massaged in to the skin will be absorbed into the blood stream.

Reasons for not using essential oils with children under twelve years of age

- The immune system of a neonate is very immature and over-use of essential oils may overwhelm an immature liver which has difficulty metabolizing these chemicals

- Essential oils are far too over-stimulating for the nervous system of the neonate

- To-date there is NO research to validate that the use of essential oils with infants is safe

- There is indeed research to indicate that the use of essential oils is potentially unsafe for pre-pubescent children, due to the oestrogenic and anti-androgenic activities of certain oils; and regular application (such as with massage) may disrupt the endocrine system

- Just because a parent likes the fragrance of particular oil does not mean that their baby will. Obviously the baby may not be able to communicate this to their parents directly. However, it may cause the baby to be unsettled, which could prompt a 'no' response to the offer of massage

- The essential oil could mask the odour of a rancid oil

- The fragrance added to oil could mask the natural scent of the parent. It is very important for the baby to smell their parent's natural smell to aid bonding

- Many products on the market intended for babies and children contain a number of essential oils. It is not uncommon to find a whole

103

array of products for the bath, the hair, massage gel, nappy rash, oils to burn for inhalation etc., each of them containing different essential oils claiming to help relax or soothe a baby. If a parent uses all these products on their young baby they could be, unwittingly, overwhelming their infant's sensitive and immature systems.

! CAUTION

Essential oils and children:

Advise parents that regular, sustained use of products containing essential oils should be avoided. Suggest to those wishing to introduce essential oils as a specific treatment that they should consult a qualified and registered Aromatherapist who specialises in treating children.

Promoting your infant massage classes successfully

Concentrating on marketing and publicising your Infant Massage Classes, will help tremendously, regardless of whether you are in an area where infant massage is still viewed with a certain amount of scepticism, or there are already well-established Infant Massage Teachers running classes locally. Working out a plan of action will help to keep you focused.

Devise a business plan

Include in your plan everything that will help you concentrate on want you want to achieve as an Infant Massage Teacher. This helps you get started and, should the going get tough, a plan can help you stay focused. Consider including in your plan:

- What you need to run your classes? For example:
  + The venue
  + The materials needed to make the classes run smoothly (e.g. baby change mats, oil, nappies, kettle, etc)
- What is your budget to get your classes up and running?
- What are you going to charge?
- Are you going to teach individuals or groups, or both?
- Do you want to teach privately, or through organisations such as Family Centres?
  - How many classes do you want to run a week?
  - How do you want to run the classes? (e.g. as a weekly drop-in, or as part of a course etc)
- How are you going to market yourself?
  + Who are you going to approach?
  + Where are you going to advertise?
  + Where are you going to give talks/presentations?
- Are there any professional development courses/study days you want to attend

Develop a network

Do not assume that the local competition is necessarily hostile.

- There are people who enjoy sharing knowledge and you may have something to offer, just as much as the next person
- There are also people who might be interested in a joint venture For example:
  - ✦ Another Infant Massage Teacher who is interested in running larger groups with a co-worker
- ✦ Another Infant Massage Teacher who only works weekends perhaps to fit in with family and you are able to offer week days
- ✦ Postnatal Exercise Teachers or Baby Yoga Instructors who would like to be involved in offering a more rounded service – their skills and yours combined

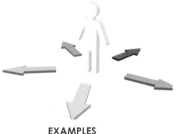

Devise an action plan

CONSIDERATION	EXAMPLES
Gather information about the area you plan to run classes in	• What is around to support parents with babies locally? • Most importantly – are there many parents with babies in that area? • Are there already Infant Massage Classes running? If so, how are they run? – by a Health Professional, or a Complementary Therapist. How much do they charge? How often do they run classes? • Are there many places to advertise/promote your classes?
Find a suitable venue that is within your budget	Consider church halls, community centres, health centres
Develop a marketing pack	• Posters • Leaflets • Compliment slips • Business cards • Letterheaded paper
Contact the 'gatekeepers' to the parents you hope to teach	• Health Visitors • Midwives • Paediatric Nurses • GPs • Family Centre Managers

CONSIDERATION	EXAMPLES
Offer to give talks and presentations	• NCT • Mother and toddler groups • Postnatal exercise groups • Antenatal groups • The 'gatekeepers'
Use your marketing material	Put up posters in community centres, health centres, village halls, libraries, churches, crèches, nurseries, local baby shops, maternity units – anywhere you can find parents with babies
Keep and maintain a professional portfolio	See below
Keep abreast of current research and keep copies of relevant articles *(helpful when dealing with professionals who wish to see proof of evidence based research concerning the benefits of infant massage)*	Keep these in your portfolio
Advertise through the local media	• Try to get the local paper to do an article, • Contact the local radio or TV station – if they have a talk show they maybe interested in covering infant massage

Be Prepared To Be Flexible and if necessary, be ready to revise your plan. What might work in one geographical area, may not in another.

Most importantly do not give up at the first hurdle

It is often tough to get started and established. Be assertive and you will get there in the end. Remember, what you can offer as an Infant Massage Teacher is so beneficial to both parent and child it is well worth the effort.

Getting known and established: the trials and tribulations

I became an Infant Massage Teacher in the mid 90s. At the time there were very few Infant Massage Teachers for me to have to compete with. This did not, however, give me any advantages, because infant massage was very much an unknown entity. Its wonderful benefits had not at that stage been enthused about through the media, so parents were unaware of what they and their babies could gain from this. Also, health professionals and other gatekeepers to the parents I hoped to gain access to, were sceptical and wary of what I was offering.

I qualified as a Massage Therapist in the early 90s, and adapted the adult massage for my three older children (all under 10 years old at the time). Then I adapted the routine further after the birth of my fourth child, so I truly understood how great a skill this was to have as a parent. This knowledge spurred me on to overcome adversity and keep 'spreading the word' as it were, about infant massage.

As soon as I qualified as an Infant Massage Teacher, I started to approach Health Visitors, Midwives (particularly those that ran postnatal groups), local National Childbirth Trust (NCT) groups and mother and baby/toddler groups in the area. I offered to give talks wherever and whenever I could; and within a few weeks of starting, I was managing to give one or two talks a week to various groups. Promoting infant massage through talks and demonstrations did not, however, necessarily mean I had lots of parents signing up for classes. In fact, to begin with, it was very hard work to actually get 'bums on seats' (or the floor) !

I advertised and promoted the classes through the local NCT newsletters, newsagents windows, community centre notice boards and the libraries nearby. I also managed to get a slot on a local radio programme.

For the first 18 months it was hard going, sometimes disheartening and even, on occasion demoralising. However, I was determined to run at least one class every week. I booked the venue (a lovely room in a community centre, with good parking and access) and promoted the courses well in advance. I never cancelled a course due to low numbers; and even ran a couple of them with only two parents and babies booked in. For the first year the majority of my courses had no more than four parents, but within 18 months, I was regularly teaching between five to seven parents that joined each course.

Why did I not give up after a few months of hard work and no results? It is because I felt it was important to focus on getting known and established in the area – and I realised that that might take time.

I knew that by getting information about infant massage into the local community, I would at some point start to reap the benefits of my hard work. Which I eventually did. I started to have referrals from parents I had already taught, repeat business from parents after they had had another baby and more firm bookings when I gave talks (because the word was beginning to get around about the benefits and what could be gained from joining one of my classes.

As infant massage became better known generally, so too did the competition increase – but as I had established myself, parents still booked with me. After about two years I decreased my advertising and promoting quite considerably, because word of mouth was doing the job instead! I was even approached by a Community College some 15 miles away, because they had heard that I taught. I then ran some courses with them – and they did all the advertising, marketing and booking (lovely!).

Pauline Carpenter

Working in different arenas

You may also wish to consider the various arenas where Infant Massage is suitable for introduction. Parents may look to health professionals and educational establishments in order to access relevant classes with their baby. The following may be of interest to you:

Infant massage via community education

You may have the opportunity to teach in a community college. If so, you may be asked to submit information about the programme and the learning outcomes. The advantage of teaching in a community college is that the marketing is usually handled by the college; and you simply have to prepare for the course and arrive there to teach. However, be warned! There is usually a lot of administrative paper work assigned to every course the college runs, even infant massage!

Infant massage and Primary Care Trusts (PCT)

You may have the opportunity to run classes for a PCT. However, beforehand, you may be expected to write a proposal. If this is the case, the following guide may help you.

In your proposal:

Include	• What it is you are proposing • How this is to be achieved • What the cost implications are • Which staff will be involved • How many hours will be allocated to the project • What sort of equipment and venue will be required • How the project is to be evaluated • How the project is to be audited • If you know of other NHS Trusts who are supporting infant massage then mention them in your proposal • Copies of your qualifications
Define	• Define infant massage • Define the benefits for the parents and the babies • Define the safety precautions and how you will be demonstrating professional accountability

Outline	• Outline current research, especially in the United Kingdom • Outline how infant massage can promote maternal and infant well-being • Give a sample of your course curriculum or scheme of work • Give a sample of a lesson plan • State your learning outcomes
Appendices	If you have a marketing pack and have professional leaflets attach them to your proposal

When writing a proposal and looking for support

- Keep the proposal simple and easy to read

- Set the proposal out in a smart design so that it is attractive to the eye

- If you are already working within the NHS, approach your manager or lead professional nurse for advice and guidance

- Consider forming a working party of similar minded people from various backgrounds. It can be useful to share ideas and produce the proposal together

When presenting your proposal

- Be prepared to do a demonstration, if required

- Take along your professional portfolio

- Devise a short statement with key points and essential information, so that you are always well briefed and prepared

Keeping a portfolio

Your marketing strategy would benefit from you designing and maintaining a professional portfolio. This needs to be concise, well presented, relevant and kept up-to-date; indicating clearly the use of research material. It should demonstrate skills, knowledge and understanding, which arise from experience, education and on-going training.

A portfolio relevant to infant massage is a useful marketing tool when approaching the 'gatekeepers' of the parents you want to teach (such as Health Visitors, Midwives and their managers) who want to see evidence of your qualifications, ability, knowledge and professionalism. You may wish to include in your portfolio:

Central diagram: **PROFESSIONAL PORTFOLIO** with connecting arrows from:
- Evaluations / Testimonials
- Course / Study day Certificates
- CV
- Audits
- Handouts
- Research and relevant articles
- Insurance and CRB certificates
- Marketing material

Writing for publication

Writing for publication may help you promote yourself as an Infant Massage Teacher. It will enlighten those who know very little about the topic and will give you further resources for your Professional Portfolio. A topic does not have to be new to be published, as editors are always looking for material and certainly appreciate a fresh outlook on any subject. If you feel you would like to take the plunge and write an article:

- Contact the journal(s) you have in mind to find out in what format they expect an article to be submitted in. They will give you guidance about the title, abstract, layout, word length and referencing style they prefer

- Once you have a title:
  + Brainstorm and jot down your initial thoughts; use a mind map
  + Have a notebook to jot things down as they pop into your head

- Be clear about the focus of the topic you are writing about. Keep to the point
- Remember, as well as the main discussion about the topic, you will need an introduction and conclusion; and you will need to remember to include references and any acknowledgements
- Think about style and content of your writing. Magazines may prefer a more informal, chatty style than a professional journal
- For extra support and guidance, take advice from a 'how to write' book, there are many on the market and it should be possible to find one that suits your needs
- It is always useful to get someone else to proof-read your work. It is so easy to miss little grammatical errors and typos when you are very close to a piece of writing

- You will need copies of your work; and if sending by post, it is advisable to use recorded or special delivery
- If the editor wishes to amend the article be sure you are happy with the changes. Do not agree to compromise unless happy to do so
- Do not give up the copyright for your work lightly. It is your intellectual property and should remain so
- Remember to find out when the publication date is; ask to be sent a copy of the issue

113

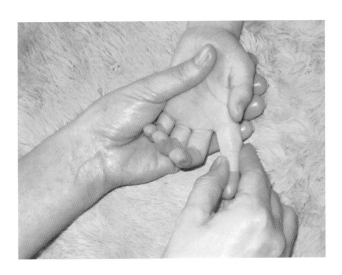

One of the best ways to market your business is to extol the virtues of infant massage by way of producing feature articles for publication.

Over the years I have written many articles that have been published in magazines, newsletters, newspapers and academic journals; I've even been paid for some. The ultimate is being asked to write a book and seeing your own words in print!

However, I wasn't always able to put pen to paper and produce a coherent piece of writing. In fact it has taken many years for my confidence to grow and for the words to flow without agonising over each sentence.

The very first article I ever wrote was to promote my infant massage courses and was printed in the magazine for the local branch of NCT. I took an essay I had written about the benefits of infant massage for my QIMT qualification, which, I have to say, was rather academic, and over which I'd agonised for many, many hours. I revamped and reworked it so that it was much more chatty and accessible to parents. Changing styles took some time but it was a good experience and left with me two styles of article to draw upon for future reference.

I also used a local newspaper to market my courses by supplying an advertorial (editorial crossed with an advert). This was great because an advertorial is educational yet you are able to market yourself at the same time thus saving on costly advertising. I contacted the editorial team and asked if they'd print my article and they were very accommodating; even sending round a photographer to take a picture of me with my demonstration doll. It made front page and half of another page inside the paper. This was fabulous exposure, but beware! I've known people supply advertorials but after they've submitted their article it has been changed beyond recognition, often with errors and omissions. Unfortunately this is accepted practice and is the editor's prerogative!

It is a good idea to have a number of articles ready in a number of different styles that you can wheel out when the situation arises. I would recommend that you write in the third person for academic style articles and in the first or second person for more chatty magazine style articles.

To begin with take one discussion topic, such as the benefits of infant massage or suitable oils for infant massage. Write your article in a fairly academic style with references, etc, and then rework your piece but in a more chatty, informal style. From experience I recommend doing it this way round so that you have the referenced piece of work should someone come back to you at a later date for more information on your less formal article.

Ensure your content is accurate and well researched. Have the good grace to reference those people who you have quoted; plagiarism is not taken lightly. An author's style is very personal and recognisable. On a number of occasions I have come across others' work where they have used my words verbatim and not referenced their source!

Make sure your article, whether a short zippy piece for the local church mag or a large article for an NHS Manager, is well structured. It should have an introduction, a middle and a conclusion to round off your piece. Finally, proof read for grammatical and spelling errors so that it is polished and editors will take you seriously.

I hope that you find my sharing some of my experiences useful and helpful when writing articles for yourself. All I would ask is don't give up at the first hurdle just because it seems like too much hard work and the bottle of Shiraz and Coronation Street are more appealing! Persevere with it and you never know, you might be writing your own book one day!

Anita Epple

Infants and Parents

Development of the brain

.....unseen forces which shape our emotional responses through life, are not primarily our biological urges, but the patterns of emotional experience with other people, most powerfully set up in infancy. These patterns are not immutable but, like all habits, once established they are hard to break. (Gerhardt, 2004. Page 15/16)

The hard-wiring of the brain

At birth, babies mainly rely on the sub-cortex to support them through the early stages of their life. Initially, the sub-cortex, which functions on a basic instinctual and emotional level, is not 'wired up' to the under-developed neo-cortex which will eventually be responsible for rational thought, regulating behaviour and dealing with social situations. During a child's first two years of life a tremendous amount of development of the rational brain occurs as a large number of connections (synapses) between the nerve cells in the neo-cortex and sub-cortex are established at a phenomenal rate. It is of great importance that these pathways are given optimum support to develop, to enable a child to grow into a rational, reasoning and caring human being.

Sub-cortex

Reptilian Brain – also known as the primitive or archipallium brain. Includes the brainstem [hypothalamus, midbrain, medulla oblongata, pons variolii and the cerebellum (see A&P section)].

Mammalian Brain/limbic system – also known as the intermediary or paleopallium brain. Includes the amygdala and the hippocampus.

The limbic system is primarily responsible for emotional life, and has a lot to do with the formation of memories. There are seven emotional systems activated by this area of the brain: rage, fear, seeking, separation distress, play, lust and nurturance.

Neo-cortex

Rational Brain – also known as the pre-frontal and neopallium brain.

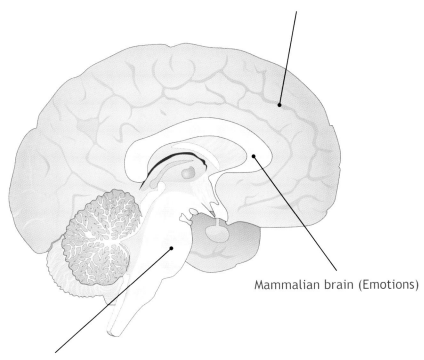

Rational brain (Higher thinking)

Mammalian brain (Emotions)

Reptilian brain (Survival)

Emotional regulation and support

An insufficient number of connections between the limbic system and frontal brain impede the newborn's ability to calm without support. Babies particularly need help to modify and regulate emotions when rage, fear and separation distress have been activated. A baby left without support to regulate their emotions is likely to experience high cortisol levels over sustained periods of time, which can be quite toxic to the brain, particularly for the development of the frontal cortex and functioning of the hippocampus. Therefore, if the parent or caregiver does not regularly help to control these emotions in a caring, nurturing manner then the effects of these negative experiences are likely to be life-long.

Cortisol is a corticosteroid hormone produced by the adrenal cortex, in the adrenal gland. It is a vital hormone, released into the system during times of stress. It increases blood pressure, blood sugar levels and has an immunosuppressive action.

An infant's need for positive life experiences

In addition to helping a baby deal with and overcome challenging emotional states, it is important during this crucial stage of development, for them to have positive input, with lots of varied experiences and stimulation in order to help promote the growth of neural pathways between the neo-cortex and sub-cortex. Lack of regulation and appropriate stimulation, similarly neglect and abuse, all impact negatively on brain development.

Unfortunately, children and adults, who do not have good experiences in infancy, struggle to control their emotions as they are inclined to negotiate their world through sub-cortical responses. This type of reaction is known as 'psycho-biochemical arrest', which effectively means that the person is functioning, or reacting like a baby. The amygdala reacts to perceived 'threats' encountered, but receives little regulation from the frontal brain. Because the pathways between the sub-cortex and neo-cortex are under-developed, the frontal lobe is unable to bring calm and control to the situation.

The Hippocampus, if damaged by regular high doses of cortisol during infancy, is also unable to help bring the amygdala in check.

The **amygdala** forms a part of the limbic system and performs a primary role in the processing and memory of emotional reactions.

The **hippocampus** forms a part of the limbic system and plays a part in long term memory, spatial navigation and managing emotional responses from the amgydala.

Massage:
A positive life experience?

Massage is an excellent way of bringing new and positive experiences into a young baby's life as they offer the opportunity for positive touch and early play, especially when accompanied with lots of talking, music and singing of nursery rhymes. Infant massage allows parents the opportunity to spend time with their baby and to have fun together; giving the baby many positive experiences. However, the experience must be baby-led.

If a baby is saying 'no' to massage they must be heard and their feelings respected if massage is to remain a positive experience.

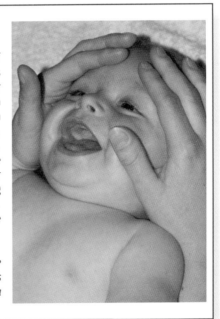

Cognitive development

The process of cognitive development during a child's early years allows them to develop the ability to think, reason, store information to memory and acquire language skills. All of these abilities, which start to develop in early infancy as the brain begins forming connections, help a child create an impression of the world around them.

Cognitive development milestones

AGE	DEVELOPMENT MILESTONE	MASSAGE AT THIS STAGE
Between 1 and 2 months	Babies become interested in new objects and will turn and look towards them. They gaze longer at more complicated objects and seem, also, to enjoy looking at many new objects as though trying to learn as much about their new world as possible.	Containment holds may help a baby feel secure. Some gentle stroking may not be too stimulating, but positive touch is usually enough at this already very stimulating stage of their life.
Around 3 months	Babies have now developed the ability to anticipate future events.	They will become excited when a parent gently lays their hands on their chest and asks if they want a massage.
Around 4 months	A baby's sight becomes more advanced and they are now able to combine what they see with what they taste, hear, and feel. Their self-aware-ness has started to develop.	Massage can help them become more aware of their legs, feet, arms and hands.
Between 6 and 9 months	Connections in the brain are increasing rapidly. Babies can recognise the appearance, sound, and touch of familiar people. Also, babies are able to recall the memory of a person, such as a parent, or a related object when that particular person is not in view.	If massaged regularly, a baby may gain comfort from a massage when feeling a little fractious. As a tool to help with this, the parent may offer massage and as they begin to ask permission, the baby may remember the signal and start to calm.
Between 9 and 12 months	Babies are constantly obser-ving the behaviour of others. They start to reveal their personality, become curious about their surroundings and begin to explore. They are also able to demonstrate many different emotions.	A baby is often too busy to want a full massage because they have too much 'to do' at this stage.

AGE	DEVELOPMENT MILESTONE	MASSAGE AT THIS STAGE
Between 12 and 18 months	Toddlers continue to explore their environment and create experiments to see how things work. They will play with anything they can find; however, at this stage they are not aware of danger so they do not realise that certain objects such as fires, sharp knives and electric plug sockets can hurt them. During this stage the ability to recognise people and objects moves on a step because not only do the babies realise that something can be hidden and still exist, but by now they will look for it too. Babies develop the capacity to build memories that incorporate all their senses. For instance children are able to see a mental picture of an object they are holding in their hand without actually looking at it. They remember the object as a whole through all their senses; they remember its texture and size in their hands, its sound through their ears, and perhaps even its smell.	As they near the end of this stage they may be able stay still long enough for just a few massage strokes. Encourage parents to involve their baby in the massage, when they do want one. E.g. letting them pour the oil into their parent's hand.
Between the ages of 18 and 24 months	Toddlers are able to create a generic image of things in their minds and retain them as examples of certain objects. They may create in their mind a picture of a teddy bear, and use it to represent other cuddly animals they play with. Because of this, babies may look for their favourite teddy bear in the toy box because they know that is where it usually lives!	A baby's concentration span is greater and the offer of a full body massage will often be accepted again.

123

AGE	DEVELOPMENT MILESTONE	MASSAGE AT THIS STAGE
Around 21 months	At this stage a child's recall and recognition also improves significantly. They can anticipate processes and understand routines, e.g. what the normal procedure is when they go to the park, from the time it is suggested to when they arrive at their destination. By now a child has began to grasp the concept of past, present and future. They also begin to understand that 'things' fit into certain categories, such as becoming capable of recognising a car as a car, even though all cars do not look the same.	When a child wants a massage they are likely to want to collect some of the equipment, such as the bottle of oil, or they may remove some of their clothes and lie on the floor in anticipation!
Around 24 months	By now a child is able to pretend and imagine things that are not in front of them. This is the first step beyond 'concrete thinking' *(only being able to think about things that are actually in front of them)*.	Introducing a simple story-time massage, for instance, about their favourite book character, or animal can help encourage their imagination.

Speech and language development

Early conversations

If parents give time to 'listen to' and 'enter into a conversation' with their baby, they will soon be able to recognise that the baby responds to their voice in a specific manner. The sounds and little noises that babies make are more structured and controlled than is immediately obvious. Babies have a definite musical ability when

A baby that is listened to as well as sung to is more likely to feel calm, respected and loved; and is more likely to develop a strong sense of well-being as they grow.

communicating with their parents; and they normally respond by imitating the sounds they hear, so they appear to be chatting, or singing along in their own way. They are able to follow simple rhythms long before they are able to speak.

> Massage allows a parent to focus on their baby, giving them the opportunity to really learn how their baby communicates with them.

The sounds uttered by a baby are in a timed, melodic sequence, particularly when trying to start the 'conversation'. The pause between each call as they try to get their parent's attention is a specific duration; as if they are politely waiting a few seconds, just to check that the parent has finished what they were saying! This can give the opportunity for a dialogue to open. It is through this type of interaction that a baby starts to learn about listening, joining in and the art of turn-taking during a conversation.

Nursery rhymes

A great way to stimulate and strengthen a baby's brain is for them to experience lots of chatter from their parents; as long as they are happy with the pace and can take part in the 'conversation'. As with any experience, it is important that a baby is comfortable with the interaction. It must be on their terms if it is to be a positive, brain developing experience for them. Some parents struggle with 'chatting' to their baby; but find they are more comfortable replacing, or supplementing talking by using nursery rhymes.

> A baby's massage time gives the perfect opportunity for parents to introduce rhymes.

Babies seem ready to tune into rhymes sung by their parents and tend to respond enthusiastically to this form of communication. But how they are sung is important to how well a baby understands or appreciates them. A flat or monotone voice will not attract

Suggested observation

- *When teaching parents,*
- *you may notice that the*
- *attention of the babies in*
- *the class is focused on 'you',*
- *the Infant Massage Teacher,*
- *because you are speaking.*
- *However, once you*
- *encourage parents to speak*
- *or sing a nursery rhyme you*
- *will have the opportunity*
- *to observe that the babies'*
- *attention will shift to their*
- *parents.*

a baby to the singer; but a soft, higher than usual pitched voice will be easier for a baby to engage with and respond to. The impact is greater if the important words or sounds are stressed and if the rhyme is repeated regularly. As the voice goes up an octave or so, the developing brain responds by sending a greater number of chemical and electrical impulses along the newly developing neural pathways. This response is indicative of how important singing to a baby really is.

Frequently repeated rhymes and songs have a very important role to play in the early development of language. In addition, the development of language influences a child's ability to think and learn. So, as well as being quite a joyful, comforting and fun experience for both parent and baby, repeating nursery rhymes, so that the baby becomes familiar with them, can actually help with a baby's cognitive development.

Fundamentally, music and language have many similarities between how they are perceived and understood when processed by the brain. To be meaningful, they both require organisation and structure, rhythm, a sense of timing, and sound frequency appreciation.

Suggested exercise for parents

- *If you find parents are*
- *unhappy/lack confidence*
- *to sing to their baby or in a*
- *group, try introducing rhymes*
- *that can also be spoken.*

- *Parents may be happier*
- *to participate this way. As*
- *long as their voices are a*
- *higher pitch than normal*
- *conversation then there will*
- *be the same benefits as if*
- *they are singing.*

Music has the ability to impact on both the conscious and unconscious mind. It can affect a person's state of arousal, provoke visual images, stimulate memories, influence feelings and emotions and have an effect on breathing and heart rate.

Speech and language development milestones

AGE	DEVELOPMENT MILESTONE	MASSAGE AT THIS STAGE
From birth	A baby enjoys interacting with their parents, being listened to and taking part in a 'conversation'.	If parents reassure a baby verbally whilst cuddling, doing gentle strokes, or a colic routine, this communication will help strengthen the attachment bond.
From about 1 month	A baby is able to make guttural sounds and coos in response to parents chatting with them.	
From 2 months	A baby is able to process and respond to emotional and tonal variation within a person's voice.	Raising the voice to pitch C whilst chatting and singing will help make the massage a positive experience and will engage a baby's attention and encourage them to interact.
At 3 months	A baby is able to vocalise their delight when parents chat and sing to them.	Encouraging parents to sing to their baby will help them focus on each other during the massage and really make it a delightful, fun-time experience.
At 4 months	A baby is capable of responding to every type of sound produced by every language in the world.	
At 6 months	A baby is able to chat tunefully, using sing-song vowel sounds. At this stage they have started to introduce double syllable sounds. They chuckle and squeal with delight when playing; and scream in annoyance when frustrated.	Repeating the same songs and rhymes helps with language and brain development.

AGE	DEVELOPMENT MILESTONE	MASSAGE AT THIS STAGE
At 9 months	At this stage a baby vocalises deliberately, such as shouting to attract attention. Their tuneful chatting has more purpose, but is still mainly for self amusement, though they are beginning to understand that they can use this as a form of communication.	A baby is able to support non-verbal cues with more vocal input, indicating 'yes' or 'no' to massage more purposefully.
At 10 months	A baby is able to distinguish sounds from their own language (or languages) and is able to start making similar sounds too.	Enhancing massage time with chatting and singing will improve a baby's understanding for language and sow the seeds for the development of speech in the coming months.

Sensory perception

Sensory development - pre-birth awareness

The development of sensory perception in the early stages of gestation allows the foetus the opportunity to experience the special rhythm and sensations of their mother's internal environment. As they near the end of their gestational period they start to become aware of the external world, that they are about to enter.

SENSE	PRE-BIRTH AWARENESS	AFTER BIRTH AWARENESS
Touch	The sense of touch is the first to develop at only three weeks gestation; and at 12 weeks gestation the whole body (except the top of the head) is sensitive to touch. It is deep pressure touch that is experienced by the foetus in-utero; they receive a continual massage within the confined space of the uterine walls, whilst their mother moves around.	Touch is a major component of how babies experience their new world. They use touch to comfort themselves and derive comfort from being touched and held by others.
Movement	In-utero the foetus is surrounded by activity. In the floating and weightless environment of the amniotic sac, they have the freedom to move, flex their joints and experience their mother's movements. Each unborn baby has its own timetable and rhythm, and mothers often notice that their baby moves more at certain times of the day than at others.	After birth, the newborn can derive pleasure from being held and rocked by their parents.
Sound	The uterine environment is a symphony of sounds and vibrations. The foetus can hear the swishing sounds of the maternal blood and heartbeat, as well as the noises in her stomach and intestines. From the third trimester, the foetus becomes aware of the sounds from the outside world. Their mother's voice will become particularly familiar to them, as it is their constant companion.	The newborn will be startled by loud noises. They will be comforted by the human voice particularly when picked up. The newborn recognises and prefers their mother's voice.

129

SENSE	PRE-BIRTH AWARENESS	AFTER BIRTH AWARENESS
Taste/ Smell	Taste cells appear at about seven to eight weeks gestation and are mature by 14 weeks. The cells are stimulated by the various chemicals circulating in the amniotic fluid, which is swallowed by the foetus whilst in-utero.	Once born a baby can find its mother's breast all by itself. The taste and smell of the amniotic fluid on the baby's hands help them to make the connection between this and the substance on the nipples, which is similar to amniotic fluid. This odour guides the infant to the breast. The newborn can distinguish between different smells. By one or two days of life, breast fed babies will recognise the smell of their mother's breast milk.
Sight	Under-developed at birth	The newborn is capable of seeing about 20 cm away – just enough to focus on their mother's face from the breast or the safe confines of her arms.

Sensory perception from birth

Information from our sensory rich world is processed through the senses. The ability to see, hear, taste, smell and touch allows us to know and understand the environment and what is happening around us. The brain processes the information received through the senses and initiates the action and regulation of the response to the stimuli.

At birth a baby already has an awareness of movement, sound, touch, taste and smell. However, they are born with limited processing and regulating abilities and need help in the early stages to manage the world at large, so that

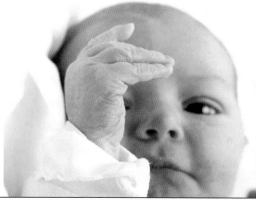

they do not become unnecessarily over-stimulated.

Habituation

In the main, adults comfortably negotiate their environment, giving attention to what they need to, whilst 'ignoring' the ordinary, mundane and everyday activities around them. This is because the entire animal world (including humans) develops the ability to habituate; enabling them to tune out the unexceptional (for example, the sound of the refrigerator motor whirring, or smell of the disinfectant in the bathroom) unless they choose to give these matters specific thought.

The capacity to deal selectively with environmental stimuli prevents us from becoming over-stimulated. We interact with our environment, give attention to a new experience/situation/object and once it is familiar we effortlessly inhibit our attention to it; preventing sensory overload thereby enabling us to deal with more important matters that require focus and concentration.

> Premature, sick and fragile infants often have a poor ability to habituate.

When presented by a noisy, stimulating environment, the (healthy, full-term) baby can avoid sensory overload by disengaging and, more dramatically, if required, feign sleep. This skill is acquired around the 34th week of gestation, but is not so apparent after three months of age, as babies gradually learn to inhibit excess stimulation from the environment more appropriately.

Habituation can be a useful tool for babies when the baby finds the environment too intrusive, such as over-handling by enthusiastic relatives at a family gathering. However, although a useful coping mechanism, it is not healthy regulation; and this skill, if used too much, can be exhausting for the baby and may have long-term effects on their emotional and social development.

Social development

During the first three years of life, a child will develop crucial social abilities. They have the potential to learn how to give and accept, become self-aware and confident, show empathy and sympathy, be curious and develop appropriate relationships with others.

Social development milestones

AGE	DEVELOPMENT MILESTONE	MASSAGE AT THIS STAGE
Up to 2 months	From birth a baby is able to grasp a finger when the palm of their hand is touched; and they will turn to regard a speaker's face. A baby will begin to smile by about four weeks old.	
At 3 months	The baby will begin to anticipate similar situations, for example, the offer of the breast or bottle. They respond by smiling, cooing and moving excitedly. They are more socially responsive, responding to friendly handling and being spoken to with interest and delight. The baby will start to model and imitate their parent.	If offered regularly, massage will be anticipated with great delight.
At 6 months	They will hold the breast or bottle when fed and reach for an object that is offered to them, such as a rattle and will shake it deliberately. The baby will begin to try to dominate their interactions with their parent. They respond to active play with delight and are beginning to become shy of strangers.	When enjoying the massage, a baby may like to hold a small toy. They are particularly receptive to interacting during the massage – particularly if rhymes and songs are included.
At 9 months	By now a baby can distinguish strangers from familiar people; and are shy of those they do not know. They like to play games, such as 'peek-a-boo' and can imitate hand clapping. A baby is able to 'offer' an object to another person, but is unlikely to give it to them. They can 'find' a hidden object, if they see it being hidden to begin with.	The face and head massage could be incorporated with a game of 'peek-a-boo' to hold the baby's attention for longer.

Physical development

Once born, changes within the infant rapidly take place to enable survival as they now commence a new stage of their life as a separate entity from their mother.

AGE	DEVELOPMENT MILESTONE	MASSAGE AT THIS STAGE
At birth	A baby has to start breathing almost immediately, getting their own oxygen supplies from the air. The kidneys and digestive systems start to function independently. The foramen ovale and ductus arteriosus close and the baby's heart and lungs become independent of the mother.	
Up to 1 month	At birth a baby's motor development is immature. In the main, they rely on a set of basic primitive reflexes, which are directed from the brainstem. They are automatic responses to specific stimuli and do not require any input from the cortex. As an infant develops and begins to control its movements, the primitive reflexes are designed to integrate into the whole body movement system; and remain inhibited throughout life *(only to reappear if postural reflexes are impeded by disease in later life).* When held in sitting position their head falls forward. They are able to focus on and follow a slow moving object with their eyes. By one week old a baby is able to recognise its mother's face.	A face massage may create upset as a baby is prompted to 'root'. Also, massaging the fingers may be difficult.

133

AGE	DEVELOPMENT MILESTONE	MASSAGE AT THIS STAGE
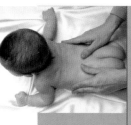 By 3 months	At this stage a baby's limbs are more pliable and their movements are becoming smoother and more controlled, as the primitive reflexes become inhibited. They are able to watch their hands and are able to alternately grasp and then release their hands – even holding a toy, such as a rattle for a few seconds. If placed in prone position, they are able to lift their head and upper chest. They have much better head control, moving their head deliberately to gaze around; are able to bring their hands to the midline; and kick their legs purposefully.	Leave teaching the back massage until one of the final classes, so that the baby is more likely to enjoy lying on the front, because they can support their upper body so much more effectively.
By 6 months	At this stage a baby explores all objects with their mouth. They can usually sit up with support. When on their back they can raise their head to look at their feet and can efficiently grasp their feet; and can roll over from front to back. Their arm movements are more controlled; for example, they can hold out their arms to indicate they want to be picked up. They stretch out their hands to grasp an object and can then pass it from hand-to-hand and examine it closely. When held in a standing position they will bounce up and down.	Consider introducing alternative positions to the parents, if the baby tires of lying on their back. Teaching the arm massage for a baby sitting between the parent's legs may help - particularly if the baby is keen to see more of the goings on in the room!

AGE	DEVELOPMENT MILESTONE	MASSAGE AT THIS STAGE
At 9 months	At this stage a baby can sit unsupported on the floor and lean forward to pick up an object within their reach, as well as turn to look sideways. They are able to apply hand-eye coordination to pick up an object with their fingers and thumb and will point at objects in the distance with one finger. By this age babies are actively rolling, commando crawling and possibly crawling. They are able to pull themselves up to a standing position with support; and can step forward with alternating feet, when supported in the standing position.	Parents who approach you about learning massage with an active crawler may find one-to-one sessions easier to manage. This allows you the opportunity to work with the individual parent and baby, whilst not disrupting a whole class of parents with pre-crawlers.
At 12 months	The primitive reflexes should have been completely inhibited and replaced by the developing postural reflexes.	

Sleeping

It is quite normal for a baby to wake at night during the early months of life. So, one of the main issues that every new parent has to cope with is not getting enough sleep.

Babies' sleep habits, in the first year of life, are influenced by their feeding requirements, as they find it difficult to go more than six hours without a feed for the first three or four months

Babies tend to double their birth weight in the first six months of life; frequent feeding during the day and night helps them to grow and develop. Some babies no longer wake for a feed

Babies who wake repeatedly at night may generally be highly reactive to noise or unfamiliar people.

from six weeks of age; others carry on for several months. It is common for babies to wake five to seven times each night even if they are not hungry. Many go back to sleep by themselves but some find this difficult, so they are likely to start to cry and fuss to gain attention.

After six to nine months there is no longer a need for the healthy baby to feed at night. By 18 months old, six

Understanding sleep patterns in babies

When young babies fall asleep they enter a light sleep called rapid eye movement sleep (REM) in which their eyes can be seen moving under their eyelids. This light sleep constitutes about 40% of their sleep. Older babies, children and adults fall asleep by entering a deep sleep called non-rapid eye movement sleep (NREM). There are regular cycles of light REM in which it is possible to be easily woken. Babies return to the REM state every 50 - 60 minutes, which is shorter than the adult cycle of 90 - 100 minutes. Like adults, babies are more likely to breathe unevenly during REM sleep and may occasionally stop breathing for a few seconds. This is natural and normal.

REM sleep plays a vital role:

- In the maturing stage of the nervous system
- For procedural types of learning (in which humans acquire motor and perceptual skills)

Newborn babies get over half of their sleep at night and this increases by the time they are twelve months.

out of ten babies sleep through the night. Some wake occasionally, others continue to wake at least once a night, but may only need comforting.

Sleep chart

Babies are individuals and like us, their sleep patterns vary, as does the amount of sleep they require.   As a general guide the following table indicates the average amount of sleep that is required by a growing baby:

AGE OF BABY	AVERAGE HOURS PER DAY
First weeks	14 -18 hours
Early months	12 -16 hours
One year	10 -13 hours
Three years	9 -12 hours
Seven years	8 -11 hours

Many babies find massage very soothing, and may even fall asleep immediately afterwards. The massage deepens and regulates the breathing, so parents may find that their baby will sleep more deeply and for longer if they receive a regular massage.

Sleep issues – support during a massage class

If you include discussion time within your massage classes, the topic of 'sleep' is very likely to come on to the agenda, as it is often a major concern for parents. The opportunity for parents to share advice is very useful.

The following tips might be useful, either as a suggestion during discussion time or as a handout:

- Suggest parents give their baby a fulfilling day with lots of different activities including calm, quiet periods. - **Fit in a massage!**

- Keep to a daily routine of play times, daytime naps and outings

- Avoid boisterous, noisy play before bedtime. Subdue the environment - tone down the lights, noise, music, TV and video

- After the evening bath, suggest parents go straight to the bedroom and feed their baby there. Once again, suggest a quiet, calm environment, gentle music and cuddles

- Place the baby in the cot awake. Babies sleep longest after a long period awake, so avoid naps before bedtime

- During the night, feed with light off and do not over-stimulate the baby. This will help the baby learn the difference between night and day

- Try not to lull a crying baby to sleep by over-soothing, over-rocking, over-feeding and taking them for night rides in the car. They will start to expect this as a normal procedure

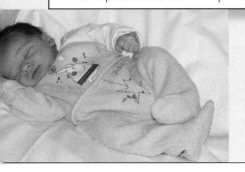
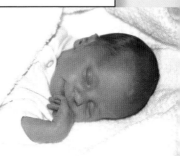

Infant cues

Babies help parents to understand what they are telling them by using non-verbal cues. There is no 'recipe' of cues, as each and every baby will have an individual method of communicating their feelings and parents need to get to know their baby's individual positive and negative cues. The positive cues are a sign that a baby is happy to engage with the environment and those around them and negative cues indicate that they either have needs to be met, or wish to disengage from their surroundings.

Not all of these cues will necessarily be displayed at once; a baby may show only one or two to begin with. However, if a baby is not being heard and responded to appropriately, the negative cues are likely to increase in number as the baby attempts to gain attention and have their needs met.

It is necessary for babies to be given the space to disengage when they need to. When a non-engagement cue is neglected, a baby will try harder to disengage. If this situation is a regular occurrence then the baby will become more withdrawn, unlike a baby whose non-engagement cues are recognised and respected. The baby who is allowed to disengage when they need to is likely to look at their parent more and experience less distress when faced with stressful situations.

Understanding cues

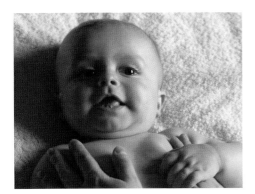

Positive cues

When babies are happy and want to engage, they are more likely to:

- Be still
- Gaze at a face
- Reach out to the person
- Raise their head
- Turn their head and eyes towards the person
- Smile
- Coo
- Have gentle and smooth arm and leg movements
- Have bright, wide open eyes
- Look alert and awake, bright and responsive

Negative cues

When babies want to disengage they are more likely to:

- Turn away
- Cry
- Become fussy
- Cough
- Hiccup
- Yawn
- Wrinkle their forehead
- Arch their back
- Breathe more rapidly
- Fall asleep (or habituate)
- Squirm
- Kick and pull away
- Become pale or red in pallor
- Have mottled skin (particularly very young babies)

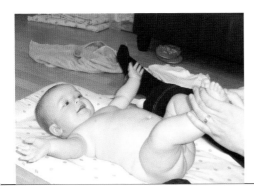

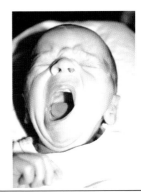

Is a baby saying 'Yes' to massage?

When deciding if a baby is saying 'yes' to massage it is important to think about their non-verbal cues, so that a parent can decide whether it is a good time for their baby to have a massage or not. Positive cues are more likely to indicate that a baby is saying 'yes' to massage and the negative cues are a sign that a baby is not willing and is saying 'no' to the activity.

It is sometimes hard to know whether a baby is saying 'yes' or 'no', particularly when the non-verbal cues are quite subtle, especially if a parent has not thought about this before. This understanding will come in time and most often, if a baby is not understood immediately they will give out even stronger signals, making it quite clear how they are feeling.

During the classes and when at home, it is vital that a baby is happy and is not forced into having a massage against their will, in order for them to learn and appreciate that this is fun and that they are respected enough that they can say 'no'. If their 'no' cues are ignored they will believe they do not have a voice and that their feelings are not worthy of attention. Also, babies that are not listened to often try harder to disengage and may, over time, become generally less responsive.

When a baby is in an alert, awake state, parents are more likely to find that a baby will say 'yes' to massage, because they are keen to engage with parents during these periods. It may be that just before a bath is a good time for both the baby and the parent; when the baby may be in the right frame of mind and the parent has the time to offer a relaxed and calming massage. May be first thing in the morning is a better time for both baby and parent and it offers the opportunity for play-time. What is important is that it is right for the baby and right for the parent; so that massage is a thoroughly enjoyable experience.

The six different (asleep/awake) states

Babies work through different states of consciousness during the day. There are six basic states that can be recognised that babies regularly go through within any given day.

State 1 - Deep sleep state
The baby's eyes are firmly closed: breathing is deep and regular with no arm or leg movement: this state gives the baby time to rest and grow.

State 2 - Light sleep state
The baby's eyes are firmly closed (though slow, circular movements of the eye can be seen under the closed eyelid). Their breathing is irregular and even shallow. They may also twitch and appearing to smile, frown and make sucking movements.

State 3 - Drowsy, in-between state
The baby's eyes may be open or closed but with a dazed appearance; arms and legs may move smoothly; breathing is regular but faster and shallower than in sleep. Babies in this state may be susceptible to being aroused to a more alert, responsive state.

State 4 - Alert, awake state
The baby's body and face are relatively quiet and they seem able to focus on their parent, or an object with bright shining eyes. Sights and sounds will produce a response; in this state a baby can be very enjoyable for parents.
The baby will be responsive to the voice of its parent. This is a good time to try singing, chatting and having fun. This is a good time to try massage.

State 5 - Alert, but fussy state
This is the baby's transitional state to crying; they may be soothed or brought to a calmer state by an attractive stimulus, if the stimulus is too much, they may break down to fussiness; movements are jerky and disorganised.

State 6 - Crying
Crying is a release of tension and a way of signalling a need. The baby communicates hunger, pain, boredom, discomfort or tiredness which sets off automatic responses of concern and responsibility in parents; this is the most effective way for the baby to attract attention. The baby is likely to be physically active.

Understanding crying

All babies are individual; some are easy going and peaceful, whilst others can be insecure and fretful. But, regardless

141

of their temperament, all babies use crying as a form of communication. Crying is an innate ability which allows them to convey their distress and their desire to be tended to. They are emotionally dependent on their parents and, it is to be hoped, they will learn from experience that if needed a parent will respond. However, even in today's society, there is still a school of thought that believes babies try to control and manipulate their parents through crying. This is not the case, as any aspect of rational thought involves activity from the rational (frontal) brain.

The hardwiring of an infant's frontal cortex is very limited, so they necessarily do not have the capacity to form a controlling thought, just as they are not capable of understanding anyone else's feelings; and therefore are not able to manipulate or 'try it on'.

Crying allows babies to express themselves and to clearly indicate that their needs (both physical and emotional) should be met (particularly when less verbal signs and cues have gone unnoticed).
Crying:

- Is an indication of negative feelings
- Can mean 'no' when a child is at the pre-verbal stage
- Allows a baby to show immediate distress
- Allows pent up stress to be released

Crying should never be ignored. Although short bouts of crying are not damaging, allowing a baby to continue crying until they are in a state of distress is potentially harmful. When a baby is regularly left to cry alone over a sustained period of time, without support, or any form of help to regulate their state, there is likely to be a negative impact on their emotional and psychological development. This utter state of despair upsets the brain's natural state and could ultimately:

- Affect, adversely, the hardwiring of the rational brain
- Maintain unnecessarily high levels of cortisol *(released when crying starts)* in the brain, which is damaging to the brain; in particular, the hippocampus
- Suppresses the levels of opiods, which play a critical role in reducing feelings of fear and stress, noradrenaline, serotonin and dopamine in the brain
- Affect, adversely, a baby's self-esteem and their belief in their own worthiness. These negative effects will have implications not only for the developing child, but also for the adult they are to become. *(Adults suffering from stress and depressive disorders are more likely to have suffered high levels of stress in infancy)*

If a baby's non-verbal cues are ignored during massage and the experience becomes over-stimulating or their needs are not being met, the experience becomes a very negative one.

It can be potentially damaging for a child's emotional and psychological development, if a parent continued to massage whilst their baby was crying ('no' cue).

Supporting parents and guiding them in a non-judgemental manner to understand when their baby is saying 'yes' to massage and that it is not suitable to massage their baby when crying, is of paramount importance.

Massage should always be a positive experience for a baby.

Recognising different cries

As with all cues, babies' cries will vary from child to child. A parent will need to learn what their baby's different cries mean; which can take time. However, even when it is not completely clear what the baby is trying to 'say', they will still benefit from their parent tending to them and trying to calm them.

How Infant Massage Classes can help

Support from the other parents in the group
Support groups, such as infant massage classes, offer parents the opportunity to share experiences and support each other. Crying is often a subject that comes up in the discussion time during a class. It is helpful for parents to be able to share their experiences and hear how other parents are coping. With support and understanding from the group, they will soon become more confident and follow their own intuition when dealing with their crying baby.

Support from an Infant Massage Teacher
Supporting parents to become confident about what their baby is 'telling' them by learning to recognise their individual cues, may help parents understand their baby's different cries. After all, crying is as much a non-verbal cue as any other, albeit a more vocal one!

The parent

Bonding

For the majority of expectant parents, there is the belief that they will have a definite feeling of love for their unborn child, either during the pregnancy or immediately at the birth. This, however, is not necessarily the case. The sense of having developed a bond with the baby is quite individual for everyone.

Some parents bond with their baby long before they are born. For others this can occur as soon as they see the baby during their first scan. Others report feelings of a bond when they experience the first kick in-utero, whilst many mothers feel bonded to their growing foetus and often talk to and massage their 'bump'. Some parents may not bond whilst their baby is in-utero, but they do almost instantly with their newborn infant. However, sometimes it may take some weeks, even months for this to happen.

Bonding stairway

3 MONTHS +

Infant massage can help to kindle the bond a parent feels for their baby or enhance an already established bond because it incorporates, touch, eye contact, smell, and sound of the mother's voice, which are integral to the bonding process.

BIRTH

GROWING BABY

FIRST KICK

FIRST SCAN

Positive approach to parenting

Every child has fundamental needs that must be met for an emotionally and physically healthy life. They should be able to feel loved, heard and respected, safe and secure and able to trust; free to be a child.

These needs must be met by their parents or caregivers. Whilst there are many ways to effective parenting, with different styles, it is widely acknowledged that all positive parenting rests upon the attribute of love.

Early communication, interaction and love between a baby and its parents

have long lasting and distinctly positive consequences. Love is absolutely essential for a baby's brain to grow healthily in the first two or three years of life.

The following points are essential when adopting a positive approach to parenting, to ensure the healthy emotional and physical development of a child:

- Comfort is the first thing a baby needs from its parents; this helps them feel secure, valued and loved
- Unconditional love and affection; parents should tell their child regularly that they love them
- Make quality time for the child; listen, share and counsel
- Empower the child to make choices within set boundaries
- Respect the child's feelings; thereby raising self-esteem
- Encourage two-way communication

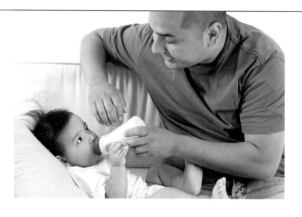

- Negotiate and compromise
- Give realistic praise (by telling the child that they are proud of their achievements)
- Always forgive and do not bear grudges
- Encourage interaction and socialisation with others
- Nurture the child by giving positive touch, hugs and kisses
- Provide opportunities for play with peers and parents
- Discipline should be fair; with love and consistency (severe physical punishment may breed violence). The effective parent offers compassionate, consistent and honest correction
- Avoid humiliation and demeaning acts
- Be an advocate
- Model a positive life by being positive; parents can use their own positive experiences as a role-model

- Encouraging the child to achieve its potential (within their own abilities and not to meet a parent's desires)
- Provide a safe environment
- Through teaching, parents help their child to learn, thereby learning to relate to others, communicate and solve problems
- In essence, wanting the child to have physical, spiritual, social and emotional health

Different styles of parenting

Everyone parents differently, with some using their own positive experiences as a child as a template when parenting their own children. Others, who were devoid of positive experiences, may opt to use their experience as a template of 'how not to parent'.

However parents choose to parent their children, they can generally be categorised according to whether they are high or low on parental demandingness and responsiveness. These categories can be placed into four parenting styles: indulgent, authoritarian, authoritative, and uninvolved.

Each parenting style reflects different patterns of parental behaviour, such as how responsive they are to the needs of their child and how demanding they are as a parent.

Four parenting styles:

- Indulgent parents tend to be more responsive than they are demanding of their child. They are not traditional parents and are lenient. They allow their children to self-regulate and avoid confrontational occurrences.

- Authoritarian parents are highly demanding and directive but not responsive. They are obedient and status-driven and expect their orders to be obeyed by their children without any explanation. This group of parents provide structured environments with clearly defined rules.

- Authoritative parents are both demanding and responsive; they monitor and communicate clear standards that their children should follow. They are assertive, but not restrictive and pushy. Their disciplinary methods are supportive, rather than penalising. They want their children to be assertive as well as socially responsible.

- Uninvolved parents are low in both responsiveness and demandingness. In extreme cases, this parenting style might include both rejecting and neglectful parents, although most parents of this type fall within the normal range.

Consequences for children

The style a parent adopts has been found to predict a child's well-being in the areas of social competence, academic performance, psycho-social development and behaviour problems. Research based on parent interviews, child reports, and parent observations consistently finds:

- Children and adolescents whose parents are authoritative rate themselves and are rated as more socially and instrumentally competent than those whose parents are non-authoritative.

- Children and adolescents whose parents are uninvolved perform most poorly in all areas.

In general, parental responsiveness predicts social competence, while parental demandingness is associated with behavioural control. These findings indicate:

- Children and adolescents from authoritarian families (high in demandingness, but low in responsiveness) tend to perform moderately well in school and show little problem behaviour; but they have poorer social skills, lower self-esteem, and higher levels of depression.

- Children and adolescents from indulgent homes (high in responsiveness, low in demandingness) are more likely to have problem behaviour and perform less well in school, but they have higher self-esteem, better social skills, and lower levels of depression.

Encouraging parental responsiveness

Infant massage can potentially promote and encourage a responsive style of parenting; thereby supporting children to become more rounded, assertive and socially responsible.

Raising parental self-esteem

Attendance at antenatal parenting classes prior to the birth of their child can help parents think positively about the baby's impending arrival, discuss hopes and fears and may help to dispel any unrealistic expectations and worries.

Becoming a new parent can be quite distressing for some parents. Having a baby is a major event affecting the lifestyle and relationship of both parents forever. Their 'once organised' life is thrown into chaos and many new parents will experience a gamut of emotions ranging from elation, utter relief that labour is over, pride at the creation of life, low self-esteem, feelings of inadequacy to sheer exhaustion!

The first few weeks of parenthood are demanding both physically and emotionally. First-time parents have to make major adjustments; there is a real need for adaptability, flexibility and good communication as the demands of the infant over a 24-hour period can be overwhelming. Parents often have great feelings of love, pride and joy, but also they feel tired, irritable, anxious, unsure, and isolated in their new role as a parent. The infant's arrival is now tangible with no negotiation! Parents suddenly realise that the responsibilities of parenthood are constant and will occupy their lives for at least the next 18 years. Real fears and anxiety can emerge at this point, and how the parents respond and adapt will affect the family relationship and their relationship with their infant.

Therefore, support in the early weeks of parenthood is vital and may come from the immediate and extended family, friends, Midwife, Health Visitor and General Practitioner. Parents need to know they have someone they can trust, share confidences with and have no fears about a breach of confidentiality.

Attendance at postnatal groups and infant massage classes can offer huge support and encourage parents to express their feelings, worries and concerns.

Self-esteem can be raised if parents:

- Feel safe and secure
- Are listened to, valued and shown respect by family, friends and professionals
- Are empowered to make their own decisions, encouraged to use their own intuition and trust their instincts
- Meet other parents and share experiences
- Are offered practical help and support without criticism
- Are praised without being patronised
- Are encouraged to accept offers of help and that to do so is not seen as an admission of failure
- Are given opportunities to relax, rest and have a break without feeling guilty
- Look after their holistic health

Perinatal illness and depression

Baby blues

In the first few days after giving birth a new mother may suffer from Baby Blues which affects around half of all new mothers. Having become a new parent, the mother may feel anxious and suffer from enormous feelings of responsibility and feel insecure and vulnerable. These feelings are normally attributed to changes in hormone levels and generally, after a day or two, they subside.

Puerperal psychosis

The causes have not been identified for this serious illness, which affects about 1 in 500 mothers. Puerperal refers to the six-week period following childbirth and psychosis is any form of mental illness in which the sufferer loses contact with reality. The symptoms include: over-activity, over-excitement, irrational behaviour and conversation, severe depression, difficulty with concentration and sleeping and eating, hearing voices and seeing things that are not there, expressing strange ideas and beliefs; also, there is an inability to care for one's self and baby. Mothers too, may have thoughts of harming themselves and/or their baby.

Puerperal Psychosis requires hospital treatment including drugs and constant assessment and the mother should make a full recovery. Family and partner support, and follow-up support from Health Visitor and GP are vital. The mother should be monitored carefully with subsequent confinements.

Postnatal illness (PNI)

Postnatal illness/depression can present itself at any point after birth. It is quite common and research indicates that up to twenty per cent of women experience postnatal depression following the birth of a child. PNI usually appears in the early months after childbirth but can occur at any time during the first year of the infant's life. If undetected a mother may suffer well beyond this period.

A study in 1997 indicated that many cases of postnatal depression remained undetected, as women who were depressed tended not to attend clinics and health care facilities. More recent observations have found that, despite much sympathetic media coverage, lack of detection was still commonplace.

The symptoms for PNI are varied and may include sleep problems, depressive mood, loss of pleasure, constant apprehension about baby's welfare and health, loss of confidence, restlessness and agitation, panic attacks, anxiety, lack of concentration, poor decision-making, loss of libido, headaches, loss of appetite, lethargy, inappropriate/obsessive thoughts about self and/or baby, physical aches and pains, avoidance of eye contact, feeling lonely and needy for company, avoiding company, feelings of going 'mad', excessive desire to clean and tidy and, in some extreme cases, thoughts of suicide.

151

Situations that increase the possibility of PNI developing

Birth trauma

It is thought that birth trauma, such as an emergency caesarean, can contribute to postnatal illness and a mother may play the difficult delivery over and over again in her mind.

Infant sleep problems

There is a strong link between infant sleep problems and postnatal depression. Infant sleep problems and postnatal depression can both impact adversely and in similar ways on the mother, on the infant, and on the mother-infant relationship.

Researchers in Melbourne surveyed 738 mothers of infants aged six to twelve months. Sleep problems were assessed by a 48-item questionnaire and maternal well-being by the EPDS. Forty-six per cent of mothers reported their infant's sleep as a problem and the same sleep patterns were associated with high depression scores and tended to increase as the depression scores increased.

The Australian research team suggest that many of the sleep problems are preventable with anticipatory guidance and can be implemented in primary care settings.

Postnatal depression and parent-infant relationship

The mother-infant relationship

Unfortunately, when a mother is suffering from PNI, the bonding and attachment process between a mother and her baby can be greatly impeded and in some cases, it may not happen at all. Very often, mothers suffering from PNI avoid eye contact with other people and often avoid communicating generally. Sadly, there can be also, a similar lack of communication with her baby.

Postnatal depression and its effect on men

When mothers suffer with postnatal illness they may have problems relating to their baby; handle them roughly or inappropriately and be under-responsive to their needs, particularly on an emotional level. This can cause behavioural and emotional problems for the child and their cognitive development may be delayed.

Men are also susceptible to post-natal depression after the birth of a child, even if their partner is not actually suffering from the condition herself. However it is seldom identified by GPs as men often hide their true feelings in an attempt to be stoical. The ratio of male depression to female depression is 1:2, however there is some indication that there is indeed some parity.

Depression for either partner can have devastating effects on a family's ability to communicate and interactions, generally can become very negative as the non-depressed parent also feels the effects of the depression.

Benefits of infant massage for fathers

The benefits of infant massage; such as one-to-one loving touch can be experienced by fathers as well as mothers. It is suggested that fathers that give their infants a daily massage show better interaction behaviour with their infants than those that do not.

Attendance at infant massage classes could give the opportunity for fathers to voice their opinions and feelings following the birth of their child.

Support and treatment for PNI

If a mother is suffering from PNI, there are various treatments that may be available to her, including:

- Attending post-natal groups, such as infant massage classes (usually available in the local community)
- Self-help strategies
- Complementary therapies such as Aromatherapy, Reflexology, Herbal remedies and Homeopathy. (These, however, may have cost implications for the parent)
- Counselling (referrals can be made by GPs, or sought privately by the individual)
- Medication (such as anti-depressants, may be prescribed by the GP)
- Hospital-based care in a Mother and Baby Unit (may be provided for severe depression)

Infant massage classes - support for mothers with PNI

If suffering from PNI it is extremely beneficial for a mother to have the opportunity to confide in someone she can trust. Attending infant massage classes allows the mother the opportunity to leave the home, where she might be feeling isolated, and benefit from being in a supportive, non-stigmatising and non-judgemental environment. Such an environment may offer the space in which an individual feels safe to discuss her concerns and feelings.

Having the opportunity to discuss fears and anxieties with other mothers may bring tremendous relief, as the depressed mother realises that she is not the only one feeling that way and that others are also experiencing the

same frustrations. It may also help raise their self-esteem and confidence if they have the opportunity to share skills and experiences and offer practical support should the situation arise.

Infant massage – supporting a developing relationship in cases of PNI

Infant massage may help break the cycle of negative, or limited, interaction between a mother and her baby. It is a highly effective way of helping mothers that are suffering emotionally, even in cases when the mother is not consciously aware that she has PNI.

By attending Infant Massage Classes, she will potentially increase her chances of bonding with her baby. The opportunity for greater interaction and communication between mother and baby may also help to enhance the baby's emotional and cognitive development.

It is recognised that kissing, cuddling and prolonged gazing at the baby support a developing bond between parent and infant.

Infant massage can ensure that a mother spends quality time with her baby; enhancing the bonding process and helping the baby to develop a strong attachment to its mother. This can promote a sense of security in the baby and the child is then more likely to grow up self-assured and self-confident.

Mothers that are having difficulty bonding and interacting with their babies also have the opportunity to observe the Infant Massage Teacher role-modelling with the demonstration doll and see how other parents interact with their babies – offering real-life role modelling.

> Mothers Suffering from PNI benefit greatly if they participate in infant massage on a regular basis because:
> - The 'feel good' hormones, Oxtocin and Serotonin, are stimulated (Oxytocin is also responsible for stimulating maternal feelings)
> - The mother's stress hormone levels are lower
>
> Also, the baby:
> - Is calmer, more relaxed and happier
> - Has less sleep problems
> - Interacts better with its mother *(helping to overcome the cycle of negative interaction that may have become normal practice within the developing relationship)*

Flexible teaching – one-to-one sessions as an option in situations of PNI

Every mother and baby is different and not everyone will experience all the benefits associated with infant massage. Similarly the severity of the PNI and the types of feelings that a mother is suffering will determine which type of infant massage session she wishes to attend. Some will prefer to go to a group and others will prefer to have one-to-one sessions.

If a mother is too ill, lethargic and depressed to attend a group then it may be more expedient to teach her infant massage on a one-to-one basis. Sessions in her own home can help the mother feel more comfortable and she may be more inclined to open up emotionally and share her anxieties; safe in the knowledge that the Infant Massage Teacher will not judge her. The one-to-one sessions allow the Infant Massage Teacher a greater opportunity, also, for working at a pace that is beneficial for the mother.

Once the mother gains confidence in her abilities during the one-to-one sessions it is worth encouraging her to attend a group also so that she can experience all the benefits associated with it.

	ADVANTAGES	CONSIDERATIONS
Merits that group sessions can offer :	Non-stigmatising environment	Mother may be too anxious or depressed to meet others
	Non-judgemental support	Mother may be too ill or lethargic to leave the home
	Gets mother out of the house	Does the teacher teach only a group of PNI sufferers or mix the group?
	Share anxieties and fears with other mothers	Would a group consisting solely of PNI sufferers be more empathetic to others in the group?
	Share good practice with each other	Discussion time may need to be extended.
	Mother will witness how other mothers interact with their babies in a mixed group	
	Teacher can role-model positive interaction with demonstration doll	
	Supportive environment	
	Chance to meet other new parents where friendships can blossom	
	Increased confidence and competence in handling their baby	
Merits that one-to-one sessions can offer :	Non-stigmatising environment	Mother can miss out on contact with others
	Non-judgemental support	Be aware of other disturbances in someone's home that may interrupt the sessions
	Enhances feelings of security when parent is in own home	Can be very intense for the Infant Massage Teacher
	Increased self-esteem enabling the mother to consider joining a group and potentially benefit from group support	It may be difficult to allocate the amount of time required for discussion as it may take time for the parent to feel comfortable discussing their feelings; conversely it may open up a 'Pandora's box'
	Teacher can work with the pace and the needs of the mother	Discussion time may need to be extended.
	Increased confidence and competence in handling their baby	

The infant - parent relationship

Infant - parent attachment

Attachment is an interactive process, which is underpinned by the baby's biological need for survival. The attachment process stimulates the need for parents to attune and respond to their vulnerable newborn baby, who is utterly dependent on them for all of their needs. From this intrinsic need to survive there is also the potential of a truly affectionate and life-long reciprocal bond developing between parent and child.

> Early, close contact (such as skin-to-skin contact, containment holds, cuddles and massage) between the parent and baby helps to establish and develop a secure attachment.

An attachment relationship is essentially based on non-verbal communication and reciprocal synchronisation, which takes place long before a baby develops speech and before they are capable of rational thought. The ability of the parents to be receptive to the baby's cues will strengthen the attachment process, as their ability to synchronise their response to their baby will in turn encourage the baby's movement and behaviour to form a 'rhythm' with them.

Rhythms or patterns of response between parent and infant form the framework for the infant's ability to regulate his own levels of physical and emotional arousal, attention and concentration, interest in the world, patterns of wakefulness and sleep.

157

John Bowlby

John Bowlby, one of the most influential Child Psychiatrists, developed an attachment theory that became very popular in the mid 20th Century. Bowlby believed that attachment is an affectionate two-way relationship that is developed between an infant and a specific individual (the mother or a permanent substitute mother). He believed that if the attachment bond is not allowed to form or is broken, emotional development will also be affected.

His ideas were subsequently adopted by the World Health Organisation and ultimately influenced the attitudes of social workers, nurseries and the health service; and from which greater rights and benefits for parents were developed.

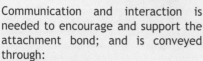

Intrinsic to Infant massage:

- Touch
- Eye contact
- Facial expression
- Timing
- Posture
- Gesture
- Body movement

Communication and interaction is needed to encourage and support the attachment bond; and is conveyed through:

- Eye contact
- Facial expression
- Timing
- Posture
- Gesture
- Body movement
- Feeding
- Touch
- Smell

The tone of voice and the 'parentese' (rhythmical, higher than normal pitched speech) that parents adopt when talking to their baby also helps to draw the baby into the interaction and further enhance the connection between them.

Forming attachment

How well an attachment is formed will ultimately have an impact on a child's future self-esteem, self efficiency, social understanding and empathy, as well as their level of autonomy and independence. Whether there is a secure, or insecure, attachment to a parent (or other significant figure) the child will develop and subsequently rely on an 'internal working model' that will affect their ability to cope with and negotiate all

future relationships. It is, therefore, of paramount importance that a baby feels secure and confident and that their emotional and physical needs are met from birth onwards.

All supported and encouraged during Infant Massage Classes.

To facilitate a healthy parent-infant attachment, the parent needs to be:

- Emotionally available
- Sensitive and responsive to their baby's needs
- Offer appropriate stimulation
- Be consistent in their care and how they respond to their baby
- Synchronise their interactions with their baby

The attachment relationship forms a secure base within the infant, providing a secure framework for the personality. Because of this the infant feels safe to explore the world around them; knowing that if scared, or feeling threatened, they can return to their parent for safety and comfort. The securely attached child understands that the parent will be available and that they can rely on support from them during times of stress.

The secure base is the internalisation of the two-way reciprocal parent/infant relationship. An infant 'internalises good parenting' which can then be called upon to continue to care for oneself throughout their life. The secure base is not the actual parent themselves, but what the infant takes in from the parent so that they can grow into a child who can separate from the parents, having internalised their care.

If there is a secure attachment a child is more likely to grow up:

- Feeling that they are worthy of love
- Believing they are effective
- To be loving, interested and responsive to others
- Confident
- Happy to investigate and explore their environment

With an insecure attachment, a child is more likely to grow up:

- Believing that they are not worthy of love
- Believing they are uninteresting, unvalued and ineffective
- Inclined to be neglectful, unresponsive and possibly hostile to others
- Detached from others
- Lacking confidence

159

Supporting a secure attachment

To help the development of a secure attachment there needs to be:

- A healthy level of reciprocal absorption and attunement
- Parent's appropriate regulation of their baby's emotional states
- Support with their developing thinking and awareness

If absorption and attunement are lacking within the relationship and a baby's emotional states are routinely neglected with little, or no, support for their developing awareness, the child will struggle to reach their full potential.

The effects of secure/insecure attachment for the developing child

SECURELY ATTACHED CHILD	INSECURELY ATTACHED CHILD
With absorption • Develops a sense of self within the relationship • Learns that they have some control within the relationship • Knows their needs will be met	**Lack of absorption** • Has a negative sense of self • Has difficulty trusting others • Does not trust in their ability to have their needs met
With attunement • Feels understood and connected to the parent • Learns to trust in the availability and responsiveness of their parent • Begins to understand how important they are to their parent	**Lack of attunement** • Has difficulties with trust (either not trusting or over trusts) • Has difficulty forming and maintaining relationships • Has difficulty feeling empathy for others

SECURELY ATTACHED CHILD	INSECURELY ATTACHED CHILD
When helped to regulate Becomes increasingly more able to regulate their own: • Emotions • Stress • Impulses • Shame • Rage	**Lack of regulation** Reacts to the lack of regulation abilities by: • Dissociation, or • Hyper-arousal Are not able to: • Soothe themselves • Regulate and control emotions • Manage anger • Assess risk appropriately • Take responsibility for their behaviour • Learn from their mistakes Are more likely to: • Inhibit their emotions, or over react emotionally • Be destructive (a danger to themselves or others) • Be socially inept and easily led • Have difficulty making and keeping friends
With support for the developing thinking and awareness • Develops the capacity to think rationally • Learns that the world and people make sense •Learns from experience	**Lack of Support with Developing Thinking And Awareness** • Lacks the ability to see the world from different perspectives • Does not understand what is an appropriate level of intimacy with others • May be disorganised • Can not clearly distinguish fact from fiction • Can not clearly distinguish 'mine' from 'yours'

161

Using infant massage as a tool to reduce insecure attachment

The necessary elements to promote a secure attachment are intrinsic to infant massage, therefore, it is a wonderful tool to help reduce insecure attachment, particularly when used to support challenging situations, for example:

CHALLENGING SITUATIONS	HOW INFANT MASSAGE MAY HELP
When a baby is admitted to special care baby units, with prolonged separation from its parents	Positive touch, containment holds and effleurage massage strokes can help a parent feel they are caring for their baby whilst they are in the highly medicalised environment, allowing them close contact and the opportunity to connect with their baby.
When the baby has special needs	Infant massage may help the parent start to recognise their baby's non-verbal cues, which can be more challenging to understand and 'read' when a baby has special needs.
Child abuse	Infant massage encourages respect for the child, as well as a connection to be formed that potentially could be loving and supportive.
If the mother suffers with postnatal illness/depression	Infant Massage can improve the relationship between parent and baby – allowing the time for the parent to focus on their baby in the safe, non-stigmatising environment of the infant massage class and during massage sessions in the home.
Due to parents own poor parenting experiences	Allows the parent to connect with their baby during infant massage sessions which stimulates the attachment process and may help to overcome inadequacies the parent may feel due to their own insecure attachment experience.
Life events and stressful family environments (e.g. poverty, bereavement, difficult relationships)	Infant massage classes allow the parent 'time-out' from the trials they may be experiencing in their life. The relaxing environment created during the massage sessions gives them the space to focus on their baby, as well as potentially receive support from the group during discussion time.
Children presenting with symptoms of ADHD (One school of thought is that ADHD is in fact a sign that a child is insecurely attached, and the presence of the parent deregulates the infant.)	As infant massage includes all the necessary facets for forming a secure attachment e.g. touch, eye contact, facial expression, timing, posture, gesture, body movement necessarily it may help prevent insecure attachment cases presenting as ADHD.

Using infant massage as a tool to encourage secure attachment

ATTACHMENT PROCESSES	HOW INFANT MASSAGE SUPPORTS THIS PROCESS
Absorption	• Communication between parent and baby is supported and encouraged • The developing relationship is nurtured as it allows a parent and baby time to focus on each other • Allows the baby to say 'yes' or 'no' giving them adequate control within the relationship • Assists a parent to meet their baby's needs because they are encouraged to listen to their baby, learn what their baby is 'telling' them and respond to their needs accordingly
Attunement	• Parents are guided to communicate with their baby through touch and eye contact • The infant receives the massage and responds accordingly to the touch and sound of their parent's voice • A trusting relationship of give-and-take and respect forms between the parent and the child • Helps a baby feel respected and important, as their parent is responsive to their needs
Regulation	• Encourages parents to respond appropriately to their baby's non-verbal cues, thus helping them to regulate their emotions • A parent who massages their infant/child is demonstrating positive and reassuring behaviour (but only if the infant is saying 'yes' to massage) • When a baby says 'no' to massage and this is responded to positively then the parent is assisting in the regulation of their baby's emotions and reducing stress levels • Massage may help prevent negative behaviour in the developing child as their emotions are regulated
Support for the developing thinking and awareness	• Helps them to relate confidently to their environment • Potentially helps with the hard-wiring of the brain as infant massage should be a positive experience

163

Anatomy and Physiology

Why Infant Massage Teachers need to learn anatomy and physiology

Infant Massage is essentially a wonderful tool for professionals to help them support parents and babies and could be considered 'parent education', as opposed to a complementary therapy. It does, however, have a physiological effect on the body. Consequently, it is necessary for all Infant Massage Teachers to have a sound understanding of the body and how it functions so that they can practise safely and professionally.

The information about anatomy and physiology that follows provides you with the necessary information you require as an Infant Massage Teacher. It includes the following body systems:

165

- Skin
- Digestive
- Urinary
- Respiratory
- Cardiovascular
- Lymphatic
- Skeletal
- Muscular
- Nervous
- Endocrine

Each system has a clear description of its anatomy and physiology including information concerning the pertinent benefits of massage, tips for teaching parents, which relate to the system, and the relevant precautions that need to be considered.

The skin

MEISSNERS CORPUSCLES

These delicate light touch mechano receptors are very tightly packed in a newborn, but slowly disperse as the child grows older. There are about 80 Meissner corpucles per square millimetre in a three year old child, 20 per square millimetre in a young adult, diminishing to just 4 per square millimetre in the elderly.

PACINIAN CORPUSCLES

A deep mechano receptor that responds to pressure, vibration and tension.

FREE NERVE ENDING

Massage can soothe or stimulate the nerve endings depending on the pressure used.

KRAUSE TOUCH RECEPTORS

A thermoreceptor that responds to cold.

RUFFINI'S TOUCH RECEPTORS

A thermoreceptor that responds to heat.

FAT CELLS

HAIR FOLLICLE

EPIDERMIS

The epidermis has five layers; the top two of which are dead.
The bottom layer of the epidermis contains melanocytes which are simulated by UV light in sunshine to produce melanin, deepening the skin's colour and protecting the deeper layers of skin. Sunlight also activates the skin to change the chemical ergosterol into vitamin D which is essential for healthy bones.

DERMIS

The dermis lies below the epidermis; it contains collagen and elastin which are tough and stretchy. It also contains capillaries which supply blood and thereby oxygen and nutrients to the skin. The dermis has a rich network of nerve endings which give us our awareness of touch, pain, temperature and pressure. Hair follicles sit in the dermis and are controlled by small muscles which make our hair stand on end, when we are cold, to keep us warm. Sweat glands in the dermis excrete sweat through the pores. Sebaceous glands in the dermis have the function of producing the skin's natural moisturiser called sebum, which makes the skin soft and supple, and helps make the skin waterproof.

SUBCUTANEOUS

The subcutaneous layer is situated below the dermis and contains fat tissue which protects us against injury and acts as a layer of insulation to keep us warm.

About the skin

The Skin is the largest organ in the body.

A third of all toxins in the body are expelled via the skin through sweat, which is why it is so vital that it is not blocked with unsuitable products, such as mineral oil.

The Chinese call The Skin the 'third lung' or 'third kidney', which highlights what an important route of elimination it really is.

Benefits of massage

Massage causes the top layer of skin to be shed (desquamation), which improves the appearance of the skin giving it a healthy glow.

Massage encourages the activity of sweat glands, thereby increasing the elimination of toxins, such as urea.

Massage increases circulation to the skin, which brings nutrients to sebaceous glands increasing sebum production.

! CAUTIONS FOR MASSAGE —————

Dry eczema may benefit from massage, provided that a suitable vegetable oil is applied so as to avoid friction on the skin. However, cracked, weeping eczema is a contraindication to massage, as massaging affected areas would cause discomfort and pain for a baby.

The use of mineral oil for massage may prevent the skin from detoxifying and consequently, is not suitable for massage. Long term use, also, can have a drying effect.

The use of a massage medium containing essential oils could possibly be harmful for prepubescent children, as such oils are potential endocrine disruptors.

Emollients (such as those for eczema) should only be applied in the direction of the hair growth; and are therefore unsuitable as a massage medium.

167

Tips for teaching parents

Encourage parents to observe their baby' cues to see whether the pressure they are using is comfortable for their baby. For example, too little pressure will tickle and may over-stimulate the sensory nerve endings in the skin.

Advise parents to do a patch test with any new oil they may be considering using for massage with their baby. If it is not an oil the parent has used before, it is advisable that they patch test it on their own skin as well as the baby's.

The digestive system

LIVER AND GALL BLADDER

The liver is the largest gland in the body that lies below the diaphragm, protected by the ribs. Bile from the liver is stored in the gall bladder from which it is ejected into the small intestine to help with the breakdown of fats. This is only one of 500 functions carried out by the liver including:

- detoxification of substances, such as drugs
- assists metabolism of proteins in infants
- storage of iron, copper and vitamins A, B12, folic acid, D, E and K
- production of plasma proteins in infants
- completes elimination of aged or damaged blood cells
- maintains blood sugar levels by releasing or storing glucoses as needed

LARGE INTESTINE

The large intestine may also be referred to as the colon. Undigested food passes into it from the small intestine, in liquid form, any remaining nutrients and water are absorbed resulting in the formation of faeces. The large intestine consists of three sections:

- The Ascending Colon (**AC**) lies on the right side of the body and travels upwards to the hepatic flexure, a valve permitting entry to:
- The Transverse Colon (**TC**) which travels across the body to the splenic flexure. This valve allows waste to enter:
- The Descending Colon (**DC**) which travels downwards and leads into the Sigmoid Colon (**SC**), Rectum (**R**) and Anus (**A**), where the faeces are finally eliminated

MOUTH

Teeth masticate / chew food. Salivary glands produce saliva.

OESOPHAGUS

Peristalsis, the wave like contraction and relaxation of the muscles throughout the gatro-intestinal tract, commences here.

OESOPHAGEAL SPHINCTER

Valve at entrance of stomach.

STOMACH

Gastric juices released to help break down food whilst muscles churn the food.

PANCREAS

As an exocrine gland, the pancreas secretes pancreatic juice into the small intestine. This contains enzymes which aid chemical digestion and alkaline fluid which help neutralise acidic stomach juices. As an endocrine gland, the Islets of Langerhans, found in the pancreas secrete insulin or glucagon to store or release glucose from the liver respectively.

SMALL INTESTINE

Cheminal digestion is completed in the small intestine which consists of three parts: the duodenum, the jejunum and the ileum.

ILEOCAECAL VALVE

The ileocaecal valve at the end of the small intestine is the entry to the large intestine.

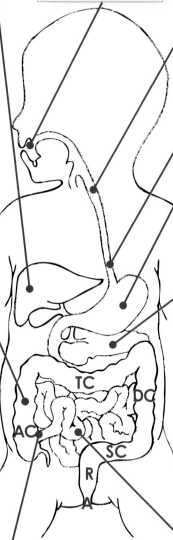

About the digestive system

The Digestive System (also known as the Gastro-intestinal Tract):
- Is more than ten metres long (from mouth to anus) in an adult
  - Changes or 'metabolises' complex food into simple molecules, which can be easily absorbed by the bloodstream and transported throughout the body to help the cells repair, grow or produce energy
- Eliminates unwanted matter in the form of faeces

Benefits of massage

Massage may improve gastric motility, thereby aiding peristalsis and helping to prevent and/or relieve constipation.

Massage may help reduce the incidence of colic. As colic can be distressing and painful, massage is a tool that helps parents feel empowered to help their baby.

! CAUTIONS FOR MASSAGE

Massage strokes applied to the abdominal area must always be carried out in a clockwise, or downwards direction, so that they follow the normal flow of the contents of the colon. This avoids the risk of pushing faecal matter back towards the small intestine; and prevents undue discomfort for a baby.

The abdominal massage strokes should be carried out below the diaphragm, so that they are effective in assisting peristalsis. If the stroke includes the lower part of the rib cage there will be no benefit for the digestive system, as the necessary clockwise pressure to the transverse colon will be omitted.

169

Tips for teaching parents

When teaching the strokes for the abdomen it is important to demonstrate the hand positioning and clockwise direction as clearly as possible.

Some suggestions for helping parents to be clear about the direction they must massage the abdomen:
- Place a cue card, with a clock face on it and arrows indicating a clock wise direction, in front of each mat when setting up the class
- Have a rudimentary diagram of the large intestine on a flip chart, with arrows indicating the direction in which the strokes should go
- Hold your doll up, facing the parents, so that they are clear about the direction of the stroke.

The urinary system

KIDNEYS

The kidneys lie in the upper back just below the rib cage. The right kidney is often lower than the left one due to the size of the liver. The functions of the kidneys can be summarised as follows:

- Filtration of the blood to remove urea, uric acid and creatinine, which are by-products of protein metabolism in the body
- Balancing the body fluids by reabsorbing water when an excess is lost through sweat or by excreting it as urine if there is too much
- Regulation of the electrolyte minerals sodium and potassium
- Releasing hormones to help vitamin D production and stimulating the production of red blood cells
- Help control blood pressure by increasing or decreasing the blood volume
- Control of the blood pH which must be maintained at pH 7.4, so that the body's enzymes can all work properly

Urine formed in the kidneys is 95% water, 3% waste products and 2% mineral salts.

URETERS

Tubes called ureters pass from each kidney to join onto the back of the bladder, through which urine is propelled to the bladder below.

URETHRA

The urethra is a small tube leading from the floor of the bladder to the outside oh the body. It is shorter in females than in males. Release of urine can be controlled voluntarily by a sphincter muscle at the bottom ot the urethra, although small children have to learn control over this muscle before dispensing with nappies!

BLADDER

The bladder is a collapsible, muscular sac used to store urine. When the bladder is sufficiently full, the desire to urinate (micturate) is felt. The bladder wall contracts, a sphincter muscle on the floor of the bladder relaxes and urine passes into the urethra for expulsion from the body.

About the urinary system

The principal organs of The Urinary System are the two kidneys, which process the blood and form urine. Urine travels from the kidneys to the outside of the body via ancillary organs:

- The two ureters
- The bladder
- The urethra

As with the skin, bowels and lungs, the kidneys are an important route of elimination.

They:

- Filter over 50 litres of blood an hour (adults)
- Maintain the all important blood pH by disposing of unwanted substances via the bladder

An adrenal gland sits above each kidney and produces some of the hormones which regulate the kidneys' functions.

! CAUTIONS FOR MASSAGE

The kidneys are protected by the ribs and muscles; and are heavily cushioned in fat. However, they are a delicate organ, so advise parents not to apply too much pressure over the kidneys during the back massage.

When massaging the lower abdomen, it is important to suggest to parents that they avoid applying heavy pressure over the bladder as this may cause discomfort.

171

Tips for teaching parents

Have spare towels and baby wipes available, so that parents feel it is 'safe' to take their baby's nappy off and are not too worried about their baby urinating during the massage routine.

Benefits of massage

Massage increases urinary output and elimination of waste products, as a result of stimulation of the circulation and lymph drainage from the tissues.

The respiratory system

PHARYNX (throat)
Food and air passage.

LARYNX
Short passageway linking the Pharynx to the Trachea.

NOSE / NASAL CAVITY
Warms the air as it is breathed in through the nostrils.

TRACHEA (windpipe)
Passageway for air to enter the lungs, which extends into the thorax (chest cavity) and branches off into two bronchi.

MOUTH
Oral cavity.

BRONCHI
Two tubes which branch off into each lung.

RIBS
Protect the chest cavity.

BRONCHIOLE
Bronchi divide off into smaller bronchioles which become progressively smaller until they become alveoli.

PLEURA
Membrane covering the lungs containing pleural fluids which allows easy movement of the lungs against the ribcage on breathing.

DIAPHRAGM
Large, dome-shaped muscle which lays directly under the lungs and separates the thoracic cavity from the abdominal cavity.

ALVEOLI
An alveolus is a miniature sac which is extremely thin walled allowing easy exchange of oxygen and carbon dioxide to and from the tiny blood capillaries that surround it.

About the respiratory system

The Respiratory System provides the route for:
- Oxygen to enter the body
- Carbon dioxide to leave the body

The process of breathing is called respiration.

Breathing in is called inhalation.

Breathing out is called exhalation.

Benefits of massage

Massaging the chest is believed to help lung function by increasing blood circulation to the area.

Additionally, relaxation deepens the breathing increasing gaseous exchange and, thereby, oxygenation of the cells.

CAUTIONS FOR MASSAGE

Hand position
When strokes for the chest area start at the bottom of the ribs and go in an upwards direction, towards the shoulders or neck, it is important that pressure to the abdomen is not included. Any upward stroke that puts pressure on the digestive tract (which is directly below the diaphragm at the bottom of the rib cage) will be working against the clockwise, downwards direction that is required for this area. An upward stroke on the abdomen would cause a baby some discomfort. When teaching, be sure to demonstrate hand positioning clearly

Positioning a baby
The effectiveness of the upper part of the respiratory system is supported by the contraction of muscles in the pharynx and larynx. When the neck is extended or flexed these muscles are compromised, which will affect the flow of air into a baby's upper airways. It is therefore important to consider the positioning of a baby for massage, especially when in the prone position.

Tips for teaching parents

When teaching the strokes for the back make sure the doll's head is turned to the side, when your doll is in the prone position, clearly indicating a free airway.

Regularly 'check in' with your doll, to remind parents to do the same.

The cardiovascular system

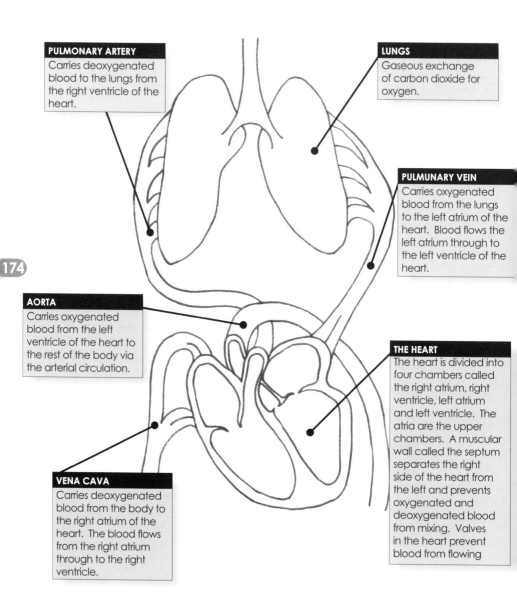

PULMONARY ARTERY
Carries deoxygenated blood to the lungs from the right ventricle of the heart.

LUNGS
Gaseous exchange of carbon dioxide for oxygen.

PULMUNARY VEIN
Carries oxygenated blood from the lungs to the left atrium of the heart. Blood flows the left atrium through to the left ventricle of the heart.

AORTA
Carries oxygenated blood from the left ventricle of the heart to the rest of the body via the arterial circulation.

THE HEART
The heart is divided into four chambers called the right atrium, right ventricle, left atrium and left ventricle. The atria are the upper chambers. A muscular wall called the septum separates the right side of the heart from the left and prevents oxygenated and deoxygenated blood from mixing. Valves in the heart prevent blood from flowing

VENA CAVA
Carries deoxygenated blood from the body to the right atrium of the heart. The blood flows from the right atrium through to the right ventricle.

174

! CAUTIONS FOR MASSAGE

Effleurage strokes should be firmer when massaging in an upwards direction, to encourage venous return (the flow of deoxygenated blood back to the heart).

When applying massage in a downwards direction, it is important to use gentle pressure to avoid putting undue stress on the valves in the veins that are helping to return deoxygenated blood back to the heart.

175

Benefits of massage

Massage may improve circulation.

Massage helps to bring oxygenated blood to the tissues and removes waste products needing elimination.

Tips for teaching parents

Role-model with your doll, when giving advice to parents. Demonstrate clearly, when gently stroking down the limbs, indicating the light pressure required.

Mention to parents that they need only keep contact – as opposed to applying pressure, as they bring their hands to the ankle or wrist on the limb that they are massaging.

The lymphatic system

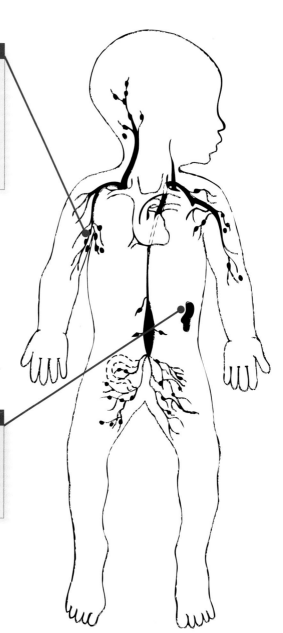

LYMPH NODES

Lymph nodes are located in groups, mainly around the neck, lower jaw, armpits, abdomen, groin and knees.

Lymph nodes filter out harmful substances, e.g. bacteria from lymph and then return it to blood circulation.

SPLEEN

The spleen is partly formed of lymphatic tissue, although lymph does not pass through it. The spleen produces lymphocytes which protect us from disease.

About the lymphatic system

Lymphatic tissue can be found in:
- The tonsils
- Adenoids in the nose
- Peyer's patches in the small intestine
- Alveoli in the lungs
- Bone marrow

Lymphatic tissue helps to destroy harmful substances, thereby assisting in prevention of infection.

Lymph is the clear, yellowy fluid part of the blood, known as plasma, which seeps through the capillary walls and enters the tissue space to become interstitial fluid. Fluid not reabsorbed by the capillaries is picked up by the lymphatic ducts and filtered through the lymph nodes.

CAUTIONS FOR MASSAGE

During times of illness (particularly when a fever is present) the lymphatic system will be working hard to clear the body of unwanted toxins. The lymph nodes are likely to be tender, so to allow the body to heal and to avoid causing pain and discomfort by putting pressure on the tender lymph nodes, advise parents not to undertake massage until the illness has passed.

Benefits of massage

Massage is believed to increase the flow of lymph, aiding the removal of waste from the tissues and transporting antibodies around the body, which, in turn, supports the immune system. Massage is supportive because unlike the blood, which is pumped by the heart, lymph does not have a pump and relies on the movement of muscles to assist its flow around the body.

Tips for teaching parents

Let parents know that a daily massage for their baby may help to boost their immune system and help keep minor illnesses and ailments at bay.

The skeletal system

AXIAL

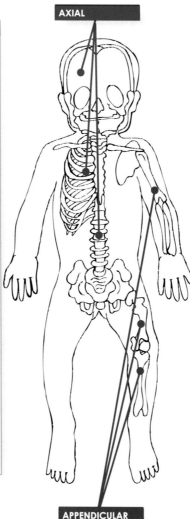

APPENDICULAR

JOINTS

Bones are too rigid to bend without damage. Joints provide the means for two or more bones to connect and/or move. There are three main types of joints.
Fibrous joints are connected by fibrous tissue; no movement is able to take place between these joints, for example, the joints of the skull.
Cartilaginous joints are able to move slightly, they are padded with fibro-cartilage, which allows slight movement, for example, between the vertebrae in the pelvic girdle.
Synovial joints are freely moveable and lubricated by synovial fluid. There are various types of synovial joints, which all have similar characteristics. For example, the hip and shoulder joints.

TYPES OF BONES

Bones are designed to meet particular needs in the body.
Long Bones have a long shaft and widen at each end. They act as levers and give the body the ability to move. For example, in the legs, the femur, tibia, fibula - in the arms, the humerons, radius and ulna.
Short Bones are often almost cube shaped. They provide strength rather than mobility. For example, the carpals in the wrists and the tarsals in the ankles.
Flat bones offer protection for the vital organs. For example, the ribs protect the heart and lungs and the skull protects the brain.
Irregular bones offer additional strength and also attachment points for muscles. Good examples are the vertebrae of the spine.
Sesamoid bones are small and curved and allow tendons to move smoothly over bones. For example, the patella, which prevents wear and tear of the thigh muscle which is attached to the tibia.

178

About the skeletal system

The Skeleton gives the body shape, provides protection for vital organs (e.g. the skull protects the brain) and it supports the weight of all the other body tissues.

Bones provide an attachment point for the tendons and store minerals, particularly calcium, which gives strength, that are available for release into the bloodstream if required. Red and white blood cells and platelets mature within the red bone marrow.

Benefits of massage

The back massage, allows a baby to become more familiar and happy with the prone position. Encouraging parents to allow them to 'play' on their front, will help prevent 'plagiocephaly' (flat head syndrome).

CAUTIONS FOR MASSAGE ————

Joints need to be handled appropriately during a massage sequence. Advise parents not to use undue pressure when travelling over joints during the massage sequence. For example, with the knees, simply glide gently over the joint.

When massaging the back, it is important to avoid placing pressure over the spine. This could cause discomfort and over-stimulation of the nerves.

At birth, the cranial bones in the skull have soft areas of membrane between them, called 'fontanelles'. It is important that parents avoid putting any pressure on the anterior fontanelle (this can be found on the front of the skull). Caution should be taken until the bones have grown together and the fontanelles disappear.

Tips for teaching parents

When massaging the limbs, advise parents to support the leg at the ankle, or the arm at the wrist, for full support and adequate control of the limb during the strokes.

Encourage parents to think about how they bend the knee joints, if they are bringing their baby's legs up towards the abdomen. The knees must be brought up in line with the hips, to avoid straining the hip joints. (Parents should be able to see their baby's umbilicus through the gap between the legs when the thighs touch the abdomen.)

Remember to role-model effectively when teaching strokes for the back, clearly place your hands/fingers either side of your doll's 'spine', which will help to remind parents to steer clear of their baby's spine.

The muscular system

SKELETAL MUSCLES

Skeletal muscles are attached to the bone and are responsible for movement of the skeleton. Massage has a direct affect on skeletal muscles.

Skeletal muscles primarily:
- Create movement
- Assist in the support of joints and posture
- Produce heat and help maintain body temperature

MOVEMENT OF SKELETAL MUSCLES

The action of a muscle is determined by the nervous system. Motor nerves transmit messages from the brain which cause the muscle to contract or relax.

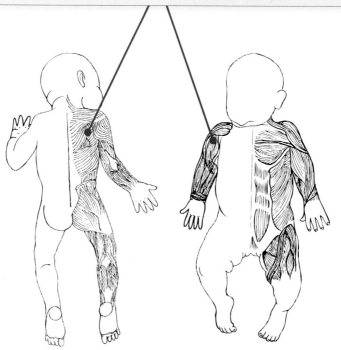

SMOOTH MUSCLES

Found lining internal organs, blood vessels and tracts of respiratory, digestive and urinary systems.

CARDIAC MUSCLE

Specialised muscle found in the heart.

About the muscular system

The main job of the Muscular System is to enable movement of the body. The body contains more than 650 muscles that are connected to the skeletal system by tendons.

There are two types of muscle in the system:
- Voluntary muscle
- Involuntary muscle

A person is able to control voluntary muscles, but involuntary muscles do not require any thought in order to function. The heart is an example of an involuntary muscle.

The Nervous System's communication network manages the Muscular System.

! CAUTIONS FOR MASSAGE ——————

With all massage routines, it is important to warm the muscles first. Effleurage strokes are the most suitable stroke to warm the muscles.

It is important to advise parents not to massage beyond their baby's point of resistance, so as not to over-stretch or put undue pressure on the muscles.

Benefits of massage

Massage increases blood supply to the muscles, bringing oxygenated blood and nutrients and carrying away waste products, reducing muscle fatigue and warming the muscles.

Regular massage helps the muscles to become firmer and more flexible, as well as pliable and more elastic. Massage is particularly useful, in cases of hypotonicity and hypertonicity.

Massage, also, may help improve motor skills.

Tips for teaching parents

Encourage parents to massage firmly over particularly muscular areas of their baby's body, for example, the thighs, but to be more gentle in areas that are less fleshy, such as, the chest.

The nervous system

THE CEREBRUM

The Cerebrum is divided into two hemispheres. Its functions include memory, judgement, reasoning, speech and work formation.
The Right Hemisphere controls the left side of the body and is responsible for creative ability.
The Left Hemisphere controls the right side of the body and is important for language, numerical and scientific skills.

(The majority of motor nerves and some sensory nerves from the cerebrum that move down into the spinal cord cross over in the medulla so that the right side of the brain controls the left side of the body and visa versa).

THE HYPOTHALAMUS

The hypothalamus links the Nervous System to the Endocrine System, via the Pituitary Gland. The Hyphthalamus is partly an Endrocrine Gland itself. It produces secretions called 'releasing hormones', which control the release of hormones from the anterior lobe of the Pituitary Gland. It is particularly important in regard to the body's response to stress. For example, in times of intense stress or severe pain, the Cerebral Cortex sends impulses to the Hypothalamus, which in turn secretes of ACTH (see Endocrine System) from the Pituitary Gland, causing cortisol production to increase from the Adrenals.

CEREBELLUM

The Cerebellum deals with movement, helps to control balance, posture and coordination of muscles during activities like walking or running.

MEDULLA OBLONGATA

The Medulla Oblongata controls activity of the heart, breathing rates, constriction and dilation of blood vessels, body temperature and the reflex actions of sneezing, coughing, vomiting and swallowing.

SPINAL CORD

The Spinal Cord runs down from the Medulla Oblongata into the protective canal formed by the vertebrae.

31 pairs of nerves, which form the peripheral nervous system, branch out from the vertebrae to the right and left sides of the body. Each nerve pair controls a particular part of the body.

MIDBRAIN

The midbrain is responsible for controlling sensory processes, eg visual and auditory; also, eye reflexes, involuntary muscle activity, motor responses of head and torso.

PONS VARIOLII

The Pons Variolii forms a bridge that transmits messages between the cerebrum, cerebellum and spinal cord.

CENTRAL NERVOUS SYSTEM

The Central Nervous System comprises of the brain and spinal cord. The brain receives and stores messages as well as transmitting them to all parts of the body to stimulate organs to do their work. The spinal cord extends downwards through the spinal column to the lumbar vertebrae.

! CAUTIONS FOR MASSAGE

If parents continually remove and then re-apply their hands during massage, their baby may become unsettled because of the assault to the peripheral nervous system. It is therefore important to encourage parents to maintain contact with their baby at all times, once they are undressed.

During the head and face massage, encourage parents not to cover their baby's eyes and ears, so they can see/ hear their parent all the time (unless they enjoy a game of peek-a-boo).

183

Benefits of massage

It is thought that, through positive interaction, baby massage encompasses the vital elements of bonding and attachment.

Infant massage develops respectful relationships, through trust and empathetic communication, which could possibly have a beneficial influence on the part of the brain concerned with emotional contentment and moral sense.

Encouraging parents to ask permission will enhance their baby's self-esteem and make them believe their feelings are respected.

Tips for teaching parents

Once your doll is undressed, keep a hand in touch with it at all times, to role-model this requirement for continuous contact with their baby to parents. Make sure you are aware of your actions and make a point of commenting when you need to break contact with your doll, so that the parents understand that they are not to follow.

Encourage parents not to massage too lightly, so that they do not tickle their baby. Tickling can be distressing to the peripheral nervous systems.

The endocrine system

PINEAL GLAND

The Pineal Gland helps to regulate body rhythms by producing melatonin during darkness, to encourage sleepiness.

THYROID GLAND

The Thyroid Gland produces the hormone thyroxine, which affects all the body's tissues and controls the metabolism. Thyroxine also has a huge influence on the body's mental and physical development after the birth.

PARATHYROID GLANDS

The Parathyroid Glands help regulate calcium levels in the blood by producing the hormones Calcitonin and Parathormone.

THYMUS

The Thymus Gland is made up of lymphoid. It is thought to delay sexual development until puberty. It releases the hormone thymosin, which is involved with the production of lymphocytes, which help fight infection in the body.

PITUITARY GLAND

The Pituitary Gland is located at the base of the brain and secretes hormones that influence the other endocrine glands. It has a posterior and anterior lobe, which between them regulate:

- Growth of the skeletal, muscles, connective tissues and organs
- Development of the reproductive organs
- Secretions from the ovaries and testes
- Stimulation of mammary glands to provide milk
- Blood pressure
- Re-absorption of water in the kidneys
- Functioning of the adrenal cortex, particularly during stress

(Many of the Pituitary Glands hormonal releases are stimulated by the activity of the hypothalamus.)

184

ADRENAL GLANDS

The Adrenal Glands consist of the cortex and the medulla. The cortex releases over 50 hormones. These 'corticoids' regulate the correct balance of minerals, quickly provide energy emergency situations and also control changes in puberty. The medulla secretes adrenalin and noradrenalin, which help prepare the body's fight and flight response.

The Endocrine System is an integrated system of glands that work together 'like an orchestra' to regulate normal body functions. These glands produce hormones and secretions that are released directly into the bloodstream and influence every cell, organ and function of the body.

(The Nervous System and Endocrine System often work in unison to help the body function properly. They are linked through the hypothalamus and its stalk-like attachment to the pituitary gland.)

CAUTIONS FOR MASSAGE

Bouts of sustained, long-term stressful situations that regularly cause a rise in cortisol levels, may:
- Shrink the hippocampus and cause cell death in the developing frontal brain
- Lower immunity
- Impair short term memory
- Disturb normal rhythms of the heart

Essential oils are potential endocrine disruptors. It is important to:
- Avoid massage mediums containing essential oils in your classes.
- Advise parents against the use of these until their child has at least reached puberty

STRESS AND CORTISOL

Stress and Cortisol
One of the main corticoids release by the adrenal cortex is cortisol, when stimulated by ACTH (adrenocorticoptrophic hormone) from the anterior lobe of the pituitary, due to stress, anger, fright or a large drop in blood sugar levels.
Cortisol:
- Helps break down glycogen into glucose ready for action
- Numbs pain during injury
- Accesses protein and fat for additional energy sources
- Is a natural anti-imflammatory
- A behavioural activating hormone (gets you going!)
- Plays a vital role in circadian rhythms. Cortisol levels are at their highest first thing in the morning (to induce wakefulness), and lowest for the three hours after midnight (to encourage sleepiness).

Stress and Adrenaline
- Makes the heart beat faster and elevates blood pressure, increasing flow to skeletal muscles
- Increases glycogen breakdown into glucose
- Dilates or widens the airways to increase lung capacity
- Stimulates ACTH to be released

Benefits of massage

Massage can be both physiologically and emotionally soothing; potentially reducing cortisol levels.

185

Tips for teaching parents

It is strongly advised, when teaching parents, that you:
- Help them understand, so that the experience does not become stressful for them, that should a baby say 'no' to massage, it is important that they do not continue until their baby says 'yes' again
- Reiterate the need for the parents to listen and respond to a baby's non-verbal cues. This allows the parent to help to regulate their baby's emotional states and potentially reduce the incidents of high cortisol levels.

Research, References And Further Reading

Research into
Infant and Child Massage

Touch research institute

Initially, research concerning the positive and negative effects of touch was carried out on animals. This research tended to look at the changes in behavioural responses that are linked to gentle handling, stroking, licking and companionship. From these early studies comparisons were made with human behaviour, but more recently studies directly investigating the effects of touch on humans has taken precedence. Over the last decade or so there have been some interesting and positive results that have come from the research carried out into the effects of infant massage.

Much of the research has come from a most prominent research team, situated at the Miami 'Touch Research Institute' in the USA. The team was headed by Tiffany Field, a renowned researcher who has helped to dramatically raise the profile of not only infant and child massage, but all aspects of positive touch. It is possible to obtain copies of the articles produced by the Touch Research Institute; so for more information about the Touch Research Institute and the work it does, visit their website at - http://www.miami.edu/touch-research/ . Or write to them at:

Touch Research Institute, Dept. of Pediatrics
University of Miami School of Medicine
PO BOX 016820 (Dept 820)
1601 NW 12th Avenue
Miami FL 33101, USA

Research in the UK

The UK has not been completely idle, where research is concerned. In the last few years, research carried out in the UK has helped to increase interest in infant and child massage and raised awareness of the benefits that this type of positive touch can bring, not only to the individual child, but also to parents, the whole family and society as a whole.

The Cochrane review

As there are a number of studies and anecdotal evidence The Cochrane Collaboration tasked a team of researchers to look at 23 current (as at 2007) studies that related to the effectiveness of infant massage in promoting physical and mental health in population samples. The Review: Massage Intervention for Promoting Mental and Physical Health in Infants Aged Under Six Months is an excellent resource for all Infant Massage Teachers, as the review is a detailed critical analysis of key research within this field.

For more information visit: www.mrw.interscience.wiley.com/cochrane/clsysrev/articles/CD005038/pdf_fs.html

Bibliography

Infant Massage

Introduction

Beaumont, B. (2005) *Baby Massage: A Loving Touch: Visual Evidence of the Benefits* Community Practitioner Vol. 78 (3)

Carpenter, P. (ed) (2005) Infant Massage: A Handbook for Teachers Touch-Learn Ltd

Carpenter, P. (2006) *Teenage Pregnancy - A Cry for Positive Touch?* Connections Vol. 2 (2)

Christensson, K. Siles, C. Moreno, L. (1992) *Temperature, Metabolic Adaptation & Crying in Healthy Full-term Newborns Cared for Skin to Skin or in a Cot* Acta Paediatrics Scandinavia Vol. 81: 488 - 493

Davis, P. (1999) The Power of Touch Hay House

Epple, A. (2007) *Healing Power of Touch* The Green Parent Dec / Jan

Fardig, A. (1980) *A Comparison of Skin to Skin Contact & Radiant Heaters in Promoting Neonatal Thermo Regulation* Journal of Nursing - Midwifery Vol. 25 (1)

Feary, A-M (2002) *Touching the Fragile Baby: Looking at Touch in the Special Care Nursery* (SCN) The Australian Journal of Holistic Nursing Vol. 9 (1)

Field, T., Schanberg, S., Davalos, M., Malphurs, J. (1996) *Massage with Oil has More Positive Effects on Newborn Infants* Pre and Perinatal Psychology Vol. 11: 73 - 78

Gray, L. Watt, L. Blass, E. (2000) *Skin to Skin Contact is Analgesic in Healthy Newborns* Pediatrics Vol. 105 (1)

Griffin, T. M. (2000) *Introduction of a Positive Touch Programme: the Value of Infant Massage* Journal of Neonatal Nursing Vol. 6 (4): 112 - 116

Gunnar, M. R., Donzella, B. (2002) *Social Regulation of the Cortisol Levels in Early Human Development* Psychoneuroendocrinology Vol. 27: 199 - 220

Heller, S. (1997) The Vital Touch Henry Holt & Co

Inman, A. (1996) *The Power of Touch: Infant Massage Therapy* The Childbirth Instructor Magazine 4th Quarter: 16 - 21

Kim, T. Shin, Y. & White-Traut, R. (2003) *Multi-Sensory Intervention Improves Physical Growth and Illness Rates in Korean Orphaned Newborn Infants* Research in Nursing and Health Vol. 26: 424 - 433

Leboyer, F (1976) Loving Hands. The traditional Indian Art of Baby Massage New Market Press

Lim, P. (1996) *Baby Massage* British Journal of Midwifery Vol. 4 (8): 439 - 440

Mercy Medical Center (2005) Health Search: Massage - What is Massage? http://beta.communityservers.com

Montagu, A. (1986) Touching: The Human Significance of the Skin Harper & Row

Moyse, K. (2005) *Baby Massage and Baby Play: Promoting Touch and Stimulation in Early Childhood* Paediatric Nurse Vol 17 (5)

Prescott (1975) *Pleasure and Violence Reciprocity Theory, the Distribution of 49 Cultures, Relating Infant Physical Affection to Adult Violence* The Futurist (April issue)

Schott J. & Henley, A. (1996) Culture, Religion and Childbearing in a Multi-Racial Society Butterworth- Heineman

Schneider, E.F. (2004) Touch Communication: the Power of Infant Massage http://beta.communityservers.com

Watson, S. (1998/1990) *Using Massage in the Care of Children* Paediatric Nursing Vol. 10 (10): 27 - 29

Weller, B. (2002) *Give a Hand to Gentle Touch* Nursing Standard Vol. 16 (31)

Whitehouse, K. (2001) *The Touch of Life* The Practising Midwife Vol. 4 (11)

Whitelaw, A. Heisterkamp, G. Sleath, K. Acolet, D. (1988) *Skin to Skin Contact for Very Low Birth Weight Infants & Their Mothers* Archives of Disease in Childhood Vol. 63: 1377 - 1381

White-Traut, R.C., Nelson, M.N. (1988) *Maternally Administered Tactile, Auditory, Visual and Vestibular Stimulation: Relationship to Later Interactions Between Mothers and Premature Infants* Research in Nursing & Health Vol. 11: 31 - 39

The benefits of infant massage

Beaumont, B. (2005) *Baby Massage: a Loving Touch: Visual Evidence of the Benefits* Community Practitioner Vol. 78 (3)

Bishop, E. McKinnon, E. Weir, E. & Brown, D. (2003). *Reflexology in the Management of Encopresis and Chronic Constipation.* Paediatric Nurse Vol. 15: 20 - 21

Clarke, C.L., Gibb, C., Hart, J., Davidson, A. (2002) *Infant Massage: Developing an Evidence Base for Health Visiting Practise* Clinical Effectiveness in Nursing Vol. 6: 121-128

Cassar (2001) Handbook of Massage Therapy: A Complete Guide for the Student & Professional Massage Therapist Butterworth – Heinemann

Cullen, C., Field, T., Escalona, A., Hartshorn, K. (2000) *Father-Infant Interactions are Enhanced by Massage Therapy* Early Child Development and Care Vol. 164: 41 – 47

Drehobl, K., Fuhr, M. (1988) *Infant Massage Helps Parents Interact With Newborn* OT Week Vol. 44 (2)

Epple, A. (2006) *The Benefits of Infant Massage* Today's Therapist Iss. 38

Epple, A. (2006) *Best For Baby* Embody Professional Summer

Epple, A. (2007) *The Benefits of Infant Massage* Midwifery Digest Vol. 17 (1)

Epple, A. (2007) *Healing Power of Touch* The Green Parent Dec/Jan

Epple, A. & Carpenter, P. (2007) Teach Yourself Baby Massage and Yoga Hodder and Stoughton

Feary, A.M (2002) *Touching the Fragile Baby: Looking at Touch in the Special Care Nursery* (SCN) The Australian Journal of Holistic Nursing Vol. 9 (1)

Ferber S.G, Laudon, M, Kuint J, Weller A, Zisapel N (2002) *Massage Therapy by Mothers Enhances the Adjustment of Circadian Rhythms to the Nocturnal Period in Full-Term Infants* Journal of Developmental and Behavioural Pediatrics Vol. 23: 410 - 415

Field, T. (1995) *Massage Therapy for Infants and Children* Developmental and Behavioural Paediatrics Vol. 16 (2)

Field,T. (2000) Touch Therapy. Churchill Livingstone

Field, T., Grizzle, N., Scafidi, F., Abrams, S., Richardson, S. (1996) *Massage Therapy for Infants of Depressed Mothers* Infant Behavior and Development Vol. 19: 109 - 114

Field, T., Hernandez-Reif, M. (2001) *Sleep Problems in Infants Decrease Following Massage Therapy* Early Child Development and Care Vol. 168: 95 - 104

Field, T., Schanberg, S., Davalos, M., Malphurs, J. (1996) *Massage With Oil Has More Positive Effects on Newborn Infants* Pre and Peri-natal Psychology Journal Vol. 11 (2)

Field, T., Schanberg, S., Scafidi, F., Bauer, C., Vega-Lahr, N., Garcia, R., Nystrom, J., Kuhn, C. (1986) *Tactile/Kinesthetic Stimulation Effects on Preterm Neonates* Pediatrics Vol. 77: 654 - 658

Fleming Drehobl, K., Gengler Fuhr, M. (2000) Pediatric Massage: For the Child with Special Needs Therapy Skill Builders

191

Fujita, M., Endoh, Y., Saimon, N., Yamaguchi, S. (2006) *Effect of Massaging Babies on Mothers: Pilot Study on the Changes in Mood States and Salivary Cortisol level* Complementary Therapies in Clinical Practice Vol. 12: 181 - 185

Glover, V., Onozawa, K., Adams, D., Modi, N., Channi Kumar, R. (March 2001) *Infant Massage Improves Mother/Infant Interaction for Mothers with Postnatal Depression* Journal of Affective Disorders Iss. 63

Glover, V., Onozawa, K., Hodgkinson, A. (2003) *Benefits of Infant Massage for Mothers with Postnatal Depression* Seminars in Neonatology Vol. 7: 495 - 500

Griffin, T. M. (2000) *Introduction of a Positive Touch Programme: the Value of Infant Massage* Journal of Neonatal Nursing Vol. 6 (4)

Gunnar, M. R., Donzella, B. (2002) *Social Regulation of the Cortisol Levels in Early Human Development* Psychneuroendocrinology Vol. 27: 199 - 220

Hart, S., Field, T., Hernandez-Reif, M., Lundy, B. (1998) *Preschoolers' Cognitive Performance Improves Following Massage* Early Child Development & Care Vol. 143: 59 - 64

Heller, S. (1997) The Vital Touch Henry Holt & Company

Inman, A. (1996) *The Power of Touch: Infant Massage Therapy* The Childbirth Instructor Magazine 4th Quarter: 16 - 21

Jewell Rich, G. (2002) Massage Therapy: The Evidence for Practice Mosby

Kelmanson, I. A. Adulas, E. I. (2006) *Massage Therapy and Sleep Behaviour in Infants Born with Low Birth Weight* Complementary Therapies in Clinical Practice Vol. 12: 200 - 205

Kim, T. Shin, Y. & White-Traut, R. (2003) *Multi-Sensory Intervention Improves Physical Growth and Illness Rates in Korean Orphaned Newborn Infants* Research in Nursing and Health Vol. 26: 424 - 433

Klaus, M. Klaus, J. (1998) Your Amazing Newborn Perseus Books

Lindrea, K. Stainton, M. A. (1997) *A Case Study of Infant Massage Outcomes* MCN-The American Journal of Maternal/Child Nursing Vol. 25: 95 - 99

Lim, P. (1996) *Baby Massage* British Journal of Midwifery Vol. 4 (8)

Livingstone, J. (2005) *Implementing Baby Massage* Independent Nurse June

Lorenz L, Moyse K, Surguy H. (2005) *The Benefits of Baby Massage* Paediatric Nurse Vol. 17 (2)

Mainous, R.O. (2002) *Infant Massage as a Component of Developmental Care: Past, Present and Future* Holistic Nurse Practitioner Vol. 16 (5)

Moyse, K. (2005) *Baby Massage and Baby Play: Promoting Touch and Stimulation in Early Childhood* Paediatric Nurse Vol 17 (5)

Payne, J. (2002) *The Benefits of Baby Massage in the Management and Prevention of Postnatal Depression* Journal of Chartered Physiotherapists of Women's Health Vol. 84: 10 - 13

Steptoe, C. *Healthy Psychology Aspects of Infant Massage* www.infantmassage.com/ benefits

Thompson, J. (2000) Infantile Colic - *What is it and are there Effective Treatments* Community Practitioner Vol. 73 (9)

Wall, A. (1998) *Baby Massage: Probably of Benefit* Professional Care Of Mother And Child Vol. 8 (4)

Watson, S. (1998/1999) *Using Massage in the Care of Children* Paediatric Nursing Vol. 10 (10)

Zealy, C (2005) *The Benefits of Infant Massage: A Critical Review* Community Practitioner Vol. 78 (3)

Precautions and contraindications

Carpenter, P. (2005) *Consideration about the Age of a Baby and the Introduction of a Massage Routine* Connections Vol. 1 (10)

Cassar (2001) Handbook of Massage Therapy: A Complete Guide for the Student & Professional Massage Therapist Butterworth - Heinemann

Epple, A. & Carpenter, P. (2007) Teach Yourself Baby Massage and Yoga Hodder and Stoughton

Sussman, W., Sussman, L. (2003) Vaccinations: Yes or No? The Merrydown Publishing Company Ltd

Teaching infant massage

A gentle introduction to touch

Epple, A. & Carpenter, P. (2007) Teach Yourself Baby Massage and Yoga Hodder and Stoughton

Gerard, CM. Harris, KA. & Thach, BT. (2002) *Spontaneous Arousals in Supine Infants While Swaddled and Unswaddled During Rapid Eye Movement and Quiet Sleep* Pediatrics Vol. 110 (6)

Murray, L. & Andrews, L (2000) The Social Baby: Understanding Babies' Communication from Birth CP Publishing

Ohgi, S. Akyama, T. Ansawa, K, & Shigemori, K. (2004) *Randomised Controlled Trial of Swaddling versus massage in Management of Excessive Crying in Infants with Cerebral Injuries* Archives of Diseases in Childhood Vol. 89 (3)

Teaching parents a massage routine

Cassar (2001) Handbook of Massage Therapy: A Complete Guide for the Student & Professional Massage Therapist Butterworth – Heinemann

Epple, A. & Carpenter, P. (2007) Teach Yourself Baby Massage and Yoga Hodder and Stoughton

Fritz, S. (2006) Mosby's Fundamentals of Therapeutic Massage Mosby

Pitman, V., McKenzie, K. (1997) Reflexology: A Practical Approach Stanley Thorns Publishers Ltd

The practicalities of teaching infant massage

Bowler (1993) *Stereotypes of Women from Asian Descent in Midwifery: Some Evidence* Midwifery Vol. 9: 716

Carpenter, P. (2004) *Using Nursery Rhymes, Singing & Music in Connection with Communication & Brain Development* Connections Vol. 1 (7)

Carpenter, P. (ed) (2005) Infant Massage: A Handbook for Teachers Touch-Learn Ltd

Carpenter, P. (2007) Music, Movement and Rhyme: Essentials for the Developing Child Touch-Learn Ltd

Carpenter, P. (2007) *A Child's Need For Music, Singing and Rhyme* Connections Vol. 2 (5)

Carpenter, P. (2007) *Music, Movement and Rhyme: The Essentials for the Developing Child* Today's Therapist Sept/Oct

Miell, D. MacDonald, R. & Hargreaves, D. (2005) Musical Communication Oxford University Press

Schott J., Henley, A. (1996) Culture, Religion and Childbearing in a Multi-racial Society Butterworth- Heineman

Sheikh, A., Gatrad, A. R. (2001) *Muslim Birth Practices* The Practising Midwife Vol. 4: 410 - 413
Small et al, (1999) *Mothers in a New Country: The Role of Culture and Communication in Vietnamese, Turkish and Filipino Women's Experiences of giving Birth in Australia* Women & Health Vol. 28: (3)

Zaidi, F. (1994) *The Maternity Care of Muslim Women* Modem Midwife March: 8 - 10

Teaching practice

Carpenter, P. (ed) (2005) Infant Massage: A Handbook for Teachers Touch-Learn Ltd

Carpenter, P. (2006) *Teaching Aids for Midwifes: Using a Realistic Demonstration Doll for a Realistic Approach* Scottish Nurse Vol. 10 (5)

Daines, J. Daines, C., Graham, B. (1998) Adult Learning, Adult Teaching Continuing Education Press

Hillen, P. (2004) *The Meaning of 'Parenting' and the Impact of Group Work* Community Practitioner Vol. 77 (11)

Mayeroff, M. (1971) On Caring Harpers & Row

Newcombe, T. (2003) *Implementing Group Work in Primary Care to Meet Client Need* Nursing Times Vol. 99 (27)

Roach, M.S. (1992) The Human Act of Caring: A Blueprint for Health Professionals Canadian Hospital Association

Transition To Parent: An Open Learning Resource for Midwives (April 1999) The Royal College of Midwives Trust

Tschudin, V. (1995) Counselling Skills for Nurses Bailliere Tindall

195

Giving guidance for special situations

Alva, M. (1999) *Getting In Touch With Children: Pediatric Massage Can Help Parents Relax and Communicate With Youngsters Who Have Special Needs* ADVANCE Vol. 3 (26)

Barlow, J., Cullen, L. (2000) Coming *Together Through Touch: The Experiences of Parents of Children with Disabilities Learning the Principles of Massage* Early Child Development and Care Vol. 161: 93 - 105

Brown, J. V. (2000) *Considerations for Touch and Massage in the Neonatal Intensive Care Unit* Neonatal Network Vol. 19 (1)

Diego MA, Field T, Hernandez-Reif M. (2005) *Vagal Activity, Gastric Motility, and Weight Gain in Massaged Preterm Neonates* Journal of Pediatrics Vol. 147 (1)

Dieter, J., Field, T., Hernandez-Reif, M., Emory, E. K., Redzepi, M. (2003) *Stable Preterm Infants Gain More Weight and Sleep Less After Five Days of Massage Therapy* Journal of Pediatric Psychology Vol. 28: 403 - 11

Epple, A. & Carpenter, P. (2007) Teach Yourself Baby Massage and Yoga Hodder and Stoughton

Feary, A. M. (2002) *Touching the Fragile Baby: Looking at Touch in the Special Care Nursery* (SCN) The Australian Journal of Holistic Nursing Vol. 9 (1)

Feijo, L., Hernandez-Reif, M., Field, T., Burns, W., Valley-Gray, S., Simco, E. (2006) *Mothers' Depressed Mood and Anxiety Levels are Reduced after Massaging their Preterm Infants* Infant Behavior & Development Vol. 3: 476 - 80

Field, T. (2001) *Massage Therapy Facilitates Weight Gain in Preterm Infants* (Review) Current Directions in Psychological Science Vol. 10: 51 - 54

Field, T., Henteleff, T., Hernandez-Reif, M., Martinez, E., Mavunda, K., Kuhn, C., Schanberg, S. (1998) *Children with Asthma have Improved Pulmonary Functions after Massage Therapy* Journal of Pediatrics Vol. 132: 854 - 858

Field, T., Schanberg, S. M. (1990) *Massage Alters Growth and Catecholamine Production in Preterm Newborns* in Gunzenhauser, N., Brazelton, T. B., and Field, T. Advances in Touch Skillman

Field, T., Schanberg, S., Bauer, C. et al (1990) *Massage Stimulates Growth in Preterm Infants* Infant Behaviour and Development Vol. 13: 167 - 188

Field, T., Scafidi, F., Schanberg, S. (1987) *Massage of Preterm Newborns to Improve Growth and Development* Pediatric Nursing Vol. 13: 385 - 387

Field, T., Schanberg, S., Scafidi, F., Bauer, C., Vega-Lahr, N., Garcia, R., Nystrom, J., Kuhn, C. (1986) *Tactile/Kinesthetic Stimulation Effects on Preterm Neonates* Pediatrics Vol. 77: 654 - 658

Fleming Drehobl, K., Gengler Fuhr, M. (2000) Pediatric Massage: For the Child with Special Needs Therapy Skill Builders

Griffin, T. M. (2000) *Introduction of a Positive Touch Programme: The Value of Infant Massage* Journal of Neonatal Nursing Vol. 6 (4)

Hansen, R., Ulrey, G. (1988) *Motorically Impaired Infants: Impact of a Massage Procedure of Caregiver-Infant Interactions* Journal of Multihandicapped Person Vol. 1 (1)

Hernandez-Reif, M., Field, T., Largie, S., Diego, M., Manigat, N., Seonanes, J., Bornstein, J. Waldman, R. (2005) *Cerebral Palsy Symptoms in Children Decreased Following Massage Therapy* Journal of Early Child Development and Care Vol. 175: 445 - 456

Hernandez-Reif, M., Field, T., Bornstein, J. Fewell, R. (2006) *Children with Down Syndrome Improved in Motor Function and Muscle Tone Following Massage Therapy* Journal of Early Child Development and Care Vol. 176: 395 - 410

Kuhn, C., Schanberg, S., Field, T., Symanski, R., Zimmerman, E., Scafidi, F., Roberts, J. (1991) *Tactile Kinesthetic Stimulation Effects on Sympathetic and Adrenocortical Function in Preterm Infants* Journal of Pediatrics Vol. 119: 434 - 440

McGrath, J. Thillet, M. & Van Cleave, L. (2007) *Parent Delivered Infant Massage: Are we Truly Ready for Implementation?* Newborn and Infant Nursing Reviews Vol 7 (1)

Scafidi, F., Field, T., Wheedon, A. et al (1996) *Cocaine-Exposed Preterm Neonates Show Behavioural and Hormone Differences* Pediatrics Vol. 97: 851 - 855

Tracey, N. (2000) Parents of Premature Infants: Their Emotional World Whurr Publishers Ltd

Watson, S. (1998/1999) *Using Massage in the Care of Children* Paediatric Nursing Vol. 10 (10)

Wheeden, A., Scafidi, F.A., Field, T., Ironson, G., Valdeon, C., Bandstra, E. (1993) *Massage Effects on Cocaine-Exposed Preterm Neonates* Journal of Developmental and Behavioral Pediatrics Vol. 14: 318 - 322

White-Traut, R. C., Nelson, M. N. (1988) *Maternally Administered Tactile, Auditory, Visual and Vestibular Stimulation: Relationship to Later Interactions between Mothers and Premature Infants* Research in Nursing & Health Vol. 11:31 - 39

Suggestions for adapting massage for the growing child

Brazelton, T. B. (1984) To Listen to a Child: Understanding the Normal Problems of Growing Up Addison Wesley Publishing Company

Epple, A. & Carpenter, P. (2007) Teach Yourself Baby Massage and Yoga Hodder and Stoughton

Field, T. (1995) *Massage Therapy for Infants and Children* Developmental and Behavioural Paediatrics Vol. 16 (2): 105-11

Hart, S., Field, T., Hernandez-Reif, M., Lundy, B. (1998) *Preschoolers' Cognitive Performance Improves Following Massage* Early Child Development & Care Vol. 143: 59 - 64

Sheridan, M (1997) From Birth to Five Year: Children's Developmental Progress Routledge

Teaching safely and professionally

Brown, A., Butcher, M. (2005) *A Guide to Emollient Therapy* Nursing Standard Vol. 10 (24)

Carpenter, P. (2003) *The Law, Complementary Therapies & Infant Massage* Connections Vol. 1 (4)

Carpenter, P. (ed) (2005) Infant Massage: A Handbook for Teachers Touch-Learn Ltd

Carpenter, P. (2007) *New Evidence to Indicate Usage of Essential Oils for Children is Unsafe* Connections Vol. 2 (6)

Carpenter, P. (2007) *GICM Standard Setting and Offering Support* Connections Vol. 2 (6)

Carpenter, P. (2007) *Henley's Essential Oil Research: Analysing The Arguments Against The Research Findings* Connections Vol. 2 (7)

Epple, A. (2006) *The Use of Emollients in Infant Massage* Connections Vol. 2 (3)

Darmstadt, G., Saha, S., Ahmed, A., Chowdhury, M., Law, P., Ahmed, S., Alam, M., Black, R., Black, M. *Effect of Topical Treatment with Skin Barrier-Enhancing Emollients on Nosocomial Infections in Preterm Infants in Bangladesh: a Randomised Controlled Trial* The Lancet Vol. 365: 1039 -1045

Field, T., Schanberg, S., Davalos, M., Malphurs, J. (1996) *Massage with Oils has more Positive Effect on Normal Infants* Pre & Perinatal Psychology Journal Vol. 11 (2)

Hambly, K., Muir, A. (2001) Stress and How to Manage it - Course Textbook Stress Education Services

Henley, D., Lipson, N., Korach, K., Bloch, C. (2007) *Prepubertal Gynecomastia Linked to Lavender and Tea Tree Oils* New England Journal of Medicine Feb.

Kusmirek, J. (2002) Liquid Sunshine - Vegetable Oils for Aromatherapy Floramicus

Price, L. (1999) Carrier Oils For Aromatherapy & Massage Riverhead

Wall (2002) *Agreeing a Standard for Infant Massage* Journal of Neonatal Nursing Vol. 8: 3

Marketing and publicity

Carpenter, P. (2004) *Marketing Suggestions for Infant Massage Teachers* Connections Vol. 1 (8)

Epple, A. (2008) *Writing For Publication* Connections Vol. 2 (8)

Harold, S. A. (2002) Marketing for Complementary Therapists How-to-Books Ltd

Johnson, C. (2003) How to be a Successful Therapist Book Guild Ltd

Infants and parents

Child development

Barlow, J., Parsons, J. (2003) *Group-Based Parent-Training Programmes for Improving Emotional and Behavioural Adjustment in 0-3 Year-old Children* Cochrane Database Systematic Review 2003 (1)

Brazelton, T. B. (1984) To Listen to a Child: Understanding the Normal Problems of Growing Up Addison Wesley Publishing Company

Brazelton, T. B. (1995) <u>Touchpoints, The Essential Reference: Your Child's Emotional and Behavioural Development</u> Perseus Books

Brazelton, T. B. & Sparrow, J. (2003) <u>Calming your Fussy Baby: The Brazelton Way</u> Perseus Publishing

Chess, S., Thomas, H. (1977) <u>Your Child is a Person: A Psychological Approach to Parenthood without Guilt</u> Harmondsworth Penguin

Cicchetti, D., Tucker, D. (1994) *Development and Self-Regulatory Structures of the Mind* <u>Development and Psychopathology</u> Vol. 6: 533 - 549

Coons, S., Guilleminault, C. (1982) *Development of Sleep-Wake Patterns & Non-Rapid Eye Movement Sleep Stages During the First Six Months of Life in Normal Infants* Pediatrics Vol. 69: 793 - 798

Feldman, R. et al (1996) *Relations Between Cyclicity and Regulation in Mother-Infant Interaction at 3 and 9 Months and Cognition at 2 Years* <u>Journal of Applied Developmental Psychology</u> Vol. 17: 347 - 365

Ferber, S. G., Laudon, M., Kuint, J., Weller, A., Zisapel, N. (2002) *Massage Therapy by Mothers Enhances the Adjustment of Circadian Rhythms to the Nocturnal Period in Full-term Infants* <u>Journal of Developmental and Behavioral Pediatrics</u> Vol. 23: 410 - 415

Field, T. (1995) *Massage Therapy for Infants and Children* <u>Developmental and Behavioural Paediatrics</u> Vol. 16 (2)

Field, T. (1998) *Maternal Depression: Effects on Infants and Early Interventions* <u>Preventative Medicine</u> Vol. 27(2)

Field, T., Grizzle, M., Scafide, R., Abrams, S., Richardson, S. (1996) *Massage Therapy for Infants of Depressed Mothers* <u>Infant Behaviour & Development</u> Vol. 19: 107 - 112

Field T., Hernandez-Reif, M. (2001) *Sleep Problems in Infants Decrease Following Massage Therapy* <u>Early Child Development and Care</u> Vol. 168: 95 - 104

Fonagy, P. (1998) *Prevention: The Appropriate Target of Infant Psychotherapy* <u>Infant Mental Health Journal</u> Vol. 19 (2)

Gerhardt, S. (2004) <u>Why Love Matters: How Affection Shapes a Baby's Brain</u> Brunner-Routledge

Gordon, Y. (2002) <u>Birth and Beyond</u> Vermillion

Gunnar, M. R. (1998) *Quality of Early Care & Buffering of Neuroendocrine Stress Reactions: Potential Effects on the Developing Human Brain* <u>Preventive Medicine</u> Vol. 27: 208 - 211

Helen, B. & Gavey, J. (2002) *Responding to Babies' Needs through Holistic Care* <u>Nursing Standard</u> Vol. 16: 33 - 37

Herring, M. & Kaslow, N. J. (2002) *Depression and Attachment in Families: A Child-focused Perspective* Family Process Vol. 41 (3)

Kelmanson, I. A., Adulas, E. I. (2006) *Massage Therapy and Sleep Behaviour in Infants Born with Low Birth Weight* Complementary Therapies in Clinical Practice Vol. 12: 200 - 205

Kilgour, T. & Wade, S. (2003) Infantile Colic Clinical Evidence

Kim, T. Shin, Y. & White-Traut, R. (2003) *Multi-Sensory Intervention Improves Physical Growth and Illness Rates in Korean Orphaned Newborn Infants* Research in Nursing and Health Vol. 26: 424 - 433

Klaus & Klaus (1998) Your Amazing Newborn Perseus Books

Lim, P. (1996) *Baby Massage* British Journal of Midwifery Vol. 4 (8)

Lipari, J. (2000) *First Impression Count with your Newborn: Early Months, Time for Emotional, Cognitive Development* Boston Herald Aug 27th

Mainous, R. O. (2002) *Infant Massage as a Component of Developmental Care: Past, Present and Future* Holistic Nurse Practitioner Vol. 16 (5)

McGlauglin, A., Grayson, A. (2001) *Crying in the First Year of Infancy: Patterns & Prevalence* Journal of Reproductive & Infant Psychology Vol. 19: (1)

Murrey, L. (1992) *The Impact of Postnatal Depression and Infant Development* Journal of Child Psychology & Psychiatry Vol. 33: 542 - 561

Murray, L., Fiori-Cowley, A., Hooper, R., Cooper, P. (1996) *The Impact of Postnatal Depression and Associated Adversity on Early Mother-Infant Interactions and Later Infant Outcome* Child Development Vol. 67: 2512 - 2526

Murray, L., Andrews, L. (2000) The Social Baby: Understanding Babies' Communication from Birth CP Publishing

Murray, L & Cooper (1997) *Effects of Postnatal Depression on Infant Development* Archive of Diseases in Childhood Vol. 77: 99 - 101

Nash, M. (1997) *Fertile Minds: From Birth* Time Magazine Vol. 149 (5)

Panksepp, J. (1998) Affective Neuroscience: The Foundations of Human and Animal Emotions Oxford University Press

Perry, B. D. et al (1995) *Childhood Trauma, the Neurobiology of Adaptation and 'Use-Dependent' Development of the Brain: How 'States' Become 'Traits'* Infant Mental Health Journal Vol. 16: 271 - 291

Preston, C., Dunton, T. (1998) Little Terror - First Six Weeks Metro Books

Preston, C., Dunton, T. (1998) Little Terror - Good Sleeping Guide Metro Books

Royal College of Midwives *A Helpful Guide to a Better Understanding of Your Baby's Behaviour* Your Baby, Your Midwife, You Bounty

Schore, A. N. (1999) Affect Regulation and the Origin of the Self: The Neurobiology of the Emotional Development Lawrence Erlbaum Associates

Schore, A. N. (2001) *Effects of a Secure Attachment Relationship on Right Brain Development, Affect Regulation and Infant Mental Health* Infant Mental Health Journal Vol. 22 (1 - 2)

Sears, W. (1993) The Baby Book – Everything you Need to Know about your Baby from Birth to Age Two Little, Brown and Company

Sheridan, M (1997) From Birth to Five Year: Children's Developmental Routledge

Solter, A. (1984) The Aware Baby Shining Star Press

Spangler, G. Schieche, M. Llg, U. Maier, U. & Ackermann, C.l (1994) *Maternal Sensitivity as an Organizer for Biobehavioural Regulation in Infancy* Developmental Psychobiology Vol. 27: 425 - 437

Steptoe, C. Healthy Psychology Aspects of Infant Massage www.infantmassage.com/benefits

Stern, D. (1985) The Interpersonal World of the Infant: A View from Psychoanalysis and Developmental Psychology Basic Books

Sunderland, M. (2006) Science of Parenting Dorling Kindersley

Tronick, E. (1989) *Emotions & Emotional Communication in Infants* American Psychologist Vol. 44 (2)

Upledger, J. E. A Brain is Born: Exploring the Birth and Development of the Central Nervous System North Atlantic Books USA

Uvnas-Moberg, U. (2003) The Oxytocin Factor Perseus Publishing

Wolke, D. (1994) *Feeding and Sleeping Across the Lifespan* in Rutter, M., Hay, D. (eds.) Development through Life: A Handbook for Clinicians Blackwell Scientific Publications

Wolke, D. (1999) *Understanding My Baby's Sleep Patterns: A Guide to Parents* Leaflet Sponsored by Johnson & Johnson

Woodhouse, S. (2003) Sound Sleep Hawthorn Press

Wright, K. (1997) *Babies Bonds and Brains* Discover: The World of Science October

Understanding the infant

Brazelton, T. B. (1984) To Listen to a Child: Understanding the Normal Problems of Growing Up Addison Wesley Publishing Company

Brazelton, T. B. (1995) <u>Touchpoints, The Essential Reference: Your Child's Emotional and Behavioural Development</u> Perseus Books

McGlauglin, A., Grayson, A. (2001) *Crying in the First Year of Infancy: Patterns & Prevalence* <u>Journal of Reproductive & Infant Psychology</u> Vol. 19: (1)

Murray, L., Andrews, L. (2000) <u>The Social Baby: Understanding Babies' Communication from Birth</u> CP Publishing

Preston, C., Dunton, T. (1998) <u>Little Terror - First Six Weeks</u> Metro Books

The Parent

Aiken, C. (2006) <u>Surviving Postnatal Depression: At Home, No one hears you Scream</u> Jessica Kingsley Publishers Ltd

Ballad, C. G., Stanley, A. K., Brockington, I. F. (1995) *Post traumatic stress disorder following childbirth* <u>British Journal of Psychiatry</u> Vol. 166: 525 - 528

Barlow, J., Parsons, J. (2003) *Group-based Parent-Training Programmes for Improving Emotional and Behavioural Adjustment in 0-3 Year-old Children* <u>Cochrane Database Systematic Review 2003</u> (1)

Chess, S., Thomas, H. (1977) <u>Your Child is a Person: A Psychological Approach to Parenthood without Guilt</u> Harmondsworth Penguin

Edhberg, M., Lundh, W., Seimyr, L., Widstrom, A. M. (2000) *The Long-Term Impact of Postnatal Depressed Mood on Mother-Child Interaction: a Preliminary Study* <u>Journal of Reproductive & Infant Psychology</u> Vol. 19 (1)

Faber A., Mazlish, E. (1998) <u>Siblings without Rivalry</u> Avon Books Inc

Faber, A., Mazlish, E. (2002) <u>How to Listen so Kids Will Talk and Talk so that Kids Will Listen</u> Harper Collins Publishers Inc

Feijo, L., Hernandez-Reif, M., Field, T., Burns, W., Valley-Gray, S., Simco, E. (2006) *Mothers' Depressed Mood and Anxiety Levels are Reduced after Massaging their Preterm Infants* <u>Infant Behavior & Development</u> Vol. 3: 476 - 80

Glover, Onozawa, Adams, Modil, Channikar (2001) *Infant Massage Improves Mother-Infant Interaction for Mothers with Postnatal Depression* <u>Journal of Affective Disorders</u> Vol. 63: 201-207

Glover, V., Onozawa, K., Hodgkinson, A. (2003) *Benefits of Infant Massage for Mothers with Postnatal Depression* <u>Seminar in Neonatology</u> Vol. 7: 495 - 500

Hambly, K., Muir, A. (2001) <u>Stress and How to Manage it- Course Textbook</u> Stress Education Services

Hillen, P. (2004) *The Meaning of 'Parenting' and the Impact of Groupwork* Community Practitioner Vol. 77 (11)

Holland, S. Postnatal Depression and Maternal Mental Health CPHVA publications

Lerner, H. (1998) The Mother Dance - How Children Change Your Life Quill

Martins, C., Gaffan, E. A. (2000) *Effects of Early Postnatal Depression on Patterns of Infant-Mother Attachment: a Meta-Analytic Investigation* Journal of Child Psychology & Psychiatry Vol. 45: 737 - 746

Murray, L. (1992) *The Impact of Postnatal Depression & Infant Development* Journal of Child Psychology & Psychiatry Vol. 33: 542 -561

Murray, L. Fiori-Cowley, A. et al (1996) *The Impact of Postnatal Depression and Associated Adversity on Early Mother/Infant Interactions and Later Infant Outcome* Child Development Oct 1996, Vol. 67 (5)

Payne, J. (2002) *The Benefits of Baby Massage in the Management and Prevention of Postnatal Depression* Journal of Chartered Physiotherapists of Women's Health Vol. 84: 10 - 13

Pritchard, P. (1999) *Helping Parents with Severe Parenting Difficulties* Community Practitioner Vol. 72: 248 – 51

Russell, S. (2005) *Helping Alleviate Social Isolation and PND* Community Practitioner Vol. 78 (2)

Steptoe, C. Healthy Psychology Aspects of Infant Massage www.infantmassage.com/benefits

Tracey, N. (2000) Parents of Premature Infants: Their Emotional World Whurr Publishers Ltd

Solter, A. (1984) The Aware Baby: A New Approach to Parenting Shining Star Press

Sved-Williams, A. E. (1992) *Phobic Reactions of Mothers to their Own Babies* Australian and New Zealand Journal of Psychiatry Vol. 142: 238 - 246

Tronick, E. Z., Weinberg, M. K. (1997) *Depressed Mothers and Infants: Failure to Form Dyadic States of Consciousness* in Murray, L., Cooper P. J. (eds) Postpartum Depression in Child Development Guilford Press

The infant-parent relationship

Anisfield, E. Casper, V. Nozyce, M. & Cunningham, N (1990) *Does Infant Carrying Promote Attachment? An Experimental Study of the Effects of Increased Physical Contact on the Development of Attachment* Child Development Vol. 61: 1617 - 1627

Anderson, G. (1989) *Risk in Mother-Infant Separation Post-Birth* Journal of Nursing Scholarship Vol. 21:196 - 99

Barlow, J., Cullen, L. (2000) Coming *Together through Touch: The Experiences of Parents of Children with Disabilities Learning the Principles of Massage* Early Child Development and Care Vol. 161: 93 – 105

Beebe, B. (2000) *Co-Constructing Mother-Infant Distress: the Microsynchrony of Maternal Impingement and Infant Avoidance in the Face-to-Face Encounter* Psychoanalytic Inquiry Vol. 20: 214 - 440

Bidmead, C. & Andrews, L. (2004) *Enhancing Early Parent-Infant Interaction: Part 1 – Observation Strategies* Community Practitioner Vol. 77 (10)

Bidmead, C. & Farnes, J. (2004) *Enhancing Early Parent-Infant Interaction: Part 2 – Positive Touch* Community Practitioner Vol. 77 (11)

Bidmead, C., Mackinder, L. (2004) *Enhancing Early Parent-Infant Interaction: Part 3 – Play* Community Practitioner Vol. 77 (12)

Bidmead, C. (2005) *Enhancing Early Parent-Infant Interaction: Part 4 – Infant Massage* Community Practitioner Vol. 78 (3)

Bowlby, J. (1990) A Secure Base: Parent-Child Attachment and Healthy Human Development Basic Books

Brazelton, T. B., Cramer, B. G. (1991) The Earliest Relationship: Parents, Infants and the Drama of Early Attachment Karnac Books

Cullen, C., Field, T., Escalona, A., Hartshorn, K. (2000) *Father-Infant Interactions are Enhanced by Massage Therapy* Early Child Development and Care Vol. 164: 41 - 47

Edhberg, M. Lundh, W. Seimyr, L., Widstrom, A. M. (2000) *The Long-Term Impact of Postnatal Depressed Mood on Mother-Child Interaction: a Preliminary Study* Journal of Reproductive & Infant Psychology Vol. 19 (1)

Feldman, R. et al (1996) *Relations Between Cyclicity and Regulation in Mother-Infant Interaction at 3 and 9 Months and Cognition at 2 Years* Journal of Applied Developmental Psychology Vol. 17: 347 - 365

Francis, D. D., Meaney, M. J. (1999) Maternal Care and the Development of Stress Responses Current Opinion in Neurobiology Vol. 9: 128 - 134

Gerhardt, S. (2004) Why Love Matters: How Affection Shapes a Baby's Brain Brunner-Routledge

Glover, V., Onozawa, K., Adams, D., Modi, N., Channi Kumar, R. (2001) *Infant Massage Improves Mother/Infant Interaction for Mothers with Postnatal Depression* Journal of Affective Disorders Iss. 63

Gutbrod, T., (1999) *Mother and Infant Relationships* International Journal of Alternative Complementary Medicine Vol. 17: 18 - 19

Herring, M., Kaslow, N. J. (2002) *Depression and Attachment in Families: A Child-Focused Perspective* Family Process Vol. 41 (3)

Karen, R. (1998) Becoming Attached: First Relationships and How They Shape Our Capacity to Love Oxford University Press

Lee, B. (2000) *Attached or Detached? Aspects of Baby-Parent Attachment* Royal College of Midwives Vol. 3: 158 - 159

Maccoby, E. E., Martin, J. A. (1983) *Socialization in the Context of the Family: Parent-Child Interaction* in Hetherington, E (Ed) Handbook of child psychology: Vol. 4. Socialization, personality, and social development John Wiley & Sons

Martins, C., Gaffan, E. A. (2000) *Effects of Early Postnatal Depression on Patterns of Infant-Mother Attachment: a Meta-Analytic Investigation* Journal of Child Psychology & Psychiatry Vol. 45: 737 - 746

Murray, L. (1992) *The Impact of Postnatal Depression and Infant Development* Journal of Child Psychology & Psychiatry Vol. 33: 542 – 561

Murray, L., Fiori-Cowley, A., Hooper, R., Cooper, P. (1996) *The Impact of Postnatal Depression and Associated Adversity on Early Mother-Infant Interactions and Later Infant Outcome* Child Development Vol. 67: 2512 - 2526

Panksepp, J. (1998) Affective Neuroscience: The Foundations of Human and Animal Emotions Oxford University Press

Penman, R. et al (1983) *Synchronicity in Mother-Infant Interaction: A Possible Neurophysiological Base* British Journal of Medical Psychology Vol. 56: 1 - 7

Poehlmann, J., Fiese, B. H. (2001) *The Interaction of Maternal and Infant Vulnerabilities on Developing Attachment Relationships* Developmental Psychopathology Vol. 13: 1 - 11

Porter, L. (2003) *The Science of Attachment: The Biological Roots of Love* Mothering July/August

Raphael-Left, J. (2003) Parent-Infant Psychodynamics: Wild Things, Mirrors and Ghosts Whurr Publishers

Schore, A. (2000) *Attachment & the Regulation of the Right Brain* Attachment & Human Development Vol. 2: 23 - 47

Schore, A. N. (2001)*The Effects of a Secure Attachment Relationship on Right Brain Development, Affect Regulation and Infant Mental Health* Infant Mental Health Journal Vol. 22: 7 - 66

Sears, W., Sears, M. (2001) The Attachment Parenting Book: A Commonsense Guide to Understanding and Nurturing Your Baby Little, Brown & Company

Spangler, G. et al (1994) *Maternal Sensitivity as an Organizer for Biobehavioural Regulation in Infancy* Developmental Psychobiology Vol. 27: 425 - 437

Sunderland, M. (2006) Science of Parenting Dorling Kindersley

Tronick, E. (1989) *Emotions & Emotional Communication in Infants* American Psychologist Vol. 44 (2)

Tronick, E. Z., Weinberg, M. K. (1997) *Depressed Mothers and Infants: Failure to Form Dyadic States of Consciousness* in Murray, L., Cooper P. J. (eds.) Postpartum Depression in Child Development Guilford Press

White-Traut, R. C., Nelson, M. N. (1988) *Maternally Administered Tactile, Auditory, Visual and Vestibular Stimulation: Relationship to Later Interactions between Mothers and Premature Infants* Research in Nursing & Health Vol. 11:31 - 39

Anatomy and physiology

Fox, S. & Pritchard, D (2001) Anatomy, Physiology and Pathology for the Massage Therapist Corpus Publishing

MacGregor, J. (2000) Introduction to the Anatomy & Physiology of Children Routledge

Upledger, J. E. A Brain is Born: Exploring the Birth and Development of the Central Nervous System North Atlantic Books

Relevant Organisations

Ditto International Ltd
7 Regent's Hall
St Mary's Avenue
Stony Stratford
Buckinghamshire
MK11 1EB
www.dittointernational.co.uk

Publishers of positive parenting, positive touch and nutrition in childhood books.

The Guild of Infant and Child Massage
22 Elder Close
Uttoxeter
Staffordshire
ST14 5UR
www.gicm.org.uk

The regulatory body for Infant Massage, Massage in Education and Baby Yoga Teachers.

Touch-Learn International Ltd
Saddler's Court
18a Carter Street
Uttoxeter
Staffordshire
ST14 8EU
www.touchlearn.co.uk

An exemplary training company offering positive touch trainings and workshops for health professionals and complementary therapists who work with parents, babies and young children.

Touch-Needs Ltd
7 Regent's Hall
St Mary's Avenue
Stony Stratford
Buckinghamshire
MK11 1EB
www.touchneeds.com

Supplies Positive Touch Teachers with the necessary resources they require to take trainings and for the classes they offer parents, babies and children.